ROUTLEDGE LIBRARY EDITIONS:
TRADE UNIONS

```
I0130733
```

Volume 8

THE GOVERNMENT
OF BRITISH TRADE
UNIONS

THE GOVERNMENT OF BRITISH TRADE UNIONS

A Study of Apathy and the Democratic Process in the Transport and General Workers Union

JOSEPH GOLDSTEIN

Routledge
Taylor & Francis Group

LONDON AND NEW YORK

First published in 1952 by George Allen & Unwin Ltd.

This edition first published in 2023
by Routledge
4 Park Square, Milton Park, Abingdon, Oxon OX14 4RN

and by Routledge
605 Third Avenue, New York, NY 10158

Routledge is an imprint of the Taylor & Francis Group, an informa business

© 1952 Joseph Goldstein

All rights reserved. No part of this book may be reprinted or reproduced or utilised in any form or by any electronic, mechanical, or other means, now known or hereafter invented, including photocopying and recording, or in any information storage or retrieval system, without permission in writing from the publishers.

Trademark notice: Product or corporate names may be trademarks or registered trademarks, and are used only for identification and explanation without intent to infringe.

British Library Cataloguing in Publication Data
A catalogue record for this book is available from the British Library

ISBN: 978-1-032-37553-3 (Set)
ISBN: 978-1-032-39222-6 (Volume 8) (hbk)
ISBN: 978-1-032-39223-3 (Volume 8) (pbk)
ISBN: 978-1-003-34888-7 (Volume 8) (ebk)

DOI: 10.4324/9781003348887

Publisher's Note
The publisher has gone to great lengths to ensure the quality of this reprint but points out that some imperfections in the original copies may be apparent.

Disclaimer
The publisher has made every effort to trace copyright holders and would welcome correspondence from those they have been unable to trace.

THE GOVERNMENT OF
BRITISH TRADE UNIONS

A STUDY OF APATHY AND THE DEMOCRATIC PROCESS
IN THE
TRANSPORT AND GENERAL WORKERS UNION

BY

JOSEPH GOLDSTEIN
PH.D.

*with a Foreword by
Arthur Deakin*

LONDON
GEORGE ALLEN AND UNWIN LTD
RUSKIN HOUSE MUSEUM STREET

FIRST PUBLISHED IN 1952

This book is copyright under the Berne Convention. Apart from any fair dealing for the purposes of private study, research, criticism or review, as permitted under the Copyright Act, 1911, no portion may be reproduced by any process without written permission. Enquiry should be made to the publishers

PRINTED IN GREAT BRITAIN
in 12 *point Baskerville type*
by SIMSON SHAND LTD
London and Hertford

To the memory of Harold J. Laski
a great and affectionate teacher

'We have more moral, political, and historical wisdom than we know how to reduce into practice; we have more scientific and economical knowledge than can be accommodated to the just distribution of the produce which it multiplies. The poetry, in these systems of thought, is concealed by the accumulation of facts and calculating processes. There is no want of knowledge respecting what is wisest and best in morals, government, and political economy, or at least what is wiser and better than what men now practise and endure. But we let "*I dare not* wait upon *I would,* like the poor cat in the adage". We want the creative faculty to imagine that which we know; we want the generous impulse to act that which we imagine, we want the poetry of life: our calculations have outrun conception; we have eaten more than we can digest.'

Percy Bysshe Shelley, *A Defence of Poetry* (Porcupine Press, London).

FOREWORD

When the author of this book came to us as a student seeking information about our Union, we gave him free access to our records and introductions to any officer or other person to whom he desired to talk. We made no reservations, either of time or subject-matter, neither did we place any conditions or prohibitions upon him.

Here is his book. It is in no sense official. He has drawn the picture as he sees it. With many of the conclusions he has drawn I am in profound disagreement and he has, I feel, misunderstood what he has seen or, at any rate, failed to assess its significance. Nevertheless, the book illustrates only too well what many of us know—that drawing up a good Constitution and providing the means by which members can make their contribution, is not of itself sufficient.

To those of us who read these pages and who may try to see how it affects his own organization and by what means his own contribution can be improved, I would suggest that any analytical examination of a structure such as the Transport and General Workers Union is worthy of thought and consideration.

I am well aware that this book may arouse some criticism of the Trade Union Movement and of this Union in particular, more especially as the author is a young man and an American, and has set down the position as he sees it, without attempting to describe its economic and social causes.

If criticism comes our way then we shall try to turn it to good account. The Union is a great organization which has been brought into being to serve the interests of its members, and I think it can be claimed, quite fairly, that it has done a great work during the years of its existence and has accomplished much for its members, and provided the type of service which is appreciated throughout the various sections of the Union and by the whole of the Union membership.

A. DEAKIN

PREFACE

This book *could* not have been written or published without the assistance of many individuals personally unknown to me. To live and to work, I, like everyone, depend on others who produce and distribute food, clothing, shelter and knowledge. I rely on the milkman, the policeman, the doctor, the docker, the scientist, the miner, the publisher, the collector of refuse and the collector of internal revenue, the lorry driver, the lumberjack, the statesman and countless others doing their jobs so each can follow his pursuit. My thanks are offered, therefore, to all the members of all the communities who have participated in this work.

This book *would* not have been written, however, without the help of certain individuals, many of whom are known to me personally.

I owe much to the inspiration, guidance, and encouragement which Harold Laski so affectionately bestowed on all of his students. Whatever merits this book may have are in large measure due to his influence. I wish to thank Mrs Laski, too, for the memorable summers we spent in their home, where much of this book was written between wonderful excursions through the libraries on all three floors.

I am grateful to Professor Arthur Wilson, Dartmouth College, who first aroused my interest in the democratic process with his inspiring course in Democratic Thought.

I feel deeply indebted to everyone, teachers, students and staff, at the London School of Economics. In particular I wish to thank Professor Lionel Robbins for the patience and understanding with which he helped me reorient myself to the discipline of academic life during my first year out of the Army at L.S.E. Professor Edward Shils was of immense help in drafting the questionnaire which was used in gathering the material for Part III. I should also like to thank Dr. Ann Bohm for the skill and kindness with which she continually solved administrative difficulties.

To all the members and officers of the Transport and General Workers Union I owe my sincere thanks. Particularly I wish to thank the members of the Branch which is the subject of a major part of this study, for their co-operation and hospitality. They and many others in Area 1 who were so helpful must go unnamed. I should like to express my gratitude to Arthur Deakin, General Secretary, for writing the Foreword and for authorizing the use of much of the material on which this book is based. I owe Ellen McCullough manifold thanks for her unfailing kindness, co-operation and wisdom. To Norman Richards, Stewart Greenhalgh, A. A. Edwards and Alf Chandler I am greatly indebted for many valuable and pleasant hours at Transport House. My thanks also go to Charles Brandon, and his associates of T.G.W.U.'s 'Woodberry' office and to E. Fletcher and Alan Winterbottom of the T.U.C.

Teddy Chester, Steve Graubard, George Halverson, Bob Picus, Ben Roberts, Jake Simmons and other members of our *ad hoc* Anglo-American labour discussion group helped me greatly with their suggestions and criticisms. Gustav Jahoda and Jim Lambek were most helpful in their suggestions for testing the adequacy of the statistical materials employed. My thanks also go to Harry Chester and Bud Mandelstam, to whose constructive criticism I owe much.

For the financial assistance provided under the G.I. Bill and the Fulbright Act, and administered in London by persons sympathetic and aware of the real needs of students, I owe my sincere thanks.

I want to thank Mr. C. A. Furth, of Allen & Unwin Ltd., for his understanding help, and my close friends Curt and Eleanor Farrar, whose interest and encouragement led to this publication.

My Mother and Dad with rare understanding have always helped and encouraged me to do work such as this which I most enjoy. They know, I am sure, how much I appreciate being their son.

Last, but most important, is my wife, who shared in every phase of the making of this book. While I am responsible for its faults, we and all those who have helped are responsible for its virtues.

Most of the material on which this book is based was approved by the University of London for the award of the Ph.D. degree in 1950.

J. G.

'Rooftop', 276 Orange Street,
New Haven, Conn.

May 1951

CONTENTS

TABLES

PART ONE

Chapter 1

INTRODUCTION

In the modern industrial civilization of the mid-twentieth century, efficiency spells division of labour. The minuteness of this division of labour has broken the psychological nexus between the industrial worker and his production. This development has taken place in an Acquisitive Society guided by the profit motive, which, like the division of labour, is no respecter of the individual human being.

At the same time, however, the basic assumption of political thought of the western democracies has been, and is, a respect for the individual as a human being whose liberty and freedom must be guaranteed. But under the prevailing economic philosophy of *laissez faire*, a front for the growth of monopolistic competition, this belief in the freedom of the individual grew amidst inequality which, in effect, made this basic assumption of little meaning in the social and economic relationships between members of the community.

Furthermore, the scope for self-fulfilment on the job has decreased as the degree of mechanization has increased. In spite of several ill-advised attempts in the past to prevent the use of a new technique or a new machine[1], the majority of workers, whether by brain or by hand, are destined to perform routine jobs during their working lives. Though it may one day be possible for many to find fulfilment in industry as it becomes even

---

[1] For example, there are the restrictive practices of the Luddites whose organized movement of machine breaking began in 1811. See G. D. H. Cole, *A Short History of the British Working Class Movement* (Allen & Unwin, 3rd Ed., 1938), Vol. 2, pp. 62–64. Sidney and Beatrice Webb, *The History of Trade Unionism*, 1666–1920 (printed by the Authors for the Trade Unionists of the United Kingdom, 1920 Ed.) Chapter II, p. 87—hereinafter cited as 'Webbs, *History of Trade Unionism*'.

more highly mechanized and technical, the average worker has, for the time being at least, been condemned to do permanent K.P.[1] for the community.

This subordinate status of the worker within the industrial organization is in part a product of advanced industrial techniques and in part a product of the form of industrial ownership, itself a product of the economic philosophy of *laissez faire*. However, a change in the form of ownership through nationalization, for example, will not necessarily alter the situation. No matter what the form of ownership, inherent in modern industrial technology of an interdependent economy is the subordinate status of the average worker in the industrial process. Here is a problem which Trade Unions and parties professing Social Democracy have not yet faced squarely. In a rather confused form the demands for worker control of industry have been and are an expression both of a sense of subordination and a craving for respect[2].

It is necessary to make a clear distinction between the subordinate status of the individual worker in industry as an expression of the hierarchy of authority which the discipline of modern industry demands, and the subordinate status of the individual in the community as a consequence of this expression. The issue of the status of the worker in the community must not be dismissed by pointing out that an ex-lorry driver can become Foreign Secretary in His Majesty's Government, for example. The status of Mr. Bevin was determined by his function as Foreign Secretary. It is the status of the lorry driver, however, as an important member of society because of the fact that he as an individual is serving a need of the community, that requires recognition.

---

[1] 'K.P.'—American Army terminology for Kitchen Police. Generally, enlisted personnel in an army unit are compelled to share the 'dirty work' of kitchen duty.

[2] See Robert A. Dahl, 'Workers' Control of Industry and the British Labour Party', in the *American Political Science Review*, Vol. XLI, No. 5 (October 1947); and 'Industrial Democracy', No. 1 in the *Towards Tomorrow* series of Discussion Pamphlets issued by the Labour Party in 1948.

The fact that most of us have been brought up to understand that the status of the worker, particularly the manual worker (e.g., lorry driver, mill hand, and agricultural labourer), is a subordinate one in the community does not in fact mean that from the community point of view this is true. In reality, the increased interdependence created by the division of labour has made the modern wage earner one of the most important members of modern economic society, particularly in a full-employment economy[1].

Even now, though to a lesser extent, property, income, family and formal education (the opportunities for the last being largely determined by the first three qualifications) have defined for most individuals in the community, particularly in economic and social spheres, their 'rights, privileges, immunities, duties, and obligations . . . and, obversely, . . . the restrictions, limitations, and prohibitions governing' their behaviour[2].

Underlying this structure, there has been and is the insecurity characteristic of an economy precariously riding a trade cycle. The worker as an individual living continually under the threat of being called up by the army of the unemployed found freedom to choose his life's work—in fact, to work at all—extremely limited[3]. This threat and its consequences to wife and family became a real incentive to work, under almost any condi-

[1] Under the photograph of a British coal miner, appearing on the front page of the *Observer*, London, Sunday, January 4, 1948, the following comment is made: 'Upon his efforts depend not only the economic well-being of the country, but also, in some measure, the stabilizing of Europe.'

[2] Chester I. Barnard, 'Functions and Pathology of Status Systems in Formal Organizations', in *Industry and Society*, edited by William F. Whyte (McGraw-Hill, 1946).

[3] Speaking in Glasgow on January 19, 1922, Mr Austin Chamberlain, Chancellor of the Exchequer, said: '. . . Nearly 2,000,000 of our people are unemployed; the trade of the country is stagnant, the purchasing power of Europe does not exist; the whole machinery of exchange and trade has been destroyed.' (As quoted in 'So Ill Remembered', Co-operative Union, Manchester, 1947.) For a specific example, see the Dockers' Inquiry, 1921, which recommended decasualization. The end of casual labour did not come, however, until the Agreement of the Dock Workers (Regulation of Employment) Scheme, 1947.

tions. From the beginning of the nineteenth century on-
wards the worker gradually learned by bitter experience
the advantage of combination to achieve bargaining
power, which he, as an individual, had long ago lost[1].
Thus, from the point of view of the rank and file member,
the Trade Union still continues primarily as a protective
agency, attempting to achieve economic satisfaction and
security for its membership through collective action.

Because the Trade Union Movement has found it
necessary to concentrate its efforts on securing these
material requisites of life above all others, the very important function of attempting to achieve status for the
worker as an individual in society, i.e., within industry,
Trade Unions and the community at large, has been neglected. It cannot be over-emphasized, however, that a
sense of security is pre-requisite to the maintenance of
respect for the individual.

The inequalities thus maintained behind the myth of
laissez faire in the economic sphere, and in the face of
Liberalism in the political sphere[2], were justified by the
acceptance of the concept of subordinate status for and by
the wage earning segment, employed or unemployed, of
the productive element in society[3].

With a recognition of the worker's vital contribution
to the successful culmination of two wars—a time when
the acquisitive character of society is placed in the background—and with a growing realization of the community's dependence on the wage earner in a full employment economy to overcome the crisis of Britain's
'Operation Export' the lie has been vividly put to the
justification of the concept of subordinate status. The
concept, however, has not disappeared, for the guiding
economic philosophy of the past has not given way. In

[1] See Webbs, *History of Trade Unionism.*

[2] See L. T. Hobhouse, *Liberalism* (Oxford University Press, 1944 Ed.).

[3] In an interview with a London housewife this attitude was clearly expressed:
'If you work with your hands you're a commoner. There's no getting away
from it.'

this respect current economic philosophy has not as yet recognized economic reality.

It is this status of the worker as a human being and as a responsible member of the community, contributing to its general welfare, that the guiding economic and social philosophies of the time can gradually adjust, within a democratic framework, to ever-changing conditions. If, to be specific, Social Democracy is to secure its hold and increase its strength it must help the individual achieve, in addition to economic security, social satisfaction and recognition. This may be done by revaluating the status of the individual on a functional basis, in a community devoted to satisfying the requirements of the general welfare. Spheres of respect must be readjusted.

The British Labour Party is pledged to the social democratic philosophy[1]. But, because of an economic crisis in addition to the day-to-day problems of the transitional period, in office, it seems to have lost sight of its goal. In any event it has failed to create continuous interest in what the future can promise. Productive efficiency, admittedly most important to maintaining an adequate standard of life, has to too great an extent obscured the main objectives of democratic socialism. These are the release of the individual as a responsible being in society, as a worker whose productive function is recognized for its contribution to the community, and as a person whose motivation is primarily found in filling the needs of the general welfare[2]. In other words, the indi-

[1] *Let Us Face the Future—A declaration of Labour Policy for the consideration of the Nation* (April 1945), p. 6:

'The Labour Party is a Socialist Party, and proud of it. Its ultimate purpose at home is the establishment of the Socialist Commonwealth of Great Britain—free, democratic, efficient, progressive, public-spirited, its material resources organised in the service of the British people.

'But Socialism cannot come overnight, as the product of a weekend revolution.'

[2] G. D. H. Cole: 'What Socialism Means to Me', in *Labour Forum*, Vol. I, No. 5, Oct.–Dec. 1947, pp. 2–3: 'Socialism, as I see it, is a means of releasing individual initiative and energy in the common service. It involves democracy, not merely in a formal sense and not merely in the form of centralised popular control, but also fused through every part of the social structure, so as to give everyone who is so disposed the fullest possible opportunity of really sharing in the work of government.'

vidual in a social democracy must be taken into consideration; he must be kept informed through a free exchange of information; he must be consulted; and he must be respected[1].

If the objective of Social Democracy is to satisfy the requirements of the general welfare, and if the security of full employment is to be characteristic of this economy, might not the danger that the most vital jobs (from a community point of view) be undermanned, become an incentive for co-operation in production? In other words, will it be possible to replace the fear-incentive of unemployment, which in the past directed labour into the Acquisitive Society's 'necessary' jobs by the danger that what the community needs most may very well be neglected under full employment? This is a real problem which confronts Britain today[2]. Ridicule of eels and butterflies, spivs and drones, and an attempt through 'Control of Engagement' Orders to direct labour is only a short-term answer to the problem of creating a real sense of social responsibility in the individual[3]. Implied in any affirmative answer that this danger may become a dignified incentive are the assumptions that the functional status of the individual in society has received recognition and that the social skill of the individual in what Elton Mayo terms the 'adaptive society' has been equally developed with individual technical skill.

In *The Social Problems of an Industrial Civilization* Mayo carefully develops the thesis that in the *established society*

---

[1] H. D. Lasswell in *The Analysis of Political Behaviour* (Kegan, Paul, Trench, Trubner & Co. Ltd., London, 1948), p. 17, expresses this idea in the term 'to be deferred', which he defines: 'to be taken into consideration, to be consulted, appreciated and clarified.'

[2] *Economic Survey for* 1948, presented to Parliament March 1948, p. 43, § 195: 'In order to reach the manpower targets laid down for agriculture, coal-mining and textiles, there will have to be a considerable movement of workers from one industry to another.' It is calculated that 241,000 workers, the majority of whom are fully engaged in activities which the nation cannot afford to work, must be transferred to production on which export plans depend.

[3] See *Control of Engagement Order*, 1947 (S.R. & O., 1947, No. 2021).

of the apprenticeship system 'stability of techniques went hand in hand with stability in companionship.' He argues that in our present *adaptive society*, in which it is no longer possible to 'assume that the technical processes of manufacture will exist unchanged for long in any type of work', many individuals do not 'sufficiently continue' association anywhere with anyone to develop as formerly a social skill'. 'Social skill', according to Mayo, 'shows itself as a capacity to receive communications from others, and to respond to the attitudes and ideas of others in such fashion as to promote congenial participation in a common task.'[1]

The obstacles to effective two-way communication have been further augmented by the economic crisis in Britain 1945 — ?, which has forced the Labour Government to make Socialist demands of a society whose economy is still essentially based on the profit motive. In appealing for voluntary control of prices and wages in the House of Commons on February 12, 1948, the Chancellor of the Exchequer said: 'And here I would emphasize that this effort must be a national effort of all sections of the people. If any one section seeks to gain an advantage over others, then those others cannot be expected to moderate their demands upon the community. No one is excluded from that national effort, whether they be farmers, small business men, or anybody else.'[2] A spirit of team work is being demanded of all members of the community to a greater extent today, in an era of peace, than ever before[3].

[1] Elton Mayo: *The Social Problems of an Industrial Civilization* (Division of Research, Graduate School of Business Administration, Harvard University, Boston 1945), pp. 13–15.

[2] The *Manchester Guardian*, February 13, 1948, p. 6. See also Ben Roberts: *Trade Unions in the New Era* (International Publishing Co. 1947), p. 15: 'Even when the plans envisaged in "Let Us Face the Future" are put into operation there will not be more than about 20 per cent of workers (excluding the Civil Service) in Government-controlled undertakings.'

[3] (i) See Herbert Morrison's address, 'Labour for Higher Production', to the 46th Annual Labour Party Conference, May 1947; the *Report*, pp. 134–137.

No country today, least of all Britain, can think seriously of returning to the era of apprenticeship to teach man to get on with his fellow worker. Only through a higher degree of industrial efficiency will Britain in the long run be able to solve its economic difficulties. Moreover, mechanization and extreme efficiency offer the individual hope that production will eventually reach a level where leisure will allow him an opportunity to achieve self-fulfilment. Thus, Britain as a nation is not faced with the choice of hindering or aiding the mechanical techniques of industrial development: she is faced with the alternative of achieving economic efficiency and sufficiency at the expense of or in conjunction with the individual. Britain has chosen the less spectacular but more significant alternative of carrying out this social experiment in conjunction with the individual within a democratic framework[1]. Consequently, the individual must be taught to adapt himself to the ever-changing personal relationships created by the demands of a social democracy in a highly industrialized economy.

It is recognized, therefore, that one of the major problems facing Britain, indeed any industrial civilization, is the recreation of the individual as a person, who is respected for what he does, who feels that he is being consulted in the determination of policy, and who is kept constantly informed of what is, in fact, policy. It is with this in mind that we focus our attention on a British

(ii) Sir Stafford Cripps on October 23, 1947, in Parliament: 'Nothing was more important for raising our industrial morale to the high pitch necessary than joint consultation among members of the team.

'We shall find our way to a brighter and more prosperous future all the quicker if we devote ourselves single-mindedly to our country's interests.' (*Daily Telegraph*, October 24, 1947.)

[1] Sir Stafford Cripps at Edinburgh, February 7, 1948, speaking with reference to the Prime Minister's announcement on 'Personal Incomes, Costs and Prices': 'It is therefore essential that we should get a general agreement amongst our people to act upon sound economic lines; the alternative is likely to prove to be some form of totalitarian government.

'The more the citizens understand of the situation, the more certain we are that they will support the right action.' (*Sunday Times*, London, February 8, 1948.)

Trade Union to determine how successfully it functions as a training ground for the development of social skills formerly provided by the apprenticeship system. A basic assumption of this study is that a Union can successfully carry out this function only if it is able to elicit a high degree of member participation in its activities.

The steady progress and growth of British Trade Unions has been recorded and brought up to date many times, with varying degrees of accuracy, since the Webbs first raised this subject to an academic level[1]. At the present time the influence of the Trade Union in Britain in political and economic affairs is greater than ever before in its history. With the development of democratic socialism, it becomes more and more important that the voice of the Trade Union accurately express the majority opinion of its membership. This too makes it essential to appraise the position of the rank and file member within a Union, to determine both the opportunity for and the extent of his participation.

The following questions are to be investigated: To what extent can the individual member of a Trade Union participate in its activities and in the formulation of its policy? To what extent does he take advantage of his opportunities to do so? Does there exist a psychological nexus between the rank and file member, his Union, and official Union policy? To what extent does Trade Union leadership consult its membership and share the responsibility of its duties? In becoming efficient, to what extent has the Trade Union been able to avoid treating its rank and file as cogs in its administrative machinery? Finally, to what extent does the organization and administration of the Trade Union help to develop the social skill of the individual and the social responsibility necessary for the democratic development of Socialism?

It is in an attempt to answer these questions that this

[1] Webbs, *History of Trade Unionism*, first published in 1894.

study is devoted to an investigation of apathy and the democratic process in the government of a British Trade Union.

Chapter 2

THE TRANSPORT AND GENERAL WORKERS UNION

ITS POWER POSITION (1947-1948) IN THE COMMUNITY IN WHICH IT WORKS

For this study I have selected for investigation the Transport and General Workers Union. I do not suggest that this Union is representative of the British Trade Union Movement, though many of the problems it confronts are common to most Trade Unions.

I have singled out this Union for three reasons: it is the largest organized group of workers in the Trade Union Movement in the United Kingdom; it faces obstacles to rank and file participation common to most Trade Unions and voluntary organizations, but magnified because of its size, national character and the divergent interests of its membership; expediency, though last, is not the least important reason. Qualifications for membership are sufficiently wide and the entrance fee plus dues are sufficiently low to have allowed me to join its ranks and participate in its Branch life.

Before turning to the Union's Constitution and Rule Book as a frame of reference in determining the structure of its government, I shall attempt to establish the power position of this Union in the community in which it works.

The Transport and General Workers Union, with a membership of 1,317,000 [December 1947], representing workers in fourteen different Trade Groups[1], is responsible for the livelihood of over 16 per cent of all

[1] The Trade Groups cover docks, waterways, passenger and commercial services, general workers, the building trades, the metal, engineering and chemical industries, administrative and office workers, Government and municipal workers, landworkers, flour-milling, fishing, chemical and power workers, and North Wales quarrymen.

organized labour in the United Kingdom[1]. The Union, a voluntary organization opposed in principle to the 'closed shop'[2], controls 300,000 positions of employment in the United Kingdom on the Docks and in Road Passenger Transport. Two examples will help to make this point clear. The General Secretary, Mr. Arthur Deakin, in reference to an agreement reached by the Union with the London Passenger Transport Board, said to the Scottish Delegate Conference in Edinburgh:

> To describe the agreement reached as providing a 'closed shop' is a gross distortion of the facts. Our members in London simply say they are not prepared to work with people who will not conform to those agreements which have been properly negotiated and approved by the vast majority of the people concerned with the agreements. (September 6, 1946.)

A rank and file docker, addressing London dockers on strike in June 1948, after urging them to return to work in response to the Prime Minister's wireless appeal of the previous evening for a resumption of work, warned:

> There is a movement afoot to get rid of the militants. Remember, Brothers, if we get kicked out of the Union we cannot work.[3]

This means that there are at least 300,000 positions in the United Kingdom that can be held only by workers who are willing to join and remain in good standing with the Transport and General Workers Union[4]. This figure

[1] *Ministry of Labour Gazette*, Nov. 1947, Vol. LV, No. 11, p. 365: 'The total membership (including members of overseas branches) of Trade Unions in the United Kingdom at the end of 1946 was about 8,714,000 . . .', and T.G.W.U. membership as of December 31, 1946 was 1,273,920.

[2] Minutes and Record of the Proceedings of the 11th Biennial Delegate Conference of the T.G.W.U. (Blackpool 1945), Resolutions 31 and 32, pp. 18–19. Resolution favouring the 'closed shop' principle was rejected.

[3] From my notes taken at a meeting convened by the Unofficial Strike Committee on June 29, 1948, in Victoria Park, London.

[4] (a) *Docks*: (i) 'We have maintained our position of 100 per cent membership in the ports where the Union is responsible for organization.' T.G.W.U. Report and Balance Sheet, year ended December 1944, Appendix V, p. 59.
(ii) The National Dock Labour Board, set up under the Dock Workers (Regulation of Employment) Scheme 1947, governs the increase or decrease of the dockers on register. According to the Assistant Financial Secretary of Area 1: 'The Board so operates that anyone being placed on the register must first be in good standing with the Union.'

does not take into account the numerous situations where the 100 per cent Union shop, a recognized objective of Trade Union policy, has been achieved. The late Charles Dukes, Chairman of the T.U.C. in 1946, said:

> It exists today in industries where unionisation is so strong that managements are constrained to recognise that the holding of a Union card is a necessary condition of employment.[1]

A leading official of one of the most important Industrial Federations in the United Kingdom, which has agreements with several of the major Trade Unions, had this to say:

> While the industry does not officially and publicly support the idea of a Closed Shop, it believes strongly in complete Union membership as far as its employees are concerned, chiefly because by this means discipline is maintained and agreements are honoured.
>
> If trouble is likely to be caused in a works by non-unionists or by members of Unions whose subscriptions to the Unions have lapsed and Union officials draw the attention of managements to the position, managements support the Unions even to the extent of suggesting to men of this kind that they would better be employed elsewhere unless they are prepared to join the appropriate Trade Union. In some cases investigations into matters of this kind reveal that a man may not have received fair treatment by his local shop delegate and such investigations sometimes result in putting right local trade union weaknesses. (1947.)[2]

Thus, for an ever-increasing number of workers, the Union is no longer a voluntary organization[3], but rather

---

(b) *Transport*: (i) 'The Union represents practically the whole of the workpeople employed in the transport services of the country, and the power which this gives, though it must never be abused, is extremely vital.' (*The Union, Its Work and Problems*, a T.G.W.U. correspondence course, Part I, p. 29.)

(ii) *Ministry of Labour Gazette*, March 1948, Vol. LVI, No. 3, p. 43: The number employed in the Tramway and Omnibus Services is 257,400. On December 31, 1947, T.G.W.U. membership figures account for 82 per cent of the Tramway and Omnibus Services listed.

[1] 78th Annual Report of the T.U.C., 1946, p. 13.

[2] The writer and Federation which he represents may not be disclosed.

[3] The State, according to H. J. Laski, writing in 1925, 'differs from every other association in that it is, in the first place, an association in which membership is compulsory'. (*Grammar of Politics*, Allen & Unwin Ltd., London 1934, Ed., p. 69.) However, in the light of the above examples, for the many workers who are unwilling to change their trade, the Trade Union is in fact a compulsory organization.

a tax collecting unit to which the individual worker must pay tribute for benefits received and services rendered. At this juncture I do not wish to pass a judgment on the Union's position or that of the individual non-Unionist. I have no other intention than to focus the reader's attention on the power position of the Union in relation to the individual worker and thus emphasize the need for democratic control. For the dynamic of this power is such that increased membership itself increases the Union's power to increase its membership and thus, in turn, its power.

Within the Trades Union Congress, the central organ of the Trade Union Movement in Great Britain, the T.G.W.U. is the most powerful single influence. The Union controls a block vote of more than 1,300,000, which represents close to 20 per cent of the entire vote of Congress[1]. In conjunction with its control of the largest vote of any one affiliated Union, the T.G.W.U. can and does claim four (more than any other single Union) of the thirty-five seats on the T.U.C. General Council[2]. In the International Trade Union Movement it has direct affiliation with the International Transport Workers' Federation and the International Metal Workers Federation. Through its affiliation with the T.U.C. the Union is associated with the World Federation of Trade Unions, of which Mr. Arthur Deakin, General Secretary of the T.G.W.U., is President[3].

[1] Total membership of the T.U.C.: 7,540,397. 76th Annual Report (Southport 1947), p. 57.

[2] T.U.C. 76th Annual Report, p. 3. Officers of the Trades Union Congress General Council 1948: Miss Florence Hancock, Chairman; Mr. A. F. Papworth and Mr. A. Deakin of the T.G.W.U. and Mr. R. J. Jones of the North Wales Quarrymen's Union. As the North Wales Quarrymen's Union amalgamated with the T.G.W.U. in 1923, and is included in Area 13 of the Union, it is legitimate to say that the T.G.W.U. holds four seats on the Council.

[3] (i) T.G.W.U. Report and Balance Sheet for the year ended December 1946, p. 14.

(ii) On January 19, 1949, however, the British T.U.C., the American C.I.O. and the Dutch N.V.V. (three non-Communist representatives) withdrew from the W.F.T.U. (*Free Trade Unions Leave the W.F.T.U.*, published by the T.U.C., 1949, p. 5.)

In the political life of the Labour Movement this Union exercises considerable influence, nationally and locally. At the 47th Annual Labour Party Conference held at Scarborough in 1948, the T.G.W.U. accounted for 17 per cent of the total party membership and for 20 per cent of the Trade Union membership represented at the Conference[1]. Of the 394 Labour members returned to Parliament in the General Election of 1945, twenty-one were officially listed and supported by the T.G.W.U. Parliamentary Group.

In addition, eighteen Union members bring to forty the Union's representation in Parliament within the Labour Party. Union members (January 1948) hold the offices of Foreign Secretary, Secretary of State for Scotland, Secretary of State for the Colonies, Civil Lord of the Admiralty, Minister of Works and Parliamentary Under-Secretary at the Home Office. Three members hold Parliamentary Private Secretaryships[2]. The Parliamentary Group meets at regular intervals and maintains close contact with the Union on matters of particular interest to Union members.

Thus, at present, it is evident that the T.G.W.U., an amalgamation of fifty-one separate Unions, has power which extends far beyond the negotiation of wages and conditions in any one factory or any particular industry.

(iii) On November 28, 1949, a 'Free World Labour Conference' convened in London to form the 'International Confederation of Free Trade Unions', of which the T.U.C. is a founding member. Mr. Arthur Deakin and Miss Florence Hancock, both of the T.G.W.U., were among the T.U.C.'s ten delegates to this conference.

[1] Report of the National Executive Committee to the 47th Annual Conference of the Labour Party (Scarborough 1948), p. 26: Total membership, December 31, 1947, 4,685,659; Trade Union membership: 4,031,434. T.G.W.U. membership affiliated to the Labour Party, December 31, 1947, is 800,000, according to the Political, Research, Education and International Department of the T.G.W.U., June 1948.

[2] 'T.G.W.U. Report and Balance Sheet for the year ended 1946' pp. 128–129, and 'The House of Commons 1945–1947' (issued January 1948 by the London *Times*): Those holding Government offices in order as listed above are: Ernest Bevin, Arthur Woodburn, A. Creech Jones, W. J. Edwards, C. W. Key, George Oliver, George Brown, W. H. Oldfield, P. L. Walls. Some of these men, though still Union members, have not maintained contact with the Union for some years.

This Union is a force which has influence and prestige not only amongst its members, but within the national and international Trade Union Movement, within the Government and the Labour Party, in the economy of the United Kingdom and, most important of all, in the every-day lives of each and every one of us.

The source of this power is primarily derived from the Union's enormous membership. It is on the source of this power that attention must, in the final analysis, be focused in order to determine whether or not it can be and is responsible for the voice which speaks and acts on its behalf.

Chapter 3

THE UNION IN THEORY

AN ANALYSIS OF THE RULES AND CONSTITUTION OF THE T.G.W.U.

Before turning to this 'state within a state'[1] in action, to determine the extent to which the lay membership participates in the government of its organization, we must first ask: *Does the Constitution of the T.G.W.U. provide for a democratic Trade Union Government?* In using the Rules and Constitution of this Union as a frame of reference to answer this over-all question[2], I shall attempt to answer the following:

I WHO CAN JOIN THE UNION?
II WHAT IS THE NATURE OF THE MEMBERSHIP WHICH THE UNION'S STRUCTURE IS DESIGNED TO SERVE?
III WHO MAKES UNION POLICY?
IV WHO EXECUTES UNION POLICY?
V WHO CAN HOLD OFFICE?
VI WHO IS ENTITLED TO VOTE?

I WHO CAN JOIN THE UNION?

Persons of either sex are admitted to the Union without regard to political affiliation, race or religion[3]. As it is common practice in industry to discriminate in the payment of wages as between men and women, the main

[1] In the preface to the 1894 edition of *The History of Trade Unionism*, p. ix, the Webbs use this phrase in the following passage: 'The history of Trade Unionism is the history of a State within our State, and one so jealousy democratic that to know it well is to know the English working man as no reader of middle class histories can ever know him.'

[2] All references to Rules, unless otherwise indicated, are taken from: 'Rules of the Transport and General Workers Union, November 1942', with amendments attached as of October 23, 1947.

[3] Rule 2, Clause 2, Sec. (*a*), p. 6; and Rule 18, Clause 2, p. 42.

scales of contributions in the Union's complex schedule of contributions and benefits authorize a lower rate of dues for women workers[1]. Though unfair in appearance, its reasonableness cannot be contested until there is nation-wide acceptance of the policy of equal pay for equal work, which the Labour Party, the T.U.C., and most Unions, including the T.G.W.U. support and are committed to[2]. The only obligation common to every member of the Union is that he pay his dues in order to remain a member.

II WHAT IS THE NATURE OF THE MEMBERSHIP WHICH THE UNION'S STRUCTURE IS DESIGNED TO SERVE?

Workers, 'semi-skilled' and 'unskilled' (though in fact possessing considerable skill and ability), from a wide variety of trades and industries throughout the United Kingdom constitute the T.G.W.U.'s membership. Within the Union's ranks are found Englishmen and Welshmen, Scotsmen and Irishmen, Cockneys and Cumbrians, Manx and Mancunians, who earn their living as dockers and dairy workers, bus conductors and builders, cab drivers and chemical workers, steel benders and ships clerks, flour millers and foresters, tram drivers and tugmen—to mention but a few.

In order to reconcile conflicting loyalties among different trades and among different areas and to compose the differences between Unions amalgamating, the structure of the organization was designed to give representation to the membership on a trade as well as

[1] Schedule of Contributions and Benefits, pp. 75–102—a highly complex system incorporating various scales and benefits of many of the Unions amalgamated with the T.G.W.U.

[2] (i) *Report of 46th Annual Conference of the Labour Party* (Margate 1947), pp. 157–9: A memorable event—Mrs E. M. White, elderly suffragette, convinced Conference to reject the advice of the National Executive. Vote for: 2,310,000; against: 598,000.

(ii) 79th *Annual Report* (T.U.C., Southport 1497), Minute 10, p. 579—'Equality of pay and opportunity.'

(iii) T.G.W.U. Minutes and Record of the Proceedings of the 12th Biennial Delegate Conference (Hastings, July 1947), Minute 99, p. 42.

geographic basis. Thus, to secure unity and sound administration, the Constitution provides adequate means
for linking Trade Group bodies with territorial bodies.
Accordingly, within each of the thirteen separate geographic areas into which the membership is divided,
fourteen different Trade Groups (of which only twelve
are active) are furnished with Committees to deal with
problems unique to workers within their particular
Group.

In satisfying the demands of divergent interests, a
large degree of decentralization of power is allowed for,
in order to create communities of interest. However, the
need for greater centralization, due in large part to the
growth of national agreements and national combina-
tions on the employers' side, as well as the general trend
to handle industrial problems on a national basis, was a
principal cause of the formation of this Union in 1922,
and had to be met[1]. For this reason, a General Council
with a lay membership representing every Territorial
Area and every Trade Group was created to exercise,
with the General Secretary, control over the entire
organization. On the administrative side an office was
set up in which each National Trade Group has its own
department, in addition to a Central Finance Department, the editorial office of the Union's Journal, a Legal
Department, and a Political, Research, Education and
International Department.

To sum up: a well designed structure has been created
in which a large degree of decentralization, devised to
satisfy the dual loyalty of the membership, is balanced by
centralization which efficiency and the extent of combination and concentration in British industry made
essential.

---

[1] Rule 3, pp. 9–11: 'The Union, Its Work and Problems', Part I: '4 T.U.C.
Documents' (approved by Blackpool Conference, 1945), No. 4, pp. 48–56.

III WHO MAKES UNION POLICY?

As a guide to the discussion of the government of the Union's body politic, an organizational chart, which appears in the *T.G.W.U. Members Handbook*, is reproduced below with slight re-arrangement.

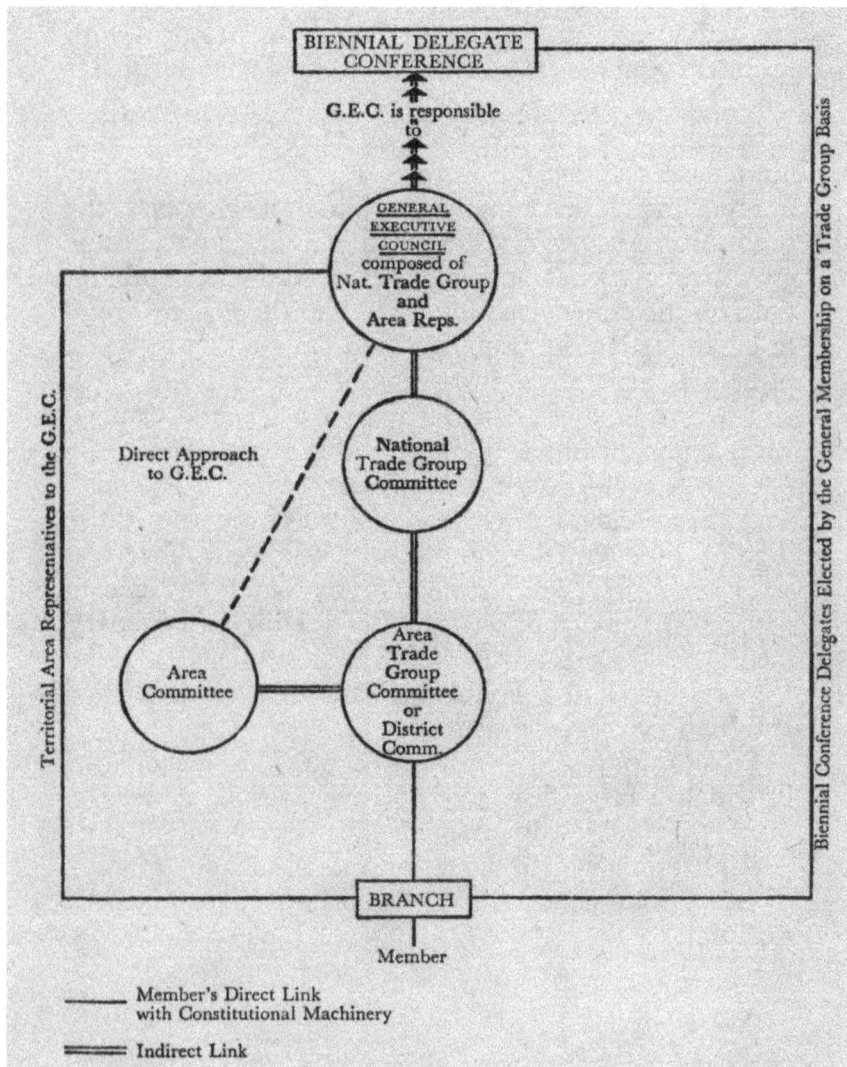

The key to the answer to the question 'Who makes Union policy?' is to be found in Clause 8 of the Constitution and Government, which reads:

> The general policy of the Union shall, subject to the Biennial Delegate Conference, be determined by the General Executive Council, but the policy of every area or trade shall, within the powers delegated to an area or national or area trade group committee by these rules or by the General Executive Council, be determined by such area or national or area trade group committee.[1]

A. *Supreme Policy-making Body—The Biennial Delegate Conference*

As in most national Unions in the United States, the supreme constitutional authority is the convention[2]. Within the T.G.W.U. this legislative body is designated the 'Biennial Delegate Conference'.

> The government of the Union and the appointment of its trustees, and the power to make, amend, and revoke the rules of the Union and its constitution, shall be vested only in a Biennial Delegate Conference. [In the event of a strike involving all the members of the Union or two or more national Trade Groups the General Executive Council must convene the Conference in special session.][3]

Essential to an understanding of the supreme authority of the Conference is its obligation to form an Appeals Committee to hear and decide appeals from the General Executive Council[4]. Decisions of the G.E.C. which are subject to appeal include cases involving the expulsion from office of a member of the General Executive Council; the suspension or dismissal of officers (excepting cases of dismissal because of an attempt to disrupt the organization by advocating, or threatening, secession, or

[1] Rule 3, Clause 8, p. 11.
[2] See Sumner H. Slichter, *The Challenge of Industrial Relations* (Cornell University Press, N.Y., 1947), pp. 103-4.
[3] Rule 4, Clause 1, p. 12; Clause 13, p. 15. It should be noted that this only applies in the event of strikes *sanctioned* by the General Executive Council, and would exclude 'unofficial' strikes. See Rule 5, Clause 15, p. 21.
[4] Rule 4, Clause 10, p. 14.

creating a rival organization[1], or because of mis-appropriation of Union funds); the removal of a Branch Chairman or Secretary from office because of mis-conduct, and the expulsion or suspension of a lay member. Decisions made by this supreme board of review are absolute. The Appeals Committee of six is elected by and from the delegates to the Conference[2].

The Conference is composed of delegates elected by ballot vote by and from the rank and file on a Trade Group basis within each Area. This representation is achieved by empowering every Branch 'to nominate a member of two years' standing who is in financial benefit' as a candidate for the office of delegate from its Trade Group or Trade Groups[3].

The number of delegates to which an Area Trade Group is entitled is in proportion to the size of its membership. The General Executive Council may be represented by only three of its members who, like full-time officials present, may 'speak upon but shall not vote on any subject'. Each delegate holds office for the two-year period between conferences, for a special Delegate Conference may be convened in any emergency if the General Executive so desires[4].

Thus, through this supreme policy-making body, in which decisions are the sole prerogative of delegates elected by popular vote, authoritative control is returned to the general membership from which it was secured. In its authority to review and make decisions on major

[1] Rule 5, Clause 10, p. 19.

[2] Rule 4, Clause 10, p. 14.

[3] The term 'in financial benefit' is defined: member who has not been in arrears for more then six weeks continuously during the two years prior to the date of nomination. (Schedule I, Clause 1, p. 52; and Schedule II, Sec. (e), p. 56.) See also Rule 4, Clause 2, p. 12.

[4] Rule 4, Clause 2: 'Every area trade group shall be entitled to one delegate at the Conference for every thousand members of that area trade group up to 5,000 members or one delegate where the membership is 1,000 or less, and where the membership exceeds 5,000 members one additional delegate for every 2,000 members.' See also Clause 4, p. 13.

issues determined by the General Executive Council it is closely linked to this unit of organization, to whose hands the real government of the Union on a national level is entrusted.

B. *National Policy-making Bodies*
1. *The General Executive Council*

The General Executive Council is charged with the overall government of Union business. Through the location of power in this national unit of organization the need for a centralized authority to determine general policy, without delaying until a statutory convening of a Biennial Delegate Conference, is satisfied. The principal functions for which the Council is responsible may be classified as follows:

(*a*) The supervision and control of the Union's finances, property and investments. (A Finance and General Purposes Committee of eight members elected by and from the Council is specifically responsible for this function and meets monthly. Actually, this committee meets more frequently and might be described as the Inner Cabinet of the Union.)

(*b*) The supervision, in general, of the business of all Union Committees and Branches to insure that the work of the Union is being administered according to the Rules.

(*c*) The authorization of strike action (with two exceptions for which the B.D.C. is responsible).

(*d*) The appointment of all permanent, full-time, paid officials of the Union (with the exception of the General Secretary, who is elected by ballot), the fixing of their powers, duties and terms of employment.

(*e*) The dismissal of any officer subject to review by the B.D.C. Committee of Appeal, except in special cases.

(*f*) The endorsement of Union Parliamentary Candidates and determination of the amount of money to be paid from the political fund in support of each endorsed candidate[1].

(g) The consideration and disposal of all appeals and resolutions addressed to it from Branches, Area and National Trade Groups, and Area Committees.

(h) The delegation of any of its powers, excluding the power to order or sanction a strike involving the whole Union membership, deemed necessary in the general interests of the Union, to the General Secretary or to any National or Area Trade Group or Area Committee. These powers may be modified or revoked[2].

The inclusion of this last function, or rather power, provides the organization with a high degree of flexibility so essential in governing a body the size and nature of which is continually changing.

The composition of the General Executive Council mirrors the dual character of the Union by merging its functional and geographic basis. The executive Councillors are lay members of the Union who are either elected by ballot vote from each Territorial Area, which is entitled to representation in proportion to the size of

[1] Under the Hastings Agreement the Labour Party set a maximum annual contribution that an affiliated Trade Union may make per constituency in which the Union has officially endorsed a Parliamentary candidate; the '1948 Report of the National Executive Committee to the 47th Annual Conference of the Labour Party', p. 7: At this Conference the maximum set at Hastings was increased from £200 in Boroughs and £250 in County Divisions to £250 and £300 respectively. From an interview with Miss E. McCullough, Officer in charge of the Political, Research, Education and International Department of the T.G.W.U. (hereinafter referred to as 'Miss E. McCullough of the T.G.W.U. Education Department'), July 1948.

[2] Rule 5, Clause 1, p. 15: Clauses 7–17, pp. 7–22 (General Executive Council). Examples of delegation of power are to be found in Members Handbook, p. 27:

(a) The Education Committee is charged with the responsibility of directing the Union's educational work.

(b) The appointment of special Committees to sit jointly with executive representatives of other Unions for the purpose of regulating relationships.

(c) The setting up of examining Committees in relation to official Union appointments.

(d) The Council refers complex issues to special sub-committees for examination and report, reserving to itself the right of final decision.

All these Committees are subject to the over-riding authority of the Council.

its financial membership[1], or are elected by and from
the National Trade Group Committees, each of which
is entitled to one representative[2]. The life of the G.E.C.
is for a two-year period. It meets quarterly for approximately a full week, at which time the representatives are
paid on a per diem basis in compensation for time lost at
work.

To sum up: The General Executive Council is the
Union's most powerful central authority responsible for
the continuous co-ordination and review of the Union's
industrial and political policy. It is ultimately responsible to the B.D.C. on the one hand; on the other it is
directly linked on a national level with the National
Trade Group Committees[3].

2. *National Trade Group Committees*
To fulfil the need for a co-ordinating body on a national
level to determine the broad outlines of industrial policy
within each of the fourteen Trade Groups provisions are
made for the creation of National Trade Group Committees. Specifically, the Rules hold these Committees
responsible for the supervision of the Union's business
relative to rates of pay and working conditions in their
respective trades. Each Committee elects one of its number to serve upon the General Executive Council.
Limitations on their authority should be noted. They

[1] Rule 18, Clause 9, p. 43: 'A financial member is a member with not less than
26 weeks' membership, having made 26 weekly payments, and who is not more
than six weeks in arrears.' Rule 5, Clause 2, Sec. (a), p. 15: 'One representative
from each Territorial Area with a membership of 50,000 or less; two representatives from each Territorial Area with a membership of more than 50,000 up to
150,000; and three territorial representatives from each Territorial Area with a
membership of more than 150,000.'
[2] Rule 5, Clause 2, Sec. (b), p. 16.
[3] The present composition of the G.E.C. is: three members each from Areas 1 and
5; one member from Area 10; and two members each from the remaining ten
Areas. There are twelve Trade Group representatives. This brings the size of the
Council to a total of thirty-nine, excluding three Trustees and three Executives
who are non-voting members.
(Interview with Miss E. McCullough of the T.G.W.U. Education Department,
1948.)

cannot authorize strike action, nor do they have any powers in relation to finance.

Members of Committees are elected by and from Area Trade Group Committees to hold office for the same period as the General Executive Council. Meetings are held quarterly[1].

Thus, while each National Trade Group Committee is subject to the over-riding authority of the General Executive Council reviewing the Union's industrial policy as a whole, it is charged with co-ordinating the activities and reconciling the divergent interests of the Area Trade Group Committees to which it is directly linked.

C. *Area Policy-making Bodies*
As on the national level, there are two major policy-making units of organization. These are called Area Committees and Area Trade Group Committees.

1. *Area Committees*
Area Committees are responsible for the administration of the general business of the Union within a Territorial Area[2]. Their work parallels to a large extent that of the General Executive Council's on a national level. Their main functions include:

(*a*) The organization of groups within the Area.

(*b*) The co-ordination of work and action taken by the Area Trade Groups within their jurisdiction.

(*c*) The supervision of such Union business as affects all sections of the membership within the Area. General industrial movements, political administration and educational work are specifically mentioned.

(*d*) The consideration of any dispute arising in the Area for the purpose of making a report with recom-

[1] Rule 6, Clause 2, p. 23: 'Where a District Committee system operates in place of Group Committees, the Area Committee shall determine the method of selecting representatives for the National Trade Group Committees.' See also Rule 7, pp. 24–25.

[2] For the thirteen Territorial Areas into which the Union is divided, see Members Handbook, Appendix III, p. 54.

mendations to the General Executive Council.

(*e*) The supervision of Area finances.

The members of Committee are elected by and from members serving on each of the Area Trade Group Committees. Each Area Trade Group is entitled to representation in proportion to the size of its membership. Members hold office for the same period as the General Executive Council (two years) during which time they meet at least once a quarter[1].

2. *Area Trade Group Committees*

Area Trade Group Committees are provided for the supervision of the trade affairs of members in each Group, within each of the thirteen Territorial Areas. These Committees are primarily concerned with the development of organization and with the over-looking of all wage movements and conditions of employment within their particular Trades[2].

They are to be consulted in 'all matters directly affecting the interests of the Group' and are to submit reports and suggestions to their National Trade Group Committee. Thus Branches send forward resolutions on trade or organizational matters for review and to determine whether or not local action is in line with national policy. Of utmost importance in the Union's system of representation is the authority to elect by and from themselves representatives to Area Committee and their National Trade Group Committee.

The size of Committee is determined by the G.E.C. Members are elected by ballot vote by and from the lay membership employed in a trade coming within the scope of the Trade Group. Members hold office for the

---

[1] Rule 7, pp. 24–25: '. . . on a basis of one representative for every thousand members . . . but no area trade group committee shall be entitled to more than three representatives on the area committee.' (Clause 2.)

[2] Under certain circumstances District Committees representative of all the trades in a particular district replace the Area Trade Group Committees and assume similar functions. Rule 5, Clause 9, Sec. (c), p. 18, authorizes the G.E.C. to establish District Committees.

life of a G.E.C. and meet quarterly.

The Area Trade Group Committees are directly linked to the National Trade Group Committee (covering workers from a particular trade in all areas) at top level, to the Area Committee on an area level, and on the other side are directly linked through ballot vote and trade communication to the Branch and thus to the individual member[1].

D. *The Branch*

Underlying this hierarchy of policy-making bodies is the Branch. This is the Union's basic unit of organization, to one of which every member is attached. In the final analysis, all higher and more centralized levels of authority draw their membership from the Branch.

Branches are required to meet at least once a month in order to fulfil their main function, i.e., to act as the main channel of (two-way) communication between the individual member and higher levels of Union organization. The work of the Branch covers a wide field and includes both policy-initiating and policy-executing responsibilities:

(*a*) The reading and consideration of all documents received from Central and Area Offices. This implies the right of the Branches to discuss any matter of Union interest and to express their views in formal resolutions to higher and the highest levels of authority in the Union's organization.

(*b*) The initiation of discussion on any matter by submitting resolutions to the B.D.C.—the supreme policy-making body of the Union—as well as to the G.E.C. and lesser Constitutional Committees.

(*c*) The nomination of candidates for delegates to the B.D.C., and representatives to the G.E.C. and the Area Trade Group Committees to be elected by ballot vote, as

---

[1] Rule 8, Clauses 1–8, pp. 25–26; T.G.W.U. Members Handbook, Chapter IV, 'The Union's Industrial Machinery', pp. 15–17.

well as the nomination of candidates for the position of General Secretary, the only permanent official to be elected by ballot.

(*d*) Subject to the approval of the General Executive Council, authorization to affiiliate itself with local Labour Parties and local Trades Councils[1].

(*e*) The election of Branch officials.

(*f*) In general, the supervision of all Branch business that may arise, including the collecting of Union moneys and the method of appointment of Shop Stewards and Collectors[2].

For the government of the Branch, Rules provide for the election by and from the Branch membership for a two-year period of a Branch Chairman, a Branch Secretary and a Branch Committee. The Chairman is primarily responsible for the conduct of meetings in accordance with the Constitution. The Branch Secretary keeps the financial accounts of the Branch, maintains the correspondence and records the Minutes of each meeting[3]. The Branch Committee, in co-operation with the Branch officers, is directly responsible for the management of the Branch.

Two types of Branch are recognized:

A. The Trade Group Branch: all members of the particular Branch belong to the same Trade Group.

B. The Composite Branch: Members of a particular Branch represent more than one Trade Group.

The Rules provide that a Branch shall consist of at

[1] A Trades Council is an organization composed of representatives of various Trade Unions operating in a given locality. Trades Councils are intended to act as local agents of the T.U.C. Detailed statistics on Trades Councils do not exist and the degree of disorganization in the Trades Councils' Movement is well known. See: 'The Final Report' of the T.U.C. entitled 'Trade Union Structure and Closer Unity' (March 1947); and T.U.C. Handbook, 'Trades Councils Guide' (May 1948).

[2] The duty of a Shop Steward or Collector is 'to collect members' contributions, record same in the book provided, and pay into the Branch the actual amounts collected at least once a week'. Rule 9, Clause 4, p. 27.

[3] Rule 10, Clause 7, p. 34: A permanent Branch Secretary may be appointed if the size of the Branch warrants.

least fifty members unless otherwise authorized by the
G.E.C. Every member is attached to a Branch[1].

Thus it can be seen that the Branch is the base upon
which the entire structure of the organization is built.
The extent to which all higher Constitutional bodies are
representative of the membership is dependent upon the
amount of participation by rank and file members in
their Branch activities. The Branch is directly connected
to the Biennial Delegate Conference, the General Executive Council and the Area Trade Group Committees on
one side; on the other stands the individual member,
who is the Branch.

IV   WHO EXECUTES UNION POLICY?

A. *Permanent Full-time Union Officials*

Corresponding to each of the Constitutional Committees
on the national and area level, provisions are made for
the appointment (not election) of permanent, full-time,
paid officials to carry out the policy determined by
these lay bodies. The only exception in method of selection is the General Secretary of the Union, who is
elected by ballot vote to hold office 'during the pleasure
of the Union'.

The Constitution provides for officials at all policy-
making levels without specifically indicating the number
of officials authorized. The required flexibility is recognized by providing the General Executive Council with
the authority to create new offices and appoint additional officers, after consulting the appropriate Constitutional Committees with reference to the nature and
conditions of any proposed appointment.

Included among the permanent paid officials specifically mentioned in the Rule Book are:

(*a*) General Secretary.

(*b*) Financial Secretary.

(*c*) Assistant General Secretary.

[1] Rules 9, 10, 11, pp. 26–36; 'The Union, its Work and Problems', Part II, pp. 5–7.

(d) National Secretaries of Trade Groups.
(e) Organizers.
(f) Area Secretaries[1].

Officers not originally mentioned but now a part of the organization include the following:

(a) National Women's Officer.
(b) Legal Officer.
(c) Political, Research, Education and International Officer[2].

The execution of Union policy is in the hands of the professional Union official. In recognition of the need for efficiency in the day-to-day administration of the Union's affairs a full-time body of officers and staff has been authorized to complement the Union's constitutional policy-making bodies at all levels.

B. *The General Secretary*

Unlike the Presidents of many American Unions, the General Secretary of the T.G.W.U. has rather limited powers[3]. According to the Rule Book the General Secretary will 'act generally under the orders of the General Executive Council'. He is to perform all duties laid down by the General Executive Council and is to supervise the work of the Union in all departments. The General Secretary has the right to speak on any business at conferences or at meetings of the General Executive Council. He has no authority to appoint officials, but can engage staff, such as shorthand typists, under the supervision of the General Executive Council[4].

It is evident that the officer holding the most im-

[1] Rule 13, p. 38; Rule 17, pp. 41–42.

[2] Minutes and Record of the Proceedings of the Twelfth Biennial Conference (July 1947), Appendix II, Lists of Delegates and Officers, p. 60.

[3] See Sumner H. Slichter, *The Challenge of Industrial Relations* (Cornell University Press, 1947), especially pp. 107–109 and Appendices D and E. In fifty-six out of eighty-eight A.F. of L. Unions the appointment of national representatives is made by the President. The power of dismissal in many cases is the prerogative of the President.

[4] Rule 14, p. 39.

portant executive and administrative position in the government of the Union must, in the final analysis, rely on the General Executive Council for his authority.

V   WHO CAN HOLD OFFICE?

Every candidate for any office in the Union, paid or unpaid, full-time or part-time, delegate to B.D.C. or representative on any Constitutional Committee, including the General Executive Council, must have been a financial member of the Union for at least two years prior to the date of nomination or application for appointment. There are three exceptions to these qualifications: Applicants for the position of Docks' Officer must have at least five years practical experience as dock workers or riverside workers. To be eligible for nomination for General Secretary, an applicant must have been a financial member of the Union for at least five years preceding the selection of candidates. The candidate for the position of Financial Secretary must have been a financial member for at least 10 years prior to making application. A financial member is one who in the period stipulated has not been more than six continuous weeks in arrears in the payment of Union dues[1].

However, there is some measure of discrimination. Rule 9, Clause 12, states:

> No member of the Union who is an employer or is keeping, managing, or assisting in managing a public-house or beer shop, or other place where intoxicants are sold, shall be eligible to hold any office in the Union without the sanction of the General Executive Council.[2]

The General Executive Council, as previously stated, may dismiss any officer, subject to review by the Board of Appeal of the Biennial Delegate Conference.

---

[1] Rules 4, 5, 6, 7, 8 and 9, pp. 12–32; Rules 13, 14, 15, 16 and 17, pp. 38–42; Schedule I, Clause 1, p. 52.

[2] Since writing this the 1949 B.D.C. extended this discrimination when it decided to amend the Rules so that no member of the Communist Party be eligible to hold any office in the Union. (Rules, Amended August 19, 1949, Schedule I (2), p. 56.)

VI WHO IS ENTITLED TO VOTE?

Any person who has been a member for at least thirteen weeks, who has paid at least thirteen weeks contributions and who is not at the time of voting more than thirteen weeks in arrears is entitled to vote by ballot.

Any member, without the above qualifications, may vote on non-ballot issues by show of hand if he is in attendance at his Branch. This covers, *inter alia*, voting for Branch officials and on resolutions[1].

Having outlined the Rules and Constitution of the Union, it is now essential to return to the question originally posed: 'Does the Constitution of the T.G.W.U. provide for a democratic Trade Union government?'

If 'democratic' means 'that everything which "concerns all should be decided by all", and that each citizen should enjoy an equal and identical share in the government'[2] the answer is quite clearly: 'No'. If, however, 'democratic' means that all qualified persons are admitted to the Union without discrimination because of political affiliation, race or religion, the answer is: 'Yes.' If 'democratic' means that there are adequate methods of securing membership representation in the government of the Union by electing policy-makers to power, the answer is: 'Yes.' If 'democratic' means that lay Committees are established at all levels of operation for consultation with and guidance of the Union's permanent, paid officials, the answer is: 'Yes.' If 'democratic' means that there are channels of communication through which the membership can be informed of Union policy and action, and through which the full-time official as well as the lay representative can be made aware of rank and file reaction, the answer is: 'Yes.' If 'democratic' means that there is equal opportunity,

[1] Rule 11, p. 36.

[2] Sidney and Beatrice Webb, *Industrial Democracy* (Longmans, Green and Co. Ltd., London, 1926), Chapter I, 'Primitive Democracy', p. 36.

within certain clearly defined limits, for all members to achieve positions of leadership in the Union, the answer is: 'Yes.'

Thus, using the Constitution and Rules as a frame of reference, it is evident that the government of the Union is that of a representative democracy. The Constitution provides a government of the membership, for the membership, and by the membership's elected representatives. The chain of action leading to positions of power in all cases starts at Branch level. The organization is so designed that the successful operation of its body politic, in contradistinction to its operation as an economic creature, depends upon a well-informed membership anxious to participate in its government. This distinction, moreover, is in the final analysis an academic one, for a Union's economic power in time of crisis depends upon its internal strength[1].

The principal points of emphasis here are that the Constitution of the T.G.W.U. provides ample opportunity for the rank and file member to participate in its activities and in the formulation of its policy, and that the success of its system of representation depends upon a high degree of member participation at Branch level. If the process of participation breaks down at Branch level, the representative character of the Union's governmental structure is open to question.

How far the actual operation of the Union departs from the formal provisions of the Rule Book and the highly idealised concept of the Union as presented in the Members Handbook, will be discussed in relation to apathy, a curse to democratic organisations and a blessing to those seeking power.

[1] The failure of the T.G.W.U. to control the activities of its London Dockers is an example of the Union's loss of influence with a section of its membership, and thus its inability to control in time of crisis the economic power it claims. Some of the implications of the London Dock Strike (June 1948), are discussed in Chapter 4.

PART TWO

Ballot-box democracy, where people go and vote—if they can be bothered and persuaded and shoved around to go and vote—every few years and do nothing much in between, is out of date. . . . Too many of our so-called democratic institutions are little better than shams which are run by small minorities in the name of large bodies of citizens who take not the least practical interest. In some cases this leads to cliques or sinister groups getting control of impressive-looking organisations and exploiting them for wrong purposes—as the Communists are so fond of doing. But even where this does not happen it is wrong and demoralising to put up with low standards of citizenship. Where such low standards prevail, corruption, or apathy, or sudden panics, or movements inspired perhaps by vested interests or irresponsible groups can find a happy hunting ground.—The Rt. Hon. Herbert Morrison.
(Report of the Forty-seventh Annual Conference of the Labour Party (Scarborough, May 1948), p. 132.)

Chapter 4

AN INTRODUCTION TO THE PROBLEM
OF APATHY

Apathy in the Trade Union Movement means nothing more nor less than a lack of interest or participation—intentional or unintentional—on the part of the individual member, in his Trade Union's activities. If the term 'apathetic' can with justice be applied to a large proportion of a Trade Union's membership, there is reason to believe that the democratic base on which the organization rests is being undermined.

Apathy is not a new problem for democratic associations; in particular it is not a new problem for Trade Unions. In the 1870's Tom Mann, one of the best-known of early Trade Union leaders, reported:

> The true Unionist policy of aggression seems entirely lost sight of: in fact, the average Unionist of today is a man with a fossilised intellect, either hopelessly apathetic, or supporting a policy that plays directly into the hands of the capitalist exploiter. . . .[1]

In the 1890's the Webbs wrote:

> Only in the crisis of some great dispute do we find the branch meetings crowded, or the votes at all commensurate with the total number of members. At other times the Trade Union appears to the bulk of its members either as a political organisation whose dictates they are ready to obey at Parliamentary and other elections, or as a mere benefit club in the management of which they do not desire to take part.[2]

News of apathy and complaints about an apathetic membership, however, are most numerous when those in power find their authority challenged by a small minority. Protestations are made and warnings are issued by men who, in fact, may have achieved positions of power by

[1] Quoted in the Webbs, *History of Trade Unionism*, p. 384. Tom Mann was at one time leader of the Dock, Wharf, Riverside and General Labourers Union, which was one of the fourteen Unions to form the T.G.W.U. in 1921.

[2] Webbs, *History of Trade Unionism*, p. 465.

60

taking advantage of this very apathy. In their *History of Trade Unionism* Sidney and Beatrice Webb describe the relationship between the Trade Union Movement and the Labour Party as one might describe, with qualifications, the situation of which the Communist Party seeks to take advantage within the Movement today:

> The very basis of the Labour Party, upon which alone it has proved possible to build up a successful force—the combination, within a political federation, of Trade Unions having extensive membership and not very intensive political energy, and Socialist societies of relatively scanty membership but overflowing with political talent and zeal—necessarily led to complications. (p. 688.)

Today, these complications appear in bold relief. To Trade Union and Labour Party leaders apathy means chiefly one thing. It means that the Communist Party may be able to gain control of that large body of organized workers from which, to a great extent, their power is derived[1]. Apathy, though at one time a stepping stone to control, has taken the shape of a headstone under which their authority might be buried. Arthur Deakin, General Secretary of the T.G.W.U., expressed this fear to the membership and nation just prior to the 1947 elections for Branch officials and representatives to the General Executive Council of the Union. In a speech at Nottingham, Deakin warned:

> We cannot afford to allow the Communists' attempted infiltration into and domination of the Trade Unions to succeed.
> It is important that members should record their votes and take their full part in making sure that their representatives are prepared primarily to do an industrial job of work.[2]

Morgan Phillips, Secretary of the Labour Party, issued

---

[1] It is of interest to note that certain types of infiltration are not at the moment considered threatening. Under the heading 'Catholic Bishops Ban Communism', the *Daily Herald*, official Labour Party National Daily Paper, printed this excerpt (on April 9, 1948) from a statement issued by the Roman Catholic Bishops of England and Wales: 'No Catholic can be a Communist, no Communist a Catholic. We urge Catholic workers to join their appropriate trade unions and help to infuse a Christian spirit into all their activities.'

[2] London *Daily Herald*, December 14, 1947.

a similar warning a few days later, on December 22, 1947:

> It would be a tragedy if the Communists, who have been rejected time and again by a free vote of the electors, were to win political power and influence through the back door of Trade Union branch meetings . . . the Communists thrive on apathy. When large numbers of Trade Unionists stay away from their branch meetings, the Communists begin to take charge.[1]

Though all this be true, emphasis has been misplaced on the Communist danger rather than on the breakdown of the democratic process within the Movement. Trade Unionists are being called on to be active against something rather than for something—an affirmative belief. A negative approach to a negative situation will not result in a positive solution to the real problem of apathy. Consequently the Trade Union leader, blinded by this negative approach, has failed to turn the spotlight on his own organization to find out why it is that a large percentage of the membership are unwilling to assume the responsibilities of citizenship in the government of the Union.

Though there are obvious signs of a breakdown in the lines of communication between the rank and file and the leaders in the T.G.W.U., Arthur Deakin is 'satisfied that the rank and file member is being heard'. However, he admits that apathy is a very big problem facing the Union. He attributes a good deal of this indifference to the fact that the pay packet is full, that hours of work have been shortened, that working conditions have improved, and that the average member has a sense of security he never before experienced. All this means that 'the Union's job is being done too well'. He hastens to add that if there were a wage issue involved or a strike pending, the membership would be flocking to the

[1] Morgan Phillips, Labour Party Secretary, 'The Communists—We Have Been Warned', (published by the Labour Party, Transport House, London). See also two T.U.C. pamphlets entitled: 'Defend Democracy—Communist Activities Defined' (1948) and 'The Tactics of Disruption—Communist Methods Exposed' (1949).

Branch. Like most Trade Union leaders, Mr. Deakin is under the impression that the Branch is the principal point of contact for the individual member with the Union[1].

Unfortunately, the Port of London dockers, members of the T.G.W.U., during the unofficial strike in June 1948, did not flock to the Branch or to the Union for advice or leadership. I attended the three principal official Union meetings held for the Docks' membership during this national emergency[2]. The total attendance for all three meetings no more than equalled the attendance at any one major meeting convened by the Unofficial Strike Committee[3].

The experience of the strike should prove at least one thing to the Union. That is that the Union cannot afford to rest on the belief that its services are now so excellent that it is no longer essential to maintain continuous communication with rank and file members and encourage their interest in the Union's affairs.

The 1948 Dock strike, however, is only a dramatic and

[1] From my records of an interview with Mr. Arthur Deakin, General Secretary of the T.G.W.U., on January 22, 1948, Transport House, London. The failure of Union officials to appreciate the importance of the Shop Stewards Movement as taking up the gap in authority and communication between rank and file and the Branch is discussed in the examination of member participation at Branch level.

[2] Under the Emergency Powers Act of 1920, the King proclaimed a State of Emergency on June 28, 1948. (*The London Gazette*, June 29, 1948, p. 3,785.) The Powers were never enforced, for the Dockers returned to work on June 30, after the Prime Minister's broadcast of the previous evening.

[3] (a) *Official meetings:* (i) Albert Hall Meeting, June 22, 1948. Attendance approximately 1,300. This figure is considerably lower than Mr. Deakin's estimate of 3,000 and was calculated only after checking the seating capacity of various sections in the Albert Hall. (ii) Southwark Park Meeting, June 25, 1948. Attendance approximately 600. (See *Manchester Guardian*, June 26, 1948.) (iii) Canada Yard, Surrey Commercial Docks Meeting, June 27, 1948. Attendance approximately 2,500 members. (See *Manchester Guardian*, June 29, 1948.)

(b) *Unofficial meetings:* (i) Victoria Park E. Meeting, June 22, 1948. Attendance approximately 5,000. Note this meeting was held at the same time as official Albert Hall Meeting. (*Daily Herald* and *Manchester Guardian*, June 23, 1948.) (ii) Victoria Park E. Meeting, June 29, 1948. Attendance approximately 5,000–6,000. (See *Manchester Guardian*, June 30, 1948.) At this meeting the resolution was passed to return to work. Thus, the men resumed work under the leadership of the Unofficial Strike Committee, and not the official Trade Union leadership.

costly example of what happens in a crisis to an organization whose leaders, satisfied with the efficiency of their administration and absorbed in the day-to-day problems confronting them, fail to maintain contact with their members. A letter by a docker to the editor of the *News Chronicle* clearly indicates how wide is the gap between some members and their Union representatives. The letter said in part:

'. . . What's wrong with the N.D.C. (National Dock Corporation)? Nothing as a board, but I think that they should have two workers as well as the employers, Union and N.D.C. on a tribunal so that the merits of a case could be thrashed out.

'You might say that we are represented by Union officials on the Board. The truth is the rank and file are suspicious of their officials. So why not have two workers on the Board to clear the air? . . .' (June 22, 1948.)

The strike in the period of transition from a capitalist economy to a socialist economy is becoming as much a means of informing the Trade Union leader of his membership's grievances, as it is a weapon against the employer. When socialist demands are being made of workers living in what is essentially a profit-motivated society in transition, the average workers must be kept more closely in touch than ever before with what leaders are thinking and doing. The strike as a means of communication between leader and rank and file is both expensive and dangerous, and one the community can ill afford.

Thus it becomes essential to look inside the Transport and General Workers Union to determine to what extent the high degree of member participation which the Constitution and Rules provide for, and on which the successful operation of this democratic structure relies, can and does take place. As was emphasized in the preceding section, it is within the Branch and at Branch level that the entire system of lay representation is initiated. However, before turning to a report on Branch life and membership participation in Area 1's AAA Branch, the material relevant to the subject and of a national character will be discussed.

Though the spotlight in this study is of necessity trained on the areas of breakdown in the democratic process within the government of the T.G.W.U., it is not intended to black out the Union's many great achievements. These are numerous and well known to many both inside and outside the Union.

Unfortunately, many of the Union's members are unaware of their organization's continuous progress in gaining recognition for the general worker in the community; of the vast improvements in conditions of work and wages; of the legal protection and action taken on behalf of the injured worker to obtain compensation; and of the general improvement for a large percentage of the unorganized workers directly and indirectly receiving the advantages of agreements negotiated by the Union on behalf of its members.

Yet, pride in one's progress and success may lead to complacency. With this in mind and with the conviction that a democratic organization welcomes a critical analysis of itself, I turn to the living body of the T.G.W.U. to determine the state of its health.

Chapter 5

THE MEMBERSHIP TURNOVER

AND SIZE, AND DISTRIBUTION IN BRANCHES OF DIFFERENT
SIZES

I SIZE

Size of membership is an interesting index of a Union's
external strength. This index is used to measure the
power position of the Transport and General Workers
Union in the community in which it works. It has been
shown that, primarily because of a large membership,
enormous influence and far-reaching powers are attributed to the Union by the Trade Union Movement, by
Industry, by Political Parties and by the Government.
Records of the change in size of membership and the net
annual decrease or increase derived therefrom are used
to measure the decline or growth of the power and prestige of an organization[1].

Between 1935 and 1947, the T.G.W.U. has registered
an average net annual increase in size of membership of
9·4 per cent. (See Table II.) Since its formation in 1922
with 297,460 members the Union has increased in size by
approximately 350 per cent, and in 1947 represented
1,317,000 workers in the United Kingdom. (See Appendix
No. 1.) This enormous development and extremely large
membership reflect the growth of power and prestige of
the T.G.W.U., which is what people have in mind when
discussing the external strength of an organization. Total
membership and change in its size as determined by net
annual increases or decreases are, however, imperfect
indices of external strength. They disclose little, if any,
information on the Union's internal stability and thus

[1] See Leo Wolman, *Ebb and Flow of Trade Unionism* (National Bureau of Economic
Research, New York, 1936).

66

of its ability to control through member participation the source of its power by which its external strength is measured. This huge membership has brought with it problems of administration and control inherent in all large organizations. It is misleading, however, primarily on the basis of size of membership to conclude that a Union is either too big or too small to allow for effective rank and file participation.

II DISTRIBUTION IN BRANCHES OF DIFFERENT SIZES

Of greater significance than size of national membership is the size of Branch membership. If the Union is to make possible the fulfilment of its claim that 'it is in the Branch that the individual member can begin to play his or her part in Union affairs'[1], the Branch must be of a reasonable size to allow individual members a genuine opportunity to participate in Union activities. Unfortunately, the Union has not considered information on the distribution of its membership in Branches of different sizes of sufficient importance since 1928 to maintain such records.

However, it has been possible to estimate the distribution of membership for 1945 by examination of the issue of ballot papers to the 4,021 Branches in the Union at the time of the election for General Secretary. Table I presents this data for the years 1924 and 1945. It is of interest to note that the distribution of membership has not varied to any large degree over the past twenty years. Approximately 30 per cent of the members are in Branches of less than 250 members, and 50 per cent of the members are in Branches of over 500 members. Three per cent of the Branches account for 26 per cent of the membership (belonging to units of more than 1,000 members). Of these 126 super Branches thirty-one have more than 2,000 members, four more than 4,000 members, and one more than 9,000 members. These

[1] T.G.W.U. Members Handbook, p. 11.

large Branches are allowed to develop without sub-
division because Area officials find them the easiest and
cheapest to administrate[1]. It is thus quite obvious that at
least 50 per cent of the T.G.W.U. members find themselves in Branches which, because of size alone, deny
them the opportunity to take an active part in Branch
life.

What this means to an individual in a T.G.W.U.
Branch will be discussed in some detail in the chapters
devoted to the 1/AAA Branch. It does not take much
imagination, however, to visualize the pandemonium
that would reign if 1,000 members of one Branch, for
example, were to attend their monthly Branch meetings
regularly.

There are insufficient data available on the 4,642
Branches of the T.G.W.U. (1947) to determine the size
or sizes of optimum Branches in given Areas and for
given Trade Groups. The Union must devote considerable time to research at Branch level to determine what
size Branch will be most favourable to a high degree of
member participation and at the same time be administratively efficient. No Branch should be allowed to exceed a certain maximum size that such an inquiry might
determine. Upon the basis of the information in Table I
it may be concluded that though the size of the Union is
not too large for effective rank and file participation,
many of its Branches are.

III   TURNOVER

Essential to an understanding of a Union's internal
strength and of the amount of rank and file participation
that can take place within the government of the organization, is an analysis of the real gains and losses in
membership, as expressed in the size of a Union's turnover. Turnover—the number of lapsed members or the

---

[1] From an interview with Miss E. McCullough of the T.G.W.U. Education
Department, May 31, 1948.

Table I

DISTRIBUTION OF THE T.G.W.U. MEMBERSHIP IN
BRANCHES OF DIFFERENT SIZES 1924 (a) and 1945 (b)

Size of Branches	Year	No. of Branches	No. of Branches as % of Total No. of Branches	Membership of all Branches	Membership of all Branches as % of Total Membership
1–50	1924	255	21·4	7,435	2·0
	1945	1,285	32·0	32,125(c)	3·7
51–100	1924	230	19·3	17,235	4·7
	1945	779	19·4	58,425	6·7
101–150	1924	139	11·7	17,317	4·7
	1945	466	11·6	58,250	6·6
151–200	1924	117	9·8	19,396	5·3
	1945	317	7·9	55,475	6·3
201–250	1924	74	6·2	16,750	4·6
	1945	212	5·3	47,700	5·5
251–500	1924	185	15·6	66,197	18·1
	1945	541	13·4	190,825	21·9
501–750	1924	92	7·7	56,254	15·5
	1945	201	5·0	121,675	13·9
751–1,000	1924	40	3·4	35,283	10·1
	1945	94	2·3	82,950	9·4
1,001 and over	1924	58	4·9	128,331	35·0
	1945	126	3·1	228,390	26·0
TOTAL	1924	1,190	100·0	364,198(d)	100·0
	1945	4,021	100·0	875,815(c)	100·0

(a) Source: Based on figures in the T.G.W.U. 3rd Annual Report, December 31, 1924, pp. 112–240.
(b) Source: Area Scrutineers' Reports in the T.G.W.U. Central Office Files—'Election of the General Secretary' November 22–23, 1945. Since 1928 no record of Branch sizes for the Union as a whole has been kept.
(c) 1945 membership figures for a given size group are an approximation which is the product of the multiplication of the mid-point in size of each group (except for Branches over 1,000 where actual figures are available) and the number of Branches within the group in question. The total membership of 875,815 excludes 35,410 Power Workers Group members and 2,858 members who make up the difference between the approximate total and the actual total of 914,083—membership eligible to vote in 1945.
(d) 1924 Annual Report gives total national membership as 372,560. The difference is attributed to the different recording of Area 6 membership as 34,485 in the summary and 26,913 in the Section on Branch membership. This leaves 790 members unaccounted for possibly attached to District and Area Offices. All calculations are based on the total of 364,198.

number of new members each year in relation to the size of total membership—is a revealing and an important index of a Union's internal stability and strength[1].

A large turnover is both evidence and a principal cause of apathy within an organization. Evidence of apathy is to be found in membership turnover as expressed in the size and rate of the annual lapsed membership. A fundamental reason for lapses in membership is the failure on the part of the individual member to identify himself with the Union to which he or she belongs. A member too often associates his Union card not with the Union but with the factory or job in which he is employed, and, upon changing employment, permits his Union card to lapse.

Large turnover, as expressed both in terms of the size of new membership and lapsed membership, is a principal cause of apathy within a Union. A high rate of turnover limits the number of members eligible to hold office and makes continuous two-way communication between leader and rank and file extremely difficult. A high rate of turnover prevents a large percentage of members classed as 'card-holders' from ever becoming Trade Unionists who identify themselves with and feel an allegiance to their Trade Union in particular, and to the Trade Union Movement in general[2]. If the annual turnover in membership is high, a large proportion of the membership has little opportunity of becoming acquainted with the Constitution, the Rules and the structure of the Union. This problem is greatly intensified by a high rate of lapses which reduces the number of old members who would be available to orient the new

---

[1] Formula: (a) $\text{Turnover} = \dfrac{\text{lapsed membership of current year}}{\text{total membership of previous year}}$

(b) $\text{Turnover} = \dfrac{\text{new membership of current year}}{\text{total membership of current year}}$

For a discussion of Labour Turnover Statistics see Riggleman and Frisbee, *Business Statistics* (McGraw-Hill, New York, 1938), pp. 489–490.

[2] 'Card-holder' is an expression used by active Trade Unionists to describe inactive members.

membership. Thus, high turnover is a danger signal for which leaders of democratic organizations must be on the look-out. For, if members are not members long enough to become thoroughly familiar with the Union's system of government, the system 'is certain, sooner or later, to be perverted by those who have the secret of its manipulation.'[1]

It is with these factors in mind that the statistics of Table II, on the Annual Changes in Size of Membership of the T.G.W.U., showing new and lapsed membership for the period 1935–1947, are to be analysed[2]. There are, however, certain qualifications that must be noted and taken into consideration in using the information presented in this table.

i *Lapsed membership* includes lapses caused by death. Death accounts for approximately 0.8 per cent of the total membership and is considered of little significance in this study[3].

ii *New membership* includes members, previously lapsed, who have rejoined the Union; i.e., amongst the new members there are some individuals who might be acquainted with the Union's structure and leaders. Unfortunately, the Central Office of the T.G.W.U. keeps no records which make a distinction between new members who once belonged to the Union and those joining for the first time. However, Area 1 Office, which is responsible for the T.G.W.U. membership in London and the Home

---

[1] H. J. Laski, *Grammar of Politics* (Allen & Unwin Ltd., London 1934, 3rd edition), p. 73—quoted out of context: 'for any governmental system not capable of being grasped by the ordinary elector is certain sooner or later to be perverted by those who have the secret of its manipulation.'

[2] Prior to this study the only figures available on the size of membership for any major Union have been total membership and the net annual decrease or increase in size. Fortunately, the T.G.W.U. has made available sufficient data to measure turnover in size of new membership and lapsed membership from 1935–47. For the period prior to 1935 figures available are both inadequate and inaccurate.

[3] The approximate number of deaths is calculated by dividing the Union's Annual Funeral Expenditure, as recorded in T.G.W.U. Report and Balance Sheets 1935–1946, by £7, the average funeral expenditure per death. (From an interview with Mr. A. J. Chandler, Minute Secretary of the T.G.W.U. (March 1948).)

Counties and which constitutes approximately 26 per cent (347,012 members) of the total membership, does make this distinction in its records. (See Appendix No. 2.) During the period 1935–1947 an average of 12·3 per cent of total new membership and 5·2 per cent of the total membership of Area 1 represented lapsed members who rejoined the Union as new members. These percentages should be noted, though they are not considered of great significance in this study. Though the turnover of membership in Area 1 over this period is slightly higher than that for the entire Union, these percentages can be applied to the 'New Membership' and 'Total Membership' columns in Table II, in order to obtain a relatively accurate picture of the size of the national membership that previously lapsed and then rejoined. For the percentages applicable for any year between 1935–1947 see Appendix No. 2.

iii *New membership* also includes members joining through amalgamation. These members are to be considered more as former Trade Unionists than as new members. For the 1935–1947 period covered in this study the percentage of new members in this category is negligible. For example, in 1935 2·3 per cent of new membership and 0·8 per cent of the total membership joined the Union via amalgamation. These percentages are the highest recorded during the 1935–1947 period. In 1941, a year in which no amalgamations took place, new membership represented 49·6 per cent of the total national membership. Thus, new membership attributed to members in this category can safely be ignored. (See Appendix No. 3.)

iv *These statistics* represent individuals playing an important part in maintaining the life of the community. In using percentages or numbers it is too often forgotten that they stand for human beings, not cogs in some administrative machine. With this word of caution, the reader's attention is drawn to Table II.

During the 1935–1947 period covered in Table II turnover, as expressed in terms of lapsed membership, has been on an average of 33·3 per cent of the total national membership of the Union. In 1935 lapses were at a minimum of 22·2 per cent (96,145 workers) of the national membership. A maximum during this thirteen-year period was registered in 1942 when 42·1 per cent (394,699 workers) dropped out of the T.G.W.U. During the past year (1947) 34·4 per cent (436,706 workers) of the membership, approximately the average for the thirteen-year period, allowed their Union cards to lapse. Though impossible to ascertain from the data presented here, a large percentage of these lapses can be attributed to indifference on the part of the individual, i.e., a failure to identify himself with the Union to which he belongs.

Though an average net annual increase of 9·4 per cent is recorded for this same period (1935–1947), an average of 38·3 per cent of each year's membership was comprised of new members. Turnover, as expressed in the proportion of new members to total national membership, was at its lowest point in 1938, when 30·2 per cent (220,326 men and women) of a national membership of 679,360 were new members. In 1942 the size of new membership in relation to the total membership of 1,113,165 workers reached an all-time high of 51·2 per cent (579,785). New members in 1947 comprised 36·6 per cent (480,628) of the total Union strength of 1,317,842. This percentage is just slightly below the average for the entire period covered in Table II.

It is worth noting that in 1942, when the entire British population was employed in the war effort, the greatest fluctuations in the turnover of membership took place: 42·1 per cent (394,699 members) lapsed and 51·2 per cent (579,785 members) joined the ranks of the T.G.W.U. The smallest fluctuations took place in 1935, when 2,000,000 insured workers (14 per cent of those registered under the Unemployment Insurance Scheme)

Table II

TRANSPORT AND GENERAL WORKERS UNION ANNUAL CHANGES IN SIZE OF MEMBERSHIP DECEMBER 31, 1935—DECEMBER 31, 1947(a)
(Showing Gains and Losses in Membership)

Year	Total National Membership	Lapsed(b) Member-ship	Lapsed Mem-bership as % of Last Year's Total	New (d) Member-ship	New Mem-bership as % of Current Year's Total	Net In-crease or De-crease (—) in Member-ship	Net In-crease or De-crease(—) as % of Last Year's Total
1934	433,816						
1935	493,266	96,145	22·2	155,595	31·6	59,450	13·7
1936	561,908	111,202	22·6	179,844	32·0	68,642	13·9
1937	654,510	141,913	25·2	234,515	36·0	92,602	16·5
1938	679,360	195,476	30·2	220,326	30·2	24,850	3·8
1939	694,474	228,729	33·7	243,843	35·2	15,114	2·2
1940(c)	743,349	266,934	38·6	315,809	42·5	48,875	7·4
1941	948,079	265,424	35·7	470,154	49·6	204,730	27·6
1942	1,133,165	394,699	42·1	579,785	51·2	185,086	19·5
1943	1,122,480	439,615	38·8	428,930	38·2	—10,685	—0·9
1944	1,070,470	394,551	35·2	342,541	31·0	—52,010	—4·6
1945	1,019,069	418,797	39·1	367,396	36·2	—51,401	—4·8
1946	1,273,920	356,793	35·0	611,644	48·0	254,851	25·0
1947	1,317,842	436,706	34·4	480,628	36·6	43,922	3·4
AVERAGE %			33·3		38·3		9·4

(a) Source: Compiled on basis of information in the Financial Secretary's Annual Membership Reports 1935–1947, addressed to the Chairman and members of the General Executive Council.

(b) Lapsed membership includes lapses through death. During the period 1935–1946 lapses through death represented 0.8 per cent of the total membership and 2.5 per cent of the lapsed membership.

(c) Total national membership figures (1940–1947) include members on military service. Though not every member entering service notified his Branch (and thus remained on the Union's books), this does not affect the figure for lapsed membership greatly.

(d) New membership includes members, previously lapsed, who have rejoined the Union. For the period 1935–1947 the averages of lapsed members who rejoined the Union in Area 1 were: 12.3 per cent of the Area's new membership and 5.2 per cent of the Area's total membership (see Appendix: Table No. 2).

were unemployed in Great Britain[1]. At that time 22·2 per cent (96,145) of the membership lapsed and 31·6 per cent (155,595) had held their T.G.W.U. cards for less than a year. Since V.J. Day, 1945, annual fluctuations in turnover have been about average.

No matter what the economic characteristics of a year in question, turnover in the membership of this Union is alarmingly high. From a *statistical point of view* a complete turnover in membership has occurred during the last three years. A total of 1,459,658 new members joined the Union, while 1,212,296 members lapsed in 1945, 1946 and 1947. This does not mean that at the end of 1947 no Union member had joined prior to 1945. There is no doubt that there exists in the Union a relatively small but stable membership of many years' standing. A clear illustration of this is to be found in the analysis of turnover figures of the 1/AAA Branch, which reveal that *statistically* a complete turnover of membership took place during 1946–1947, while in fact only 70 per cent of the membership were composed of members who joined during that period. (See Table XIX.) At the end of 1947 the total national membership of 1,317,842 was 141,826 short of the number of new members during these three years. Whatever the causes of these startling fluctuations, the fact is they exist.

What does this material on turnover mean in relation to apathy, or lack of member participation, in the T.G.W.U.? It means that at all times the Union is composed of a large number of workers, new to the organization, who have had little time to identify themselves and their interests with the T.G.W.U.; little time to become acquainted with Union leaders, their problems, their personal characteristics and their policy; little time to become conversant with the Constitution and Rules and thus become aware of their right to take

[1] 'Annual Abstract of Statistics', No. 84, 1935–1946 (H.M. Stationery Office), Table 131, p. 107 and Table 136, p. 113.

an active part in the government of their Union. It means that the responsibility of maintaining the continuous operation of the Union must rest on a relatively small nucleus of men. The speed with which new members join and old members lapse prevents the creation of a large body of members capable and desirous of making the new members feel a sense of belonging to the organization which collects their 7d. a week. Because one must be a member in good standing for at least two years before becoming eligible to hold any office in the Branch or at higher levels in the Union, it means that a very large percentage of the membership is automatically deprived of the opportunity of official participation. Furthermore, it means that large numbers of members never become well enough acquainted with those running for office to feel that an election affords them an opportunity to make a knowing choice.

It is difficult for any organization with this annual member turnover to become unified into a well-disciplined body, aware of Union policy and capable of communicating approval or disapproval through the channels provided in the Constitution. The fact that this high turnover deprives the Union of a large membership capable of joining in and making a contribution to the formation of policy is self-evident. It must be emphasized that in the long run participation must mean more than an expression of approval or disapproval by voting or non-voting on policy already formulated by the few. It must mean that each member takes part according to his capacity to make a contribution in the unit of the organization to which he belongs. For participation of rank and file Union members a much more stable membership is required than is found in the T.G.W.U.

It would be wrong to assume from the statistics presented in Table II that the apathy-carrier member turnover has infected all sections of the Union's body politic equally. However, no section appears to be im-

mune. In Table III the average annual member turnover figures for the 1936–1947 period, as expressed in
percentages of lapsed and new members for each of the
T.G.W.U.'s National Trade Groups, are presented. It
should be noted that the heavy turnover of labour due
to the seasonal nature of the work in the building
industry[1] is reflected in the member turnover of the
T.G.W.U.'s National Building Trade Group. Over the
twelve-year period covered in Table III the National
Building Trade Group has registered an annual average
of 84·0 per cent lapses and 85·7 per cent new members.
This high fluctuation in member turnover is attributed
to the nature of the work. An organizer will go to a
building site and sign up all the building labourers, who,
on completion of work on a particular site, will allow
their cards to lapse[2]. Though this be a valid explanation, it is equally valid and much more to the point for
Union leaders to realize that these lapses are an indication of the Union's failure to make building labourers
feel a sense of belonging to the organization which they
have joined as a condition of employment.

It is of interest to note that the National Docks Group
is the most stable unit in the T.G.W.U. There has been
an average member turnover, as expressed in lapsed and
new members, of approximately 11 per cent. In view of
the Unofficial Dock Strike of 1948, these data appear to
refute the argument that apathy or lack of participation
is to be attributed to high member turnover. In fact,
these statistics do nothing more than show that apathy in
an organization can have more than a single cause. This
information does suggest, for example, that the embarrassment and loss of prestige suffered by the official
Union leaders and the Union as a result of the 1948

[1] See Ministry of Labour and National Service Report for the years 1939–1946
(H.M. Stationery Office, London, September 1947), p. 203, 'Unemployment in
the Building and Civil Engineering Industries.'
[2] From an interview with Mr. A. J. Chandler, Minute Secretary of the T.G.W.U.
(March 1948).

Table III

TRANSPORT AND GENERAL WORKERS UNION AVERAGES
OF ANNUAL PERCENTAGE CHANGES (a) IN SIZE OF MEM-
BERSHIP OF ALL TRADE GROUPS (b) FOR PERIOD 1936–1947 (c)

National Trade Group	Average Annual New Member- ship %	Average Annual Lapsed Member- ship %	Average Annual net Increase or De- crease (—) %	1947 Member- ship	1947 Mem- bership as % of Total Union Member- ship (d)
Docks	11·8	11·6	—0·1	86,458	6·5
Road Transport Pas- senger—Tram Section	19·5	19·6	—0·4	44,054	3·4
Waterways	20·1	17·8	2·9	10,766	0·8
Road Transport Pas- senger—Bus Section	25·8	21·5	6·6	165,992	12·5
Road Transport Pas- senger—Cab Section	25·4	28·5	—3·3	2,888	0·2
Agricultural	27·8	17·5	15·5	31,415	2·4
Milling	28·0	22·2	8·7	16,310	1·2
Road Transport Com- mercial	32·8	27·3	8·7	156,026	11·7
Supervisory	33·6	25·3	13·3	24,957	1·9
Municipal Workers (c)	44·2	25·0	40·5	38,317	2·9
General Workers	44·5	39·6	10·1	305,900	23·2
Government Workers(c)	46·8	49·7	—16·1	74,415	5·6
Engineering	51·1	46·1	17·8	207,631	15·7
Chemical (c)	53·8	41·0	33·5	34,824	2·6
Building	85·7	84·0	11·0	64,602	4·9
Miscellaneous (b)	—	—	—	53,287	4·5
TOTAL				1,317,842	100·0

(a) Source: Compiled on basis of information in the Financial Secretary's Annual
Membership Reports 1936–1947, addressed to the Chairman and Members of the
General Executive Council. More comprehensive Tables for each Trade Group
may be found in the author's original manuscript entitled 'Apathy and the
Democratic Process in the Government of a British Trade Union' in the library of
the London School of Economics.

(b) Except for: Fishing, Power Workers and Marine Sections, which are listed as
Miscellaneous, and for which data are inadequate.

(c) Except for: Municipal Workers, Government Workers and Chemical Groups,
which were established as separate Trade Groups in 1945, 1943 and 1945 respectively.

(d) Total Union membership in 1947 was 1,317,842.

Dock Strike could hardly have occurred in the Building Trade Group through unofficial strike action. On the other hand, the same embarrassment and loss of prestige might result if Union officials called a strike in the Building Trade Group. It would be difficult in such a crisis to get this highly unstable membership to hold together and act in unison, though a strike can be used as a means of creating a sense of unity among men.

Although apathy and a breakdown in the lines of communication between rank and file member and leader are not eliminated by reducing to nil a high member turnover, a high degree of member participation in a Trade Union cannot take place if the member turn-over is large. It is thus argued that a high degree of member turnover does of necessity create apathy in a Trade Union organization, and, like the termite, can destroy from within that which looks solid and strong from without.

If the problem of member turnover is to be recognized and faced as the very serious threat to the democratic functioning of the Union's body politic that it is, a very detailed investigation must be made by the Union in order to locate and thus isolate for special consideration areas and units of the organization in which the greatest degree of member turnover occurs. If the Union is to achieve its object of securing 'a real measure of control in industry and participation by the workers in the management, in the interests of labour and the general community'[1], it must be made to encourage member participation in the control of Union activities at all levels of its government. For, training in participation through participation in one's Trade Union's activities is essential to the development and maintenance of democratic control in industry.

A statistical analysis of member turnover in the National Trade Groups, of which Table III is a sum-

[1] T.G.W.U. Rules, Rule 2: Objects, Section 2, Clause (i), pp. 7–8.

mary, must be further refined by isolating units of apathy within Areas and Groups of highest member turnover, right down to the Branch. Every unit should be kept constantly informed of its member turnover. The ratio of Union officers to the number of members must bear some relation to the extent of turnover within each Group or Area. In March 1948, there was an average of four full-time paid officers and four clerks to every 10,000 members in each Area of the Union (Appendix No. 4). This appears to be extremely low in view of the enormous turnover in membership, but because data available are extremely limited it has not been possible to make an analysis of the number of paid officials assigned to each National Trade Group in relation to turnover. The Union must redirect the energies of its organizers and its members in all units of organization from the task of getting new members to that of making those already members aware of that fact and into active Trade Union citizens.

To sum up: Member turnover is a significant index of apathy in a Trade Union organization. The high degree of member turnover, as expressed in size of lapsed and new membership, is both evidence and cause of lack of rank and file participation in the government of the Transport and General Workers Union. A high degree of member turnover is of necessity accompanied by a low degree of member participation. The reverse of this statement, however, is not valid. If participation is to mean more than consent of the individual member as expressed in voting or non-voting, the Union must devote a good deal of its efforts to the reduction of member turnover, in order to create a stable body of rank and file members who can assume responsibility for the continuous operation of the government of the Union.

Chapter 6

THE ARREARS POSITION OF THE MEMBERSHIP

WITH SPECIAL EMPHASIS ON THE SIZE OF MEMBERSHIP IN RELATION TO TOTAL NATIONAL MEMBERSHIP ELIGIBLE TO HOLD OFFICE

To the Financial Secretary of a Union 'arrears' means that which is unpaid and overdue. To a member of the T.G.W.U. who is six weeks in arrears the term means in addition to this that he is no longer entitled to Union benefits[1]. As for member participation, to be in arrears for six consecutive weeks or more means to deprive oneself of the right to apply for University scholarships offered by the Union[2], of the right to be a candidate for any elected office and of the right to apply for any official position in the Union for a two-year period subsequent to rejoining the ranks of members in good standing. To fall into arrears for thirteen consecutive weeks is to forfeit one's right to vote in Union elections by ballot[3]. Thus the arrears position of Union membership can be used both as evidence of and as a cause of lack of member interest in Union activities. Arrears are another index of apathy which can be used by a Union to determine the state of its health.

Table IV presents the arrears position of T.G.W.U. membership for the years 1935 through 1947. The following deficiencies and limitations on the data should be noted:

i This Table indicates the arrears position of Union members for the final quarter (October, November,

[1] T.G.W.U. Rules: Rule 18, Section 9, p. 43. Also in bold type on every T.G.W.U. member's card.

[2] Letter, March 1947, from Miss E. McCullough of the T.G.W.U. Education Department to members.

[3] Rule 11, p. 36.

F

December) only of each year. Thus, the statistics do not include the total number of members who were 7–13 weeks in arrears during an entire year, for example, but rather include only those in arrears during the final quarter of each year under review.

ii The number of members in arrears in the final quarter of a year is normally at a minimum for the entire year. This is accounted for by the fact that a concerted effort is made during the last quarter of the year to bring as many members as possible into financial benefit. Thus, except for the fact that a single member may be counted more than once as falling into arrears, a conservative estimate of a year's total would be four times as great as that found under the '7–13' and 'over 13 weeks in arrears' columns in Table IV.

iii As of December 1947, more than 300,000 members (23 per cent) of the T.G.W.U. were employed in positions that could be held only by workers who were willing to join and remain in good standing with the Union. The effect on the arrears position of the membership is evident and is, of course, reflected in member turnover figures.

iv Union contributions are collected from rank and file members by Union lay officials, called Collectors. Because in practice members have failed to accept their responsibility, the keeping-up of the payment of Union dues is in large part the responsibility of the Collector rather than of the individual. Because of the system of collection in operation and because the 100 per cent shop covers such a large percentage of the membership, it would be invalid to conclude on the basis of statistics indicating a low proportion of total membership in arrears that the rank and file member, generally speaking, is not apathetic.

At the close of each year during the thirteen year period covered in Table IV an average of 82·2 per cent of the membership has been in benefit. This means that

Table IV

TRANSPORT AND GENERAL WORKERS UNION ARREARS POSITION OF MEMBERSHIP
DECEMBER 1935–DECEMBER 1947 (a)

Year	Under 7 Weeks in Arrears	7–13 Weeks in Arrears	Over 13 Weeks in Arrears	Total Membership	Under 7 Weeks in Arrears as % of Total Membership	7–13 Weeks in Arrears as % of Total Membership	Over 13 Weeks in Arrears as % of Total Membership	Total %
1935	392,665	53,117	47,484	493,266	79·6	10·8	9·6	100·0
1936	452,875	60,189	48,844	561,908	80·6	10·7	8·7	100·0
1937	533,692	70,288	50,530	654,510	81·6	10·7	7·7	100·0
1938	545,348	76,542	57,470	679,360	80·3	11·3	8·4	100·0
1939	565,702	74,210	54,562	694,474	81·5	10·7	7·8	100·0
1940	599,898	85,579	57,872	743,349	80·7	11·5	7·8	100·0
1941	779,305	104,322	64,452	948,079	82·2	11·0	6·8	100·0
1942	939,298	125,139	68,728	1,133,165	82·9	11·0	6·1	100·0
1943	907,537	136,244	78,699	1,122,480	80·9	12·1	7·0	100·0
1944	870,818	124,693	74,959	1,070,470	81·4	11·6	7·0	100·0
1945	850,692	111,795	56,582	1,019,069	83·4	11·0	5·6	100·0
1946	1,107,953	111,900	54,067	1,273,920	87·1	8·7	4·2	100·0
1947	1,131,481	130,878	55,483	1,317,842	85·9	9·9	4·2	100·0
AVERAGE %					82·2	10·8	7·0	100·0

(a) Source: Compiled on basis of information in the Financial Secretary's Annual Membership Reports 1935–1947, addressed to the Chairman and members of the General Executive Council of the T.G.W.U.

an average of one out of every five members listed on the Union books has not been entitled to Union benefits. As of December 31, 1947, of the total national membership of 1,317,842 members, 1,131,481 were in good standing and approximately 1,262,359 (96 per cent of the national total) were eligible to vote. To the extent that this figure includes members who have been in the Union less than thirteen weeks, it is an overestimate of those eligible to vote by ballot.

In view of the size and national character of the membership and in view of the high member turnover that plagues the T.G.W.U., the low percentage of membership in arrears at any time is a credit to the Collectors. It should not be overlooked, however, that though these statistics give the arrears position of the Union at the close of each year, approximately four times as many members per year fall into arrears 7–13 weeks or more. It is of interest to note that, between 1942 and 1947, lapses in membership (see Table II) have been between six and eight times the size of membership designated as over thirteen weeks in arrears at the end of the year. Thus, the number of members thirteen weeks in arrears might be used by the Union to make a rough prediction of the size of member turnover, as expressed in lapsed membership, that is likely to occur annually.

It is suggested parenthetically that the Union might, on the basis of more detailed information of a similar nature, establish contact by letter or personal interview with those members on the verge of lapsing, in order to determine some of the major causes of apathy[1]. Moreover, making each of those many thousands realize that he or she is thought of by the Union as an individual rather than as a card number might in itself help reduce

[1] Mr. Wisker, Financial Secretary of T.G.W.U.'s Area 1, has used the letter, on occasion, to inform members of their arrears position. He claims that the returns in back dues are considerable and regrets that the Union has neither the time nor the staff to do this as a matter of policy. (From an interview with Mr. Wisker, April 1948.)

apathy among rank and file members. The Union might consider, too, ways and means of making the payment of Union contributions more the responsibility of the individual member than that of the Collector. In order to create a sense of personal participation in new members as soon as they join the Union 'the idea that it is *up to them* to share in the burdens and benefits of the Union' should be stressed, as it has been by the International Ladies' Garment Workers Union in the United States[1].

From the arrears statistics in Table IV alone, little can be ascertained in relation to the size of membership eligible to hold office or to apply for an official position in the Union. However, by using these data in conjunction with those in Table II on the size of membership and the turnover in membership as expressed in the percentage rates of lapses, an estimate can be computed.

Union Rules provide that every candidate for any office in the Union, paid or unpaid, full-time or part-time, delegate to the Biennial Delegate Conference or representative on any Constitutional Committee, including the General Executive Council, must have been a financial member of the Union for at least two years prior to the date of nomination or application for appointment[2]. On the basis of these qualifications a formula has been devised to estimate the number of members in relation to total membership eligible to run for·or apply for official Union positions at any given time. The difficulties in devising a valid formula were numerous; most have been overcome though some have not been completely eliminated. If the statistics derived are in any way distorted, their bias is in the direction of over-

[1] Herbert Harris, *American Labor* (Yale University Press, 1939) p. 220.

[2] In some cases even more stringent requirements limit the size of membership eligible to hold office. For example, the Transport Bus section requires a member to attend twelve Branch meetings in the year preceding an election, before he becomes eligible to stand or apply for Union office. (From an interview with Mr. Charles Brandon, Secretary of T.G.W.U.'s Area 1, April 1947.)

estimating the number of members eligible to hold office. Additional comments on the formula and sample calculations are to be found in Appendix No. 5.

Table V presents statistics on the size and proportion of the total national membership eligible to hold official positions in the Union during its election years 1937, 1939, 1941, 1943, 1945, 1947[1]. For each of these six years an average of 21 per cent of the total membership has been eligible for office. Though the actual number of those eligible has progressively increased between 1935 and 1947, the ratio of eligible to total national membership has tended, with some fluctuations, to run in the opposite direction. This is a reflection of the high member turnover expressed both in the larger size of lapsed and new members and the general increase in the total membership.

In 1937, 26 per cent (168,149) of a national membership of 654,510 were eligible to hold office in the Union. In 1947 only 19 per cent (255,274) out of a total membership of 1,317,842 members were qualified under the Rules for office in the Union. What this means, is that four out of every five members, in total 1,062,568 men and women workers, were in 1947 ineligible to stand as candidates or apply for any office, paid or unpaid, at Branch level and at all higher levels, in their Union. This means that of a total membership of 1,019,069 members in 1945 more than 788,000 thought so little of the Union and the right to hold office in the government of the Union that they either lapsed from the Union or allowed themselves to fall into arrears for at least six consecutive weeks sometime between December 1945 and December 1947.

These figures also represent the number of members

---

[1] It must not be overlooked that these were years when evacuation, direction of labour and general war-time controls caused a maximum of disturbance to Trade Union membership.

No election was held in 1939 as a result of a decision of the 1939 B.D.C. (See T.G.W.U. Annual Report and Balance Sheet for 1939 and 1940.)

eligible to apply for University scholarships offered by the Union.

Furthermore, it is of interest to note that in the 1945 election for General Secretary approximately 2 per cent

Table V

TRANSPORT AND GENERAL WORKERS UNION SIZE OF MEMBERSHIP ELIGIBLE TO HOLD OFFICE IN RELATION TO TOTAL MEMBERSHIP FOR THE YEARS 1937, 1939, 1941, 1943, 1945 and 1947 (a)

Year	Total National Membership	Membership Eligible to Run or Apply for Office in the Union (b)	Eligible Membership as % of Total National Membership
1935	493,266		
1937	654,510	168,149	26
1939	694,474	163,222	24
1941	948,099	142,264	17
1943	1,122,480	166,777	15
1945	1,019,069	230,236	23
1947	1,317,842	255,274	19
			—
AVERAGE %			21

(a) Source: Compiled on basis of information in the Financial Secretary's Annual Membership Reports 1935-1947, addressed to the Chairman and members of the General Executive Council (see Tables II and IV).

(b) Determined by the following formula in which E is the membership eligible to hold office in the year of election (see Appendix No. 5 for sample calculations and comments on formula).

$$1.\ E_2 = a - b$$
$$x = c\% \cdot E_2$$
$$2.\ E_1 = E_2 - x$$
$$z = d\% \cdot E_1$$
$$3.\ E = E_1 - z$$

Key: a Total national membership as of December 31 of the base year (i.e., 2 years prior to date of election). See Table II.

b Total membership 7-13 weeks in arrears in the base year. See Table IV.

$c\%$ Total percentage rate of lapses in membership and of falling into arrears for 7-13 weeks in base year plus one year. See Tables II and IV.

$d\%$ Total percentage rate of lapses in membership and of falling into arrears for seven weeks or more in base year plus two years (i.e., the year of election). See Tables II and IV.

of a membership of more than 1,000,000 were eligible to run for that office. In other words, only 20,000 members in 1945 had been in the Union for five years without falling into arrears for six consecutive weeks or more.

These figures are a startling index of apathy within the T.G.W.U., which must be brought to the attention of Union members if the democratic structure of the Union is to be preserved. The fact that so few members can ever look forward to holding office in the Union, whether at Branch level or national level, limits automatically the number of members actively interested in Union affairs. 'Only 20 per cent of the total national membership' is the answer to the question 'Who can hold office?' originally posed in Chapter 3.

Unfortunately, sufficient data are not available to refine this analysis in order to identify the Areas, Trade Groups and Branches where the number eligible to hold office in relation to their respective membership is extremely small. There is no doubt, however, that the ratio of eligible members to the size of membership in the Building Trade Group, for example, where member turnover is extremely high, is much lower than in the stable Dock Workers Trade Group. (See Table III.)

It is not within the scope of this study, nor is it possible on the basis of this information alone, to make detailed recommendations for changes in the rules of eligibility in order to increase the size of member potential qualified to hold office in the Union. Some might suggest that the Union consider the advisability of reducing the length of membership and the rigid arrears requirements for candidates for offices at Branch level at least. This suggestion is, at best, only a temporary expedient to increase the opportunity for participation in this apathy-ridden body politic. It takes into account the present arrears position of the membership and the present rate of member turnover which automatically limit eligibility for official participation, and from which immediate relief is essential. From a long-run point of view drastic changes in qualification requirements for office in the Union will not solve the problem. Union efforts must be engaged in the reduction of the rate of member turnover as expressed in lapsed membership, and in the education of this more stable body of members to the responsibility of Trade Union citizenship.

Thus, the arrears position of a Union's membership is another index, though an inadequate one, of apathy, and a possible measure of future lapses in membership. This measure can and should be used by the Union to locate areas threatened by apathy and to reduce the rate of member turnover by establishing contact with rank and file members about to lapse. The 100 per cent Union shop, Union benefits, and an efficient system of collection are responsible for maintaining approximately 80 per cent of the membership in benefit. On the other hand, 80 per cent of the total national membership at any time between 1935 and 1947 were found to be ineligible for official position in the Union. This is but another indication of the extent to which the democratic process has broken down or failed to develop in the Transport and General Workers Union. It is difficult to create a willingness to participate in an association in which, during the past thirteen years, approximately 80 per cent of the members have deprived themselves of eligibility for office. So to deny over one million of the T.G.W.U.'s one million three hundred thousand members the right to hold office is disqualification on a scale that no democratic organization can afford.

Chapter 7

ELECTIONS IN RELATION TO MEMBER PARTICIPATION

An institution characteristic of democratic government is the election of representatives by popular vote in a free and secret ballot. The election provides the citizens of a state or the members of an organization with a peaceful and effective means of supporting and thus re-electing, or dismissing and thus replacing their leaders, i.e., those in policy-making positions. An election, to have meaning to the individual in a free society, must provide an opportunity for making a choice. Choice, to have meaning, must imply the right of opposition. The right of opposition, to have meaning, implies the right and opportunity of a free exchange of and easy access to information and ideas that any member of the society might consider relevant to an informed decision. The underlying assumption upon which the success of the election as an instrument of democracy depends is the provision of adequate educational opportunities for the elector. Finally, an election is an instrument of democratic society only to the extent that it gives the individual—citizen of a state or member of a group—a genuine sense of being able to participate, if he wishes, in the control of his government.

Election statistics are thus another index frequently used to measure the degree of participation that takes place within a state or organization[1]. However, election returns, like written constitutions, must not be taken at face value, for they can be and are used to disguise the true nature of governments which are not in the political

[1] See: C. E. Merriam and H. F. Gosnell, *Non Voting—Causes and Methods of Control* (University of Chicago Press, 1924); H. F. Gosnell, *Why Europe Votes* (University of Chicago Press, 1930); and H. Tingsten, *Political Behaviour—Studies in Election Statistics* (Stockholm Economic Studies No. 7, 1937).

sphere at least, democratic. Though the election in the
T.G.W.U. is not intended as a sham to disguise what
might not be considered, on examination, a democratic government, it is with this caution and the above
comments on the election in a free society as a frame of
reference that an analysis of member participation in
elections by ballot in the T.G.W.U. is to be made.

I THE CIRCUMSTANCES UNDER WHICH T.G.W.U. ELEC-
TIONS ARE HELD
Though the extent to which an individual member of the
T.G.W.U. feels a genuine sense of being able to participate in Union activities through the system of elections is,
in the final analysis, what must be determined, this matter
will not be dealt with specifically until the results of
personal interviews with rank and file members of the
1/AAA Branch are discussed. However, the circumstances under which elections are held on a national and
Area level must be described before attempting an
analysis of the statistics available.

Thus it is essential to ask and answer the following
question:

*Do elections in the T.G.W.U. offer members an opportunity
to make an informed decision and thus a real choice in the
selection of representatives in the government of their Union?*

Though the answer to this question will be given, for
the most part, in reference to elections for Territorial
representatives to the General Executive Council, it applies to all elections held by the Union, with the exception of those for Branch officials—i.e., at Branch level.
The latter are discussed in the study of the 1/AAA
Branch.

Contrary to what might be expected from the information in Table V on the size of membership eligible to
hold office in the Union, in the last five elections, covering eighty contests for Territorial Representatives to
the General Executive Council, a T.G.W.U. member

had an average of twelve candidates from whom to select his favoured one. (See Table X.) This does not mean, however, that a real choice was offered to the electorate, for little, if any information was available upon which a decision could be made.

Though the right of opposition is guaranteed in the Rules of the Union, custom and practice have prevented it from becoming real or effective. For the voice of opposition, which in an organization of this nature might best be designated the 'voice of constructive criticism', has inadequate communication facilities through which it can be heard by rank and file members in general. To be specific, no regular publications or journals are published by Area organizations to keep members in a given territory informed not only of official policy, but also of criticism and of those critical of official policy.

On a national level, moreover, the official Journal of the T.G.W.U., the *Transport and General Workers' Record*, is nothing more nor less than an official publication presenting official policy from an official point of view. It is a one-way channel of communication. There is no space available for letters to the editor, nor is there any column provided for critics of Union policy or those responsible for it, to present their views to the membership. During and after the Unofficial Dock Strike of 1948, for example, the Union was faced with many critics from within and without of its policy. Though the *Record* devoted considerable space to this subject, all of it was taken by Arthur Deakin, General Secretary, in defence of the Union's attitude and actions[1]. The membership was provided with the facts only as the Union official saw them, or at least only as he wished the membership to see them. By the end of 1947, 160,000 copies of the *Record* were being published, i.e., one copy for every eight members. Because of an unsatisfactory system of distribution and because of a lack of member interest it is

[1] See T.G.W.U. *Record*, July and August 1948; and Appendix No. 6.

doubtful if there are as many readers as there are copies published[1]. The *Record*, which is the only regular publication of the Union, cannot claim to reach a majority of the membership or to present the facts upon which the electorate can make an intelligent judgment.

Though a right of opposition undoubtedly exists within the confines of meetings, for example, of the General Executive Council, the rank and file member is kept completely ignorant of how his representative stood or voted on particular issues in the Council. It is thus impossible for a member of the T.G.W.U. to judge an elected representative by his voting record as a member of the G.E.C. To my knowledge, a decision of the First Annual Delegate Conference of 1923 defeating a resolution to the effect 'that a copy of the minutes of the meetings of the General Executive Council be forwarded to all Branch Secretaries, Area and Trade Group Committees' has never been reversed by a Conference[2]. Certainly it has not been reversed in practice. Minority reports, if made, are not available to rank and file members. There is absolutely no easily accessible information on what an individual's representative really thinks about Union policy in general or on specific issues.

It might be argued that members of the G.E.C. are in the same position as the members of a Cabinet and, like them, must appear in public as supporters of official policy or resign. If this be true, it is equally true that the T.G.W.U.'s 'Cabinet', unlike the Cabinet in His Majesty's Government, sits on a front bench faced not by a virile opposition, whose remarks and criticisms are

[1] The limited publication is in part the result of war-time paper cuts, imposed in May 1940. In April 1940 a peak of 169,000 copies were being published, approximately two copies for every nine members. (Source: T.G.W.U. Education Department.)

A more detailed description of the system of distribution, the contents and make-up of the *Record* and of member interest in its contents is to be found in the study of the 1/AAA Branch.

[2] Minutes and Record of the First Annual Delegate Conference, 1923, Minute 103, p. 41.

made public, but by an incoherent mass whose voice is inarticulate. Moreover, no back-benchers are to be found in the rear to support or criticize the Union's policy. The fact of the matter is that when a member of the T.G.W.U. takes the initiative to cast his vote, he has little information about the member standing for re-election and less about the candidates in opposition. A voter may favour the G.E.C.'s policy, if he knows any-thing about it, yet cast a vote to re-elect a representative who has been in opposition to official policy within the G.E.C., since voting records are not available[1].

Nor can it be argued that matters of policy are first formulated at Branch level, and thus the right of opposi-tion can be effective in the government of the Union. Though the right of opposition is safeguarded at Branch level, the main flaw here is that there is no official chan-nel of communication through which rank and file mem-bers of one Branch can contact those of other Branches who are of like mind, or who are at least anxious to dis-cuss the issues at hand. It is no longer possible to limit the airing of opinions to Branch level and believe the right of opposition has been adequately safeguarded. Critics of policy must have, and are at present denied, a practical and recognized means of communicating their views to rank and file members in all Branches, Trades and Areas of the Union. By thus denying the voice of opposition an opportunity to be heard within the Union but outside the Branch, the T.G.W.U. has forced critical discussion to take place among members of different Branches at meetings convened by outside bodies, only too glad to lend a helping hand.

One last comment in evidence of the fact that material

---

[1] Some interesting light was thrown on this problem at the 1933 B.D.C., where a resolution proposing that the names of movers of motions and the names of those voting for and against be inserted in all Area Trade Group, Area Committee, National Trade Group and General Executive Council Minutes of meetings, was declared 'LOST'. Excerpts from the debate are presented in Appendix No. 7, to illustrate the opposing views of rank and file and officials anxious to hold on to their power. (1933 B.D.C. Verbatim Reports, Minute 22, pp. 214–218.)

essential to making an informed decision is not available
to the rank and file member: No verbatim reports of the
debates at the Union's Biennial Delegate Conferences
are published. Thus it is impossible for a member to hear
the case as presented by his representatives and all other
schools of opinion on issues of vital interest to members
of a democratic organization. It is true that the Union
publishes the 'Minutes and Record' of each Biennial
Delegate Conference, but the amount of information
available therein is limited to a statement of the resolution, immediately followed by 'at the close of the ensuing
debate . . . the question being submitted to the vote of
conference, the motion was Declared . . .' 'Lost', 'Carried', or 'Carried Unanimously.' There is no way of
determining from these publications how close the vote
in most cases, nor is it possible to consider the arguments
of debate or to compare changes of opinion on a given
issue from year to year until a change in a Conference
decision actually takes place.

Thus, elections in the T.G.W.U. are not fought on
issues. Candidates are not provided with any inexpensive
means of communicating their views and plans to their
constituents[1]. The *Record* carries little if any news of a
forthcoming election, and announces, after elections,
only the names of winning candidates, without publishing the size of the poll or the number of votes for each
candidate[2]. Election campaigns are non-existent and
there is no attempt to arouse in the rank and file member a genuine interest in this instrument of democratic
control. The closest thing to an election issue in recent
years is to be found in the elections of 1947 when the
General Secretary called on members to reject Com-

[1] An exception was the distribution of 105,000 folders containing 500-word
Election Addresses by the six candidates for the office of General Secretary in 1945.

[2] Exceptions were the two announcements in the T.G.W.U. *Record* in September
and October 1945 of the forthcoming election of the General Secretary. Some
Areas issue Memoranda, to Branches only, announcing dates for nominations and
times of elections.

munist candidates—if they recognized one when they saw one—on ballot papers that contained as many as fifty-four names and never less than six from which to take their pick. (See Table IX and Appendix No. 8.)

At best, the elections in the T.G.W.U. can be contests of personalities, though the rate of membership turnover is so great that there is little opportunity for the membership to get acquainted with leading personalities. Even this type of choice, with justification, was denied the membership in their very first election for President and General Secretary of the Union in 1921. Though versions of the story differ, the fact remains that Ben Tillett, Dockers' leader and a principal organizer of the T.G.W.U., was effectively deprived of the right, though nominated as a candidate, to run for the office of President of the T.G.W.U. against Harry Gosling, of the Watermen and Lightermen's Union[1]. The reason for this was that the amalgamation would have suffered if two leaders from the same Union of the fourteen original Unions amalgamating held major posts in the new Organization; Ernest Bevin, also a Dockers' leader, was to be General Secretary. The membership, thus deprived of the right to choose between popular personalities, participated in an election held to confirm what had already been decided[2].

A negative answer must be given to the question: 'Do elections in the T.G.W.U. offer members an opportunity to make an informed decision and thus a real choice in the selection of representatives in the government of their Union?' Though the Rules and Constitution of the T.G.W.U. provide for the election as an instrument of democratic control, the conditions under which the

[1] With the death of Harry Gosling in October 1930 the office of President ceased to be a popularly elected position. A Chairman or President of the G.E.C. is elected by and from the members of the G.E.C. (See T.G.W.U. Report and Balance Sheet, 1930, p. 14.)

[2] See Trevor Evans, *Bevin*, a Biography, especially pp. 88 and 89. (Allen & Unwin Ltd., 1946.)

electoral system operates prevent, through custom and practice, the effective exercise of the right of opposition, and an easy access to facts and information essential to making a knowing choice. There is no reason to believe that the concept or the practice of elections in the T.G.W.U. arouses member interest in Union affairs to the extent of giving a member a genuine sense of participation in the activities of his Union.

Before turning to an analysis of election returns certain limitations, qualifications and sources of error must be noted in the material available in relation to rank and file participation in elections.

A Records of election returns on file in the Central Office are limited and often inadequate. Except for the election of General Secretary in 1945 no election returns have been published by the Union for the last ten years or more.

B Plural voting in some Areas allows each voter two votes. No record is kept of the actual number of voters participating and thus only an estimate can be made.

C No record is kept of the size of membership eligible to vote at a given election. An estimate of members eligible to vote is calculated in these statistics by deducting from the total membership those members thirteen weeks in arrears or more in the quarter preceding an election. This is a slight over-estimate, for members of less than 13 weeks' duration should be excluded as well.

D Size of membership in Areas, in accordance with which the number of Territorial representatives to the General Executive Council is determined, may be inaccurate. For example, book membership, which in some Areas includes members who occasionally pay dues or who are hopelessly in arrears, may be greater than financial membership. If the discrepancy between book membership, upon which representation is generally based, and financial membership is great an Area may

have more representatives than it is in fact entitled to[1].
Furthermore, and more relevant to this study, it becomes
impossible for the Union to measure with accuracy member participation in the election of representatives.

E While methods of administration of ballot voting
vary considerably from Area to Area, the differences in
procedure do not alter the conclusions drawn in the
analysis of election statistics that follows[2]. Evidence of a
less detailed nature than that to be described in the
study of elections at Branch level indicates that malpractices if not corruption at the ballot box are not
uncommon in some Areas. Because some malpractices
no doubt go unnoticed, statistics may record a higher
degree of participation than in all likelihood occurs[3].
Though scrutineers' reports indicate the care taken
officially by the Union to secure fair elections, they also
indicate an absence of a tradition of respect, at Branch
level at least, for the individual member's right to use his
ballot. Scrutineers have reported and disqualified, for
example, block voting at ballot elections as well as ballot
papers showing marks of duplicated voting[4]. Occasionally, scrutineers, fearing adverse publicity for the Union,
merely report malpractices to the Area Committees
concerned, without actually disqualifying the votes so
cast[5]. In the Areas in which such malpractices do occur,
they make questionable the system of representation and
should be considered symptoms of breakdown in the
democratic process.

[1] Rule 5, Clause 2 (*a*) p. 15. See Chapter 3.
[2] T.G.W.U. Memorandum 'Ballot Voting', 12/9/44. Files of the Minute Secretary,
Transport House.
[3] A vote of 104 per cent of those eligible was recorded without comment in Area 11
election of Territorial Representatives to the G.E.C. in 1943 (see Table VI). As
the result of a similar ballot in 1945, a Committee was appointed by the G.E.C.
to conduct an investigation into ballot arrangements in the Area. (Council Minute
No. 1212, December 6, 1945.) See also Minute 338 of the Statutory Meeting of
the T.G.W.U. Finance and General Purposes Committee, April 11, 1946.
[4] Letter January 18, 1946, from an Area Secretary to the General Secretary.
[5] From a Scrutineers' Report on voting for Territorial Representatives to the
G.E.C., January 17, 1938.

Thus these factors must be borne in mind in an examination of election statistics in relation to member participation in the T.G.W.U.:

i Elections do not offer members of the Union an opportunity to make an informed choice.

ii There is evidence that the size of membership used as a basis for representation may be inaccurate. Thus, participation in certain Areas may, in fact, be greater than it appears to be in the Tables below.

iii Evidence of corruption at the polls is not uncommon. In some, but not in all cases ballots are disqualified where malpractices are noted. There is no means of estimating the number of violations of election rules that have passed by unnoticed.

However, I do not believe that these factors alter to any significant degree the conclusions reached in the analysis which follows. At best (or worst) these conclusions are strengthened.

II   MEMBER PARTICIPATION IN T.G.W.U. ELECTIONS

An examination of the statistics in Table VI reveals that in eighty election contests held between 1937 and 1947 for Territorial Representatives to the General Executive Council of the T.G.W.U. an average of only 37 per cent of the total eligible membership participated. Eligible membership has averaged 93 per cent of total national membership. (See Table IV.) In the five elections held in Area 12 an average of only 11 per cent of those eligible took the trouble to cast their vote. At the other extreme, Area 11 (the only territory which shows an average of more than 50 per cent membership participation) registered an average 62 per cent poll. However, because of the not uncommon practice of block-voting in Area 11, which resulted in the impossible 104 per cent vote which was recorded in 1943, and which no doubt contributed to the highly unlikely, though possible, polls of 98 per cent and 86 per cent in 1937 and 1941 respectively, there is good reason to discredit these statistics as a measure of member participation. A more reliable index of apathy in this Area is found in the percentage figures for the 1945 and 1947 elections in which disqualifications for stuffing the ballot box were rigidly enforced. During these two contests an average of only 10 per cent of the member-

Table VI

MEMBER PARTICIPATION BY AREAS IN FIVE ELEC-TIONS FOR TERRITORIAL REPRESENTATIVES TO THE GENERAL EXECUTIVE COUNCIL OF THE T.G.W.U. (a) PERCENTAGE OF ELIGIBLE MEMBERSHIP VOTING

Area	1937	1941 (b)	1943	1945	1947	Aver. %
1	45†	26†	38†	30†	32†	34
2	38	24	38	21	86*	42
3	14	14*	17*	17*	36*	20
4	49	42*	47*	33*	51*	44
5	44	39	49	47	65†	49
6	46	40*	43*	40*	34*	41
7	40	34	35	29	32	34
8	51	33	66	36	58*	49
9	39	28	45*	41*	59*	42
10	25	32	19	34	42	30
11	98	86	104‡	2*(c)	18*	62
12	12	11	9	8	16*	11
13	32	19	51	23	18	29
AVERAGE %						37

(a) Source: Scrutineers' Reports in T.G.W.U. Central Office Files for the years 1937, 1941, 1943, 1945 and 1947.
(b) No election was held in 1939 because of the war.
(c) The original ballot represented a 70 per cent poll with a disqualification of 90 per cent of the votes cast. The election was declared null and void. In the second election, of a 43 per cent poll 44 per cent of the votes cast were disqualified.
* Each member is entitled to two votes. Assuming that some but not all voters register both votes, three-quarters of the total vote recorded is arbitrarily taken as the number of individual voters participating in the election.
† Some members are entitled to two votes—others to one. The three-quarter rule* to determine the number of individual voters participating is applied only to the ballot in which members are allowed two votes.
‡ Each member was entitled to two votes. Because of large poll it was assumed that every member registered two votes. In spite of this assumption the impossible poll— 4 per cent larger than the eligible membership—was recorded. There are no queries in the Scrutineers' Report.

ship polled. Thus eliminating Area 11 from the comparisons, Areas 5 and 8 tie for the highest average poll of 49 per cent of those entitled to vote.

In the only two elections held for the office of General Secretary, participation has been no greater than in those for Territorial Representatives to the G.E.C. (Table VII). In 1921 only 35·6 per cent (107,003) of the 300,000 electorate participated in the contest which resulted in the election of Ernest Bevin. Though the 1945 election was preceded by two announcements in the T.G.W.U. *Record*[1] and by the distribution of 105,000 folders containing 500-word election addresses by the six candidates, only 38 per cent (347,523) of 914,619 members eligible to vote, did so. Only three Areas, representing 11·5 per cent of the eligible membership, registered as much as a 50 per cent poll, with a maximum poll of 64·2 per cent in Area 4. Compared with an average vote of 29 per cent in Area 13's territorial contests, 55 per cent voted in this election. Ninety per cent of these voters favoured winning candidate Deakin from Area 13, Branch No. 36. Thus, in spite of the attempt to whip up member interest in the General Secretary's election of 1945, member participation was only 1 per cent higher than the 37 per cent average in the five elections for Territorial Representatives to the G.E.C.

Though the data are incomplete, there is no evidence of a trend towards a higher or lower degree of member participation in elections held by the Union. There is sufficient evidence, however, to indicate that the degree of member participation in elections is shockingly low, particularly in a country where, as citizens, an average of 74·1 per cent of the electorate have participated in the last seven General Elections[2].

[1] T.G.W.U. *Record*, September 1945 (p. 61) and October 1945 (p. 77).

[2] Figures for 1922–1931 from H. Tingsten, *Political Behaviour* (Stockholm, 1937), p. 219. Figures for 1935 and 1945 from R. B. McCallum and A. Readman, *The British General Election of* 1945 (Oxford University Press, 1947), p. 293: 1922—71·3 per cent; 1923—70·8 per cent; 1924—76·6 per cent; 1929—76·1 per cent; 1931—80 per cent; 1935—71 per cent; 1945—73 per cent. Average: 74·1 per cent.

At the Biennial Delegate Conference held in Blackpool in 1945 a resolution was carried to the effect that 'Representatives to the T.U.C. and the Labour Party in the Areas shall be elected by ballot.' Prior to that time all

Table VII
MEMBER PARTICIPATION BY AREAS IN THE ELECTION FOR GENERAL SECRETARY OF THE T.G.W.U. 1945 (a)

Area	Eligible to Vote	Total Vote (b)	% of Eligible Membership Voting	Total Vote for (c) Winner	Vote for Winner as % of Total Vote	Vote for Winner as % of Eligible Vote
1	242,363	82,297	33·9	40,179	48·9	16·5
2	34,242	15,198	44·3	11,495	75·7	33·5
3	69,116	17,812	25·8	12,433	69·8	18·0
4	35,034	22,539	64·2	15,725	69·8	44·8
5	125,323	51,546	41·7	28,507	55·3	22·8
6	75,260	34,537	45·9	24,534	71·0	32·6
7	65,947	30,307	46·0	7,654	25·3	11·6
8	41,085	18,856	45·8	11,708	62·2	28·5
9	44,663	22,987	51·4	10,962	47·9	24·6
10	23,760	6,976	29·4	4,337	62·0	18·2
11(b)	49,553	4,043	8·1	2,921	72·9	5·9
12	35,340	3,422	9·7	1,767	51·6	5·0
13	26,665	14,718	55·1	13,397	90·9	50·2
Power	35,410	17,433	49·2	13,630	78·1	38·5
Misc(d)	10,858	4,852	44·7	4,065	83·9	37·5
Total(e) and	914,619	347,523		203,314		
Average %			38·0		58·5	22·2

(a) Source: Area Scrutineers' Reports in the T.G.W.U. Central Office Files—'Election of the General Secretary' November 22, 23, 1945.
(b) Excluding spoilt papers. Total number of spoilt papers—19,201. (Of these 11,081 were spoilt in Area 11, where the practice of block voting is not uncommon.)
(c) Mr. Arthur Deakin elected.
(d) Miscellaneous includes Central Office and North Wales Quarrymen's Section.
(e) For purposes of comparison: In the only other election for General Secretary of the T.G.W.U. in December 1921, out of approximately 300,000 eligible voters 107,003 votes were cast, i.e., 35·6 per cent of the electorate voted. (Source: Statistics compiled by Mr. H. J. Laski, based on information in the T.G.W.U. Journal 1923.)

T.G.W.U. delegates to the T.U.C. and Labour Party Conferences were chosen by Area and Group Committees. In seconding the resolution, J. Gibson, a delegate, told the Union's supreme policy-making body that 'the interest that will be taken in the Trades Union Congress and the Labour Party, if the members of the Union should each one of them get a ballot paper, will be much greater if they have the right to put a cross behind one to represent them at their Trades Union Congress. I feel that there will be much more interest in these members when the delegates come back.'[1] The argument defeated the opposition from the platform. However, two years later (1947) this decision was reversed by the B.D.C. and election by ballot of T.G.W.U. representatives to the T.U.C and Labour Party Conference was abandoned[2].

It is worth noting parenthetically that the T.G.W.U., unlike the National Union of Mine Workers, for example, does not normally send its full complement of delegates to T.U.C. Conferences. For example, the Union sent a delegation of 75, rather than 225 members to the 1949 T.U.C. Conference. A third of that small delegation were permanent paid officials[3]. The more rank and file representatives there are at Congress, the more first-hand reporters are available to return to the Branches and the men at work to explain T.U.C. policy—for example the necessary though unpopular policy of wage restraint. Furthermore, the rank and file are entitled to full delegations not only to help determine Union and T.U.C. policy, but also to provide the membership with every opportunity available to develop and train the leaders both the T.G.W.U. and the T.U.C. so urgently need.

The Central Office of the T.G.W.U. has on file the

[1] 1945 B.D.C. Verbatim (unpublished) Reports (Blackpool), Minute 98, p. 400.
[2] Minutes and Record of the Proceedings of the Twelfth Biennial Delegate Conference of the T.G.W.U., July 1947, Minute 106, p. 45.
[3] See T.U.C. Report, Bridlington, 1949, particularly pp. 21–23; and T.G.W.U.'s Report and Balance Sheet for 1948, especially pp. 3–4.

returns from only six Areas out of the thirteen for the
election held under the 1945 plan. The degree of member participation was extremely low. In Areas 2 and 10,
where each member was entitled to one vote, a 22 per
cent and 34 per cent poll respectively was registered. In
Areas 1, 4, 5 and 6, even on the assumption that each
vote cast represented one member, though each member
was entitled to two votes, an average of 39 per cent of the
membership participated. If each voter used two votes,
an average of 20 per cent on the eligible members participated[1]. A valid figure lies somewhere between 20 per
cent and 39 per cent. Though these data are incomplete,
there is no doubt that member interest was low. The
experiment, however, should have been given a longer
trial, for Mr. Gibson's argument remains a valid one for
any organization anxious to increase member participation and purporting to be a democratic body.

As for other elections by ballot conducted by the
Union, there is little information available or recorded.
Unfortunately the Central Office of the Union does not
file returns of elections for Area Trade Group Representatives. In the few cases where the vote was recorded
measurement of participation was impossible, for there
was no way of determining the size of the electorate
within the constituencies of each Trade Group in a given
Area. There is no reason to suppose, however, that member interest in general, has been greater in these elections
than in those for Territorial Representatives to the
G.E.C.

Since the T.G.W.U.'s foundation, however, there have
been at least thirty ballot votes held by the Union in
which not less than 50 per cent of the members have apparently participated. I refer to twenty-nine ballots
conducted by the T.G.W.U. under the Trade Union

[1] Scrutineers' Reports on the Union Delegation to the Annual Conference of the
Labour Party 1946—for Areas 1, 2, 4, 5, 6 and 10 only—in the Files in the office
of the Minute Secretary of the T.G.W.U.

(Amalgamation) Act, 1917, during the period from 1923 to 1939, and to one ballot in 1946[1]. This law requires that 50 per cent of the membership of each Union vote, in order to effect amalgamation. In addition, those voting 'For' amalgamation must exceed by 20 per cent those voting 'Against.' The Act makes no provision as to the length of time a ballot may remain open. Some T.G.W.U. ballots have remained open for as long as nine months[2]. Since the passage of the Societies (Miscellaneous Provisions) Act, 1940, there has been an alternative means of achieving amalgamation: the absorbing Union need not conduct a ballot to effect amalgamation if the smaller transferring Union obtains the consent of two-thirds of its membership.

In favouring the proposal for amalgamation with the 8,000 members of the Liverpool and District Carters' and Motormen's Union in 1946, 57·8 per cent of the 961,915 T.G.W.U. members cast their votes, as provided in the Act of 1917. Though no pamphlets were issued to them showing good cause for supporting the proposal, 96·2 per cent of this relatively large percentage of members voting favoured amalgamation[3]. In comparing the participation in this ballot with that for the General Secretary a year earlier, it is of interest to note that while ten of the thirteen Areas registered as much as a 50 per cent poll in the ballot for amalgamation, ten out of the thirteen Areas failed to register as much as a 50 per cent poll in the election for General Secretary. It is, moreover, difficult to find a satisfactory explanation, no matter how long the ballot may have remained open, for the 93·2 per cent poll in North Wales' Area 13 or the

[1] See *The Union, Its Work and Problems*, and Appendix No. 3.

[2] Letter to the author from Miss E. McCullough of the T.G.W.U. Education Department, June 1, 1950.

[3] Pamphlets favouring amalgamation were mailed with an announcement to all members of the Liverpool and District Carters' and Motormen's Union demanding that they vote. (Source: File, 'Liverpool Amalgamation, 1946', in the office of the Minute Secretary, T.G.W.U.)

86·2 per cent vote in Ireland's Area 11, while only 53 per cent in Liverpool's Area 12 took the trouble to record their votes on an issue with which they were more directly concerned.

These amalgamation statistics were the only ones made available. The T.G.W.U. records, upon investigation, will no doubt indicate a better than 50 per cent poll in at least 30 amalgamations. However, these data are not suitable for measuring member participation in the T.G.W.U. To believe that more than half of the T.G.W.U.'s membership voted in an election for amalmagation with, for example, a Union having as few as 150 members, is to place oneself in that large audience Mr. Barnum relied on to make his fortune.

III   VARIATIONS IN MEMBER PARTICIPATION IN BRANCHES OF DIFFERENT SIZES

Unfortunately, no record is kept of membership participation in individual Branches and in Branches of different sizes for T.G.W.U. elections. It has been possible, however, after examining the returns of 4,021 Branches in the election for General Secretary (1945), to show the variation in membership participation in Branches of different sizes. Though no conclusions of general application can be drawn from the statistics presented in Table VIII, which covers one election only, it is of interest to note that an over-all average of 18·5 per cent of all Branches failed to record a vote. An average of 24·5 per cent of all Branches with no more than 100 members did not participate in the election. That is, one out of every four Branches in this group, which accounts for 51 per cent of all the T.G.W.U. Branches, but only 10·4 per cent of the entire membership (see Table I), failed to take part in the election for General Secretary. The percentage of Branches not recording any vote appears to decrease as the size of Branch membership increases until a minimum of 5 per cent for Branches of over 1,000 (representing 26 per cent of the membership) is reached.

Of all the Branches recording a vote, those with a membership of 201–250 registered the highest degree of member participation, i.e., 47 per cent of the eligible

Table VIII

VARIATION IN MEMBERSHIP PARTICIPATION IN THE ELECTION FOR GENERAL SECRETARY OF THE T.G.W.U. 1945—IN BRANCHES OF DIFFERENT SIZES (a)

Size of Branches	Total No. of Branches	No. of Branches not Recording Any Vote	% of Branches not Recording Any Vote	% of Membership Voting in all Branches (b)	% of Membership Voting in all Branches (b) Recording a Vote
1–50	1,285	310	24·0	29·0	38·0
51–100	779	198	25·0	34·0	46·0
101–150	466	65	14·0	39·0	45·0
151–200	317	49	15·0	37·0	44·0
201–250	212	28	13·0	41·0	47·0
251–500	541	71	13·0	37·0	42·0
501–750	201	14	7·0	37·0	40·0
751–1000	94	5	5·0	30·0	32·0
1001 and over	126	6	5·0	36·0	37·0
Total	4,021	746(c)			
Average %			18·5	36·0	41·0

(a) Source: Area Scrutineers' Reports in the T.G.W.U. Central Office Files— 'Election of the General Secretary' November 22, 23, 1945.

(b) These percentages are calculated as a proportion of the number of votes cast to the number of ballot papers issued to each of the 4,021 Branches. As ballot papers are in packets of fifty, these percentages underestimate to a slight extent the degree of participation. Thirty-eight per cent of the eligible membership voted in the election. The 36 per cent recorded above is the average vote cast in all Branches. The 2 per cent difference is thus the extent of under-estimation, for example, in this column.

(c) Includes sixty-eight Branches disqualified for violation of Rule 11 on Ballot voting.

membership in the voting Branches of that category. Branches with a membership of 751–1,000 workers recorded the minimum (32 per cent) poll. It is rather surprising to find that Branches having 1–50 members registered only a 1 per cent greater vote than Branches of the 1,001–and–over Group, which registered a 37 per cent poll of Branches recording a vote. A scrutiny of these data shows that no category of Branches registered as high as a 50 per cent poll. There is insufficient evidence available to determine the size of the optimum Branch, i.e., the Branch size most favourable to a high degree of member participation and at the same time administratively efficient. There is but an indication that the optimum Branch size, if selected on the basis of voting frequency alone, might be about 225 members.

IV   MEMBERSHIP SUPPORT FOR WINNING CANDIDATES

Do elected representatives enjoy the support of a majority of the membership? Table IX presents statistics on the proportion of the total vote registered for winning candidates in eighty election contests for Territorial Representatives to the G.E.C. The most marked feature of these figures is that in fifty-eight out of the eighty contests the leading candidates received less than a majority of the total vote cast. In thirty-seven of these contests the elected representatives failed to capture more than 35 per cent of the vote. In only two of the eighty contests did winning candidates poll as much as 50 per cent of the eligible membership. One of these two exceptions is to be found in doubtful Area 11. What does all this mean? It means that in 72 per cent of the election contests held for representatives to the T.G.W.U. General Executive Council over the last ten years, winning candidates received the support of only a minority of the voters who cast a ballot, and in 97 per cent of these contests received the support of less than 50 per cent of the eligible membership.

Table IX

PROPORTION OF TOTAL VOTE REGISTERED FOR WIN-
NING CANDIDATE(S) IN EIGHTY ELECTION CONTESTS
FOR T.G.W.U. TERRITORIAL REPRESENTATIVES TO
THE GENERAL EXECUTIVE COUNCIL IN FIVE ELEC-
TIONS—1937, 1941, 1943, 1945 and 1947 (a)
(Showing the number of candidates contesting) (b)
Vote for Winner(s) as % of Total Vote Cast

Area	1937	1941 (c)	1943	1945	1947	Aver. %
1 A	23·4 (61)*	30·0 (24)*	20·4 (43)*	36·5 (49)*	35·9 (54)*	29·2
1 B	16·6 (16)	33·6 (14)	34·5 (20)	22·5 (21)	26·7 (17)	26·8
2	82·0 (2)	21·2 (10)	19·1 (16)	40·2 (18)	68·1 (27)*	46·1
3	73·0 (11)	60·2 (13)*	60·0 (11)*	33·3 (24)*	27·9 (32)*	50·9
4	55·0 (13)	38·8 (19)*	38·8 (23)*	55·8 (16)*	51·4 (19)*	48·0
5 East	42·3 (8)	34·4 (13)	30·8 (11)	29·4 (19)	31·6 (15)	33·7
5 West	51·2 (6)	58·2 (10)	52·5 (13)	34·8 (19)	36·3 (27)*	46·6
6	29·5 (12)	44·1 (20)*	36·0 (30)*	33·6 (20)*	46·1 (19)*	37·9
7 West	31·8(d) (12)	57·6 (7)	63·5 (8)	56·8 (11)	37·5 (10)	49·4
7 East		17·8 (10)	21·8 (12)	31·0 (12)	22·9 (11)	25·1
8	53·7 (12)	76·9 (8)	23·4 (12)	23·5 (18)	32·4 (21)*	42·0
9	42·9 (14)	20·7 (16)	33·2 (22)*	28·6 (23)*	58·4 (22)*	36·8
10	38·3 (7)	52·9 (7)	26·9 (11)	24·4 (10)	59·7 (8)	40·4
11	42·2 (8)	50·7 (6)	66·6 (7)*	60·4 (6)*	48·8 (10)*	53·7
12	38·3 (9)	35·9 (8)	39·6 (7)	27·2 (8)	25·0 (24)*	33·2
13 West					36·6 (7)	39·5
13 East	80·5(d) (3)	36·5(d) (10)	18·9(d) (18)	25·4(d) (16)	39·0 (6)	

(a) Source: Scrutineers' Reports in T.G.W.U. Central Office Files for the years
1937, 1941, 1943, 1945 and 1947.
(b) All figures in parentheses indicate the number of candidates standing for
election.
(c) No election was held in 1939 because of the war.
(d) Area 7 was not divided into two electoral districts until 1941 and Area 13 not
until 1947.
* Two representatives elected. In all other cases—one representative elected.

In the Summary Table X, it is to be noted that the votes cast for 106 representatives elected to office in these eighty contests accounted for only 17·1 per cent of the eligible membership and 38·8 per cent of all voting members. Thus, approximately eight out of every ten members in the T.G.W.U. have not voted for the winning candidates in elections held between 1937 and 1947. Of those members taking the trouble to vote during this period six out of ten cast their votes for losing candidates. In the 1945 election for General Secretary, though 58·5 per cent of those voting favoured Arthur Deakin, only two out of every ten eligible members cast their vote for him. (See Table VII.)

A partial explanation for this peculiar breakdown in the election system, whereby the minority of voters and in turn electors is all that is required to secure a territorial seat on the G.E.C., is to be found in the Union's frequent ultra-multi-candidate contests. An average of twelve members fight every territorial seat on the G.E.C. In no election since 1937 have there been less than six names on a ballot paper. In 1947, Area 1's foot-and-a-half long ballot sheet contained the names of fifty-four candidates for two seats on the G.E.C. (See Appendix No. 8.) Between 1937 and 1947 inclusive, 1,292 members stood for 106 vacancies on the General Executive Council. By this spreading of the vote the majority of representatives are elected by a minority of votes.

As this system operates, control by a group issuing orders from within or without is made easy, not only by the failure of most members to take an active part in the elections, but also by the minority support of voters which is all that a representative requires to win a seat in these ultra-multi-candidate contests. If the Conservative, Labour or Communist Parties were, for example, anxious to gain control of all seats held by Area Representatives to the General Executive Council of the T.G.W.U. in 1945, their energy, time and money would have been best spent in only 118 strategically selected Branches of the 4,021 Branches then in existence. By gaining control of the vote in less than 3 per cent of all the Branches of the T.G.W.U., any infiltrating organization would have had control of more than enough votes to do the job under present circumstances. Thus, with relative ease, a very important, and indeed powerful, public institution could, when apathy-ridden, fall prey to a group determined on control.

Though it is not within the scope of this study to give a detailed plan for reviving member interest in this basic instrument of participation, it is obvious that the facts

Table X

SUMMARY OF TOTAL VOTES CAST FOR WINNING CANDIDATES IN EIGHTY ELECTION CONTESTS FOR T.G.W.U. TERRITORIAL REPRESENTATIVES TO THE GENERAL EXECUTIVE COUNCIL AS PERCENTAGE OF TOTAL VOTES CAST AND OF MEMBERSHIP ELIGIBLE TO VOTE IN FIVE ELECTIONS—1937, 1941, 1943, 1945 AND 1947 (a)

(Showing the number of candidates contesting and the number of representatives elected)

Year	Votes Cast for Winners as % of Total Votes Cast	Votes Cast for Winners as % of Eligible Membership	No. of Candidates	No. of Representatives
1937	37·4	17·7	194	16
1941(b)	41·4	14·6	195	20
1943	38·6	20·4	264	21
1945	35·1	11·8	300	22
1947	41·7	20·8	339	27
Total			1,292	106
Average %	38·8	17·1		

(a) Source: Scrutineers' Reports in T.G.W.U. Central Office Files for the years 1937, 1941, 1943, 1945 and 1947.
(b) No election was held in 1939 because of World War II.

warrant a full-scale inquiry into the electoral system of the Union. Though it is recognized that the difficulties and physical obstacles to increasing participation are greater than it might appear in theory, it is suggested parenthetically that the Union give consideration to:

i The development of an authorized and inexpensive system of communication by which members can contact each other within the Union but outside the Branch. In this way the voice of constructive criticism may be allowed to create member interest and discussion in the operation of the Union. As a first step, the Union should open the columns of the *Record* to critics of Union leaders and their policies.

ii The publication in some detail of the meetings of Constitutional Committees at all levels with the voting records of elected representatives.

iii The standardization of the basis of territorial representation by eliminating the discrepancies between book and financial membership.

iv The supervision, if need be by an outside body, of all ballot elections to prevent mal-practices at the ballot box and to add to their stature in the eyes of the membership. Such an outside body could be introduced to the organization with the same status as the public auditor who checks its financial records.

v The maintenance of adequate election statistics, so as to enable the Union to locate units in which the electoral system has broken down.

vi The elimination of the election for choosing the General Secretary or, alternatively, election of a General Secretary for a limited term only. If the position of General Secretary is to be a permanent one, that official should not be allowed to defend his policy by claiming that he is the members' elected representative. If he is to make this claim, it must be justified by giving the membership periodic opportunities to express or with-

hold their support by re-electing or unseating him in a
ballot vote.

In summary: It is apparent that the T.G.W.U.'s
electoral system is not working well. The election does
not give the member an opportunity to make an informed
choice, nor can it be claimed that rank-and-filers feel a
genuine sense of being able to participate in the control
of their Union's government. Though all members are
entitled to vote, very few do. In fact, the T.G.W.U.'s
electoral system is in practice as much a cause of apathy
as election returns are an index of it. The Union is so
diseased by apathy that corruption at the ballot box may
go unnoticed by a large majority of rank and file members. Thus, though the Rules and Constitution provide
for a democratic Trade Union government in theory, the
administration of elections and the circumstances under
which they are actually held provide the organization
with but the facade of popular control.

H

Chapter 8

MEMBERSHIP RESPONSE TO THE UNION'S EDUCATIONAL SCHEME

Another index of participation available to the T.G.W.U. is the membership's response to offers of scholarships and correspondence courses under the Union's Educational Scheme. Though the Union has expended some funds and energy on educational programmes since its inception in 1922, no records were kept of membership response prior to 1936[1].

The Educational Scheme of the Union offers numerous facilities to the membership for non-vocational studies by means of correspondence courses, week-end and summer schools, and scholarships for University courses. These facilities are widely advertised throughout the Union on every T.G.W.U. membership card, on the back cover of every Union Rule Book (one of which every worker is to receive on joining the Union) and by frequent announcements issued to all branches.

Admittedly, these facilities have a limited attraction for the membership. But the extent of this limitation should be of vital concern to Union leaders and officials responsible for maintaining communication with rank and file members. A low response to these offers is both a sign of apathy and a sign that written communications—whether the announcement of a course, the course itself, the Union's Rule Book, the Members Handbook or the Union's Journal—cannot be relied on as the means of keeping in touch with members.

Of limited appeal but of considerable importance to a Union in need of University-trained personnel are the

[1] Report on Education to the General Secretary and Members of the Education Committee of the General Executive Council 1936–1947

nine full-time scholarships to Coleg Harlech, Ruskin College and the London School of Economics for a year's study. All expenses, including tuition, room and board and family allowances, are paid by the Union. These scholarships are open to members between the ages of 20 and 45 who have been in financial benefit for at least two years prior to making application.

Because of the high rate of arrears and turnover in Union membership and because of the many obstacles to leaving family and job for a year, the number of members both eligible and able to apply for these scholarships is of course low. In relation to member qualifications above, not more than one out of every five members has been eligible to apply at any time since 1945 when the full-time scholarship scheme went into operation. (See Table V.) Since that time 151 applications have been completed by members of the Union. Of the eighty-nine applicants for scholarships for the academic years 1946 and 1947, sixty-five (73 per cent) were Branch officials[1]. Of the eighty-nine only four were under the age of twenty-five. In 1947, sixty-two applications were made for the 1948 academic year.

It would be difficult to draw any conclusions on the basis of this scanty evidence. However, in view of a worker's natural reluctance to start again his formal education, the Union should consider the advisability of modifying conditions of eligibility. For example, by easing financial membership requirements and by arranging with the Universities to reduce the age minimum, the Union might induce greater participation. If such adjustments can be arranged, a large number of applicants with experience in industry, but not tied to the job, without family responsibility and not too removed from the discipline of school to be reluctant to

[1] Branch Chairmen, 20; Branch Secretaries, 10; Shop Stewards, 19; Branch Committees, 15; Collectors, 1; Total, 65. (From an analysis of all applications, 1945 and 1946.)

renew study, will become eligible to apply for the Union's University scholarships.

Of more general interest, and thus a better index of member participation, is the Union's own correspondence course entitled 'The Union, Its Work and Problems.' Any member can enrol in this course, which presents to the member-student information about the formation and development of the Union, its Constitution and structure, how it works, and the problems with which it has to deal. The course is divided into six parts and is designed to cover a period of six months' work. For a student to proceed from one part to another, he must submit an essay to the Education Department's examiners for comments and suggestions.

In Table XI statistics are presented on membership response to and staying power through this course. From its inception in 1939 to December 31, 1947, 6,930 members applied for the course; of these, 5,748 decided to enrol. During the past four years (1944–1947) an average of approximately 575 members have completed enrolment forms to start the course annually. Even under the highly unlikely assumption that each of the 623 members signing up for the correspondence course in 1947 was from a different Branch, a maximum of 14 per cent of the Union's 4,642 Branches had a representative in the course[1].

Though the number of members enrolling during this nine-year period is considerable, it would be misleading to conclude that all 5,748 student-members participated in these studies. Over 70 per cent (4,053) withdrew before completing their course of study. Only 17·7 per cent (1,018) showed enough interest in 'The Union, Its Work and Problems' to complete the six parts assigned. Of the withdrawals 498 (i.e., 12 per cent of all withdrawals)

[1] Number of Branches in T.G.W.U. in 1947, 4,642, according to information from Mr. Edwards, Assistant to the T.G.W.U.'s Minute Secretary. Unfortunately no record is kept for previous years.

were due to claims of National Service. The stages at which members dropped out are indicated in Table XI. It should be noted that approximately 50 per cent of all correspondence course students withdrew before starting the course. Thus, while response to the offer of the course of study is not low, the number of withdrawals is alarmingly high and an indication that the course is not doing its job. The suitability of the course and the efficiency of its administration should be the subject of a detailed inquiry.

Table XI

TOTAL MEMBER PARTICIPATION IN T.G.W.U. CORRESPONDENCE COURSE 'THE UNION, ITS WORK AND PROBLEMS' SINCE ITS INCEPTION IN 1939 (a)

	No. of Students	% of Total Enrolments
WITHDRAWING BEFORE COMPLETING PART (b)		
I	2,718⎫	47·0⎫
III	893 ⎬4,053	15·6 ⎬70·3
VI	442⎭	7·7⎭
COMPLETING OR PURSUING THE COURSE		
Completing the Course	1,018⎫	17·7⎫
Actively pursuing the Course as of December 31,	⎬1,695	⎬29·7
1947	677⎭	12·0⎭
TOTAL ENROLMENTS	5,748(c) 5,748	100·0 100·0

(a) Source: Based on a table of statistics entitled, 'The Union, Its Work and Problems' from the T.G.W.U. Education Department's Files: 'Correspondence'.

(b) Includes 498 withdrawals (i.e., 12 per cent of the total of 4,053 withdrawals) due to claims of National Service.

(c) 6,930 applications for the Course resulted in only 5,748 enrolments. That is, 1,182 members—17 per cent of all applications—failed to enrol after making application. This figure, plus the 2,718 enrollers who withdrew before completing Part I bring to 3,900 the number of members failing to start the Course—i.e., 55 per cent of all applications.

Though the Education Department is well aware of these facts and figures, it is interesting to note that in the T.G.W.U. Report and Balance Sheet for 1946 the rank and file member and Union official are informed: 'We are also pleased to report a very considerable advance in connection with our correspondence course on "The Union, Its Work and Problems." Up to the end of 1946, 5,125 students enrolled for this course, while 8,649 essays were written and 121 certificates awarded.' (P. 121) Though these figures are accurate, they present an inaccurate picture of the degree of member participation in this course. This misleading report betrays a lack of confidence on the part of Union officialdom in the ability of rank and file members to play an active as well as informed part in the government of their organization. In like vein is a statement by the General Secretary in the June 1947 *Record:* 'We would suggest to our critics . . . that instead of allowing their judgments to be influenced by incidents which are dramatised out of all proportion to their importance in the Press, they should make a proper study of the work and educational methods of the Union.'

Both the report and the article serve to lull lay members and officials into complacency and thus reduce to a minimum the degree of member participation in the operation of the T.G.W.U.

Table XII presents statistics of the annual membership response to all major facilities made available under the Union's Educational Scheme for the years 1936 to 1947 inclusive. These figures, in addition to the number of applicants for University scholarships and the number of enrolments for 'The Union, Its Work and Problems', include the enrolments for correspondence courses with Ruskin College and the National Council of Labour Colleges and the number of students attending summer and week-end schools. It should be noted that these statistics may count the same member more than once, for a member may enrol in more than one course; that, as has been pointed out, there are a large number of withdrawals before completing the Union's most popular course; and that only nine members are accepted out of each year's applications for University scholarships. These statistics thus overestimate T.G.W.U. member

Table XII

MEMBER PARTICIPATION AS EXPRESSED IN THE NUMBER OF ENROLMENTS IN T.G.W.U. EDUCATIONAL SCHEMES FOR THE YEARS 1936–1947 (a)

Year	Total National Membership	No. of Members Enrolling in Union Educational Schemes (b)	No. of Members per 10,000 Participating
1936	561,908	172	3
1937	654,510	149	2
1938	679,360	159	2
1939*	694,474	2,087	30
1940	743,349	621	8
1941	948,079	915	10
1942	1,133,165	1,186	10
1943	1,122,480	1,043	9
1944	1,070,470	1,740	16
1945†	1,019,069	1,667	16
1946	1,273,920	1,807	14
1947‡	1,317,842	4,800	36

(a) Based on information in the Annual Reports of the Education Department to the General Secretary and members of the Educational Committee of the General Council 1936–1947. No records of these data kept before 1936.

(b) From 1936–1938 the figures only include enrolments for Correspondence Courses with Ruskin College and the National Council of Labour Colleges and for Summer Schools.

* From 1939, in addition to the above, the figures include enrolments in the Union's Correspondence Course, 'The Union: Its Work and Problems'. (See Table No. XI.)

† From 1945–1947, in addition to all of the above, the figures include the number of valid applications made for University Scholarships.

‡ T.G.W.U. Report and Balance Sheet (1948), p. 142. This figure includes entries at day and weekend schools not available for other years.

participation in the Educational Programme. They will, however, throw a little more light on rank and file interest and willingness to participate than the response figures previously discussed in relation to University scholarships and the Union's correspondence course.

In 1939, when the Union introduced its own correspondence course, an all-time high of thirty members out of each 10,000 responded to the offers of the Education Department. Prior to that year, an average of two in 10,000 indicated an interest in Union education, and during the past four years (1944–1947) an average of only fifteen members out of every 10,000 (e.g., 1947, 2,029 out of 1,317,842 members) showed enough interest in the Educational Scheme to apply for a scholarship or enrol in a course.

If this analysis does nothing more, it shows that the Union is barely scratching the surface of its educational problem. The low response is both a sign of apathy and, to a certain extent, indicates the limitation of the written word as a means of maintaining constant two-way communication between leader and rank and file. It is not within the scope of this study to make a detailed inquiry into the facilities offered and their administration. But it is suggested that on the basis of this analysis there is good reason for the Union to examine itself carefully, in order to devise a programme, now obviously lacking, that will meet the needs of its membership. Not since 1920–1921, when Ernest Bevin toured the country giving lantern slide lectures, setting forth the structure and functions of what was to become the T.G.W.U., has any real effort been made by the Union to explain by audio-visual techniques to an ever-changing membership the nature of the organization and its problems[1]. The Union's Education Department should explore the possibilities of using the sound film and the film strip as an aid in teaching this large membership something of

[1] 'The Union: Its Work and Problems', Part I, p. 11.

the Union's work and problems. Though the age of pamphleteering has not, I hope, come to a close, the Trade Union Movement would be ill-advised to neglect the educational advantages of radio communication and audio-visual aids to reach its membership.

In response to Press criticism that followed the Unofficial Dock Strike of 1948, Arthur Deakin defended his claim that the T.G.W.U. is 'a really democratic organization' by stressing: 'Our educational facilities—unrivalled in their variety and extent—give every member the means of making an informed contribution.' (See Appendix No. 6.) Mr. Deakin attempted to answer charges against the organization in practice by telling the members about the T.G.W.U. in theory. Though his statement is true, it is extremely misleading, and reveals, in the light of these statistics, an inability to overcome the apathy which renders unsound the claim that the Union is democratic.

The purpose of this analysis would be ill served if the reader received the impression that the Union's Educational Scheme has been a complete failure. Its contribution to providing members with social and economic tools has been valuable though, as shown above, limited. However, deliberately to ignore the facts is a futile policy. By blinding the membership to the real problems confronting the Union's Education Department, the organization is weakened rather than strengthened.

Chapter 9

MEMBERSHIP AFFILIATION TO THE LABOUR PARTY

BEFORE AND AFTER THE REPEAL OF THE TRADE DISPUTES AND TRADE UNIONS ACT OF 1927, IN RELATION TO MEMBER PARTICIPATION

An interesting and indeed a revealing index of apathy in a British Trade Union is to be found in a comparison between the size of a Union's membership affiliated to the Labour Party before and after the repeal of the notorious Trade Disputes and Trade Unions Act of 1927. On May 22 the Trade Disputes and Trade Unions Act of 1946 received the Royal Assent and thereby repealed, *inter alia*, Section 4 of the 1927 Act which 'made the right to obtain contributions to the Political Fund from a member of a Trade Union conditional on a contracting-in agreement in each case'.[1] Under the new Act of 1946 an individual Union member desiring exemption from his Union's Political Levy must sign a contracting-out form[2].

What this means in relation to participation is that the responsibility for taking positive action has now been shifted from the Union member wishing to subscribe to the Union's Political Fund to the Union member preferring not to. Thus, if a large percentage of a Union's membership is composed of members who do not care one way or the other about their Union's political activities or who have been too lazy in the past to declare definitely their wish to contribute to their Union's Political Fund, a large net increase in the Union's membership affiliating to the Labour Party in 1947 will be recorded.

[1] H. Samuels, *The Law of Trade Unions*. (Stevens, London, second edition, 1947), p. 2.

[2] See the Trade Disputes and Trade Unions Act, 1946, as reprinted in the Amendments to Rules as of October 23, 1947, Rule 23, Clause 3, p. 7.

It is with this hypothesis in mind that I draw the reader's attention to Table XIII, showing the annual changes in size of T.G.W.U. membership affiliation to the Labour Party for the period 1935–1947 inclusive. During the twelve years (1935–1946) prior to the repeal of the Act of 1927 the highest net annual change in the size of the T.G.W.U.'s membership contracting into affiliation to the Labour Party was a 14 per cent increase (50,000 members) registered in 1944. For this entire period there was an average net annual increase of 6 per cent.

Table XIII
TRANSPORT AND GENERAL WORKERS UNION ANNUAL CHANGES IN SIZE OF MEMBERSHIP AFFILIATION TO THE LABOUR PARTY 1935–1947

Year	Total (a) National Membership	Member-ship (b) Affiliated to the Labour Party	Affiliated Member-ship as % of Total National Member-ship	Net Increase or De-crease (—) in Affiliated Membership	Net Increase or De-crease (—) as % of Last Year's Affiliated Membership
1934		225,000			
1935	493,266	247,715	49·0	22,715	10·0
1936	561,908	274,454	49·0	26,739	10·0
1937	654,510	301,000	46·0	26,546	9·7
1938	679,360	337,000	50·0	36,000	12·0
1939	694,474	380,000	55·0	43,000	12·7
1940	743,349	373,177	50·0	(—) 6,823	(—) 1·8
1941	948,079	350,000	37·0	(—)23,177	(—) 6·2
1942	1,133,165	350,000	31·0	—	0·0
1943	1,122,480	350,000	31·0	—	0·0
1944	1,070,470	400,000	37·0	50,000	14·0
1945	1,019,069	400,000	39·0	—	0·0
1946	1,273,920	450,000	35·0	50,000	12·5
1947	1,317,842	800,000	60·0	350,000	77·5

(a) Source: From the Financial Secretary's Annual Membership Reports, 1935–1947 addressed to the Chairman and members of the General Executive Council.
(b) Source: Reports of the Annual Conference of the Labour Party, 1934–1947. 1947 Affiliations—figures from the Political and Education Department of the T.G.W.U. June 1948.

The effect of the new Act of 1946 is reflected in the 77·5 per cent increase (350,000 members) in the size of the T.G.W.U. membership affiliating to the Labour Party in 1947. During this same year the net increase in the total membership of the T.G.W.U. was only 3·4 per cent (43,922)—though 480,628 new members joined the Union. Unfortunately, figures are not available to indicate what proportion of the 800,000 T.G.W.U. members contributing to the Union's Political Fund are doing so for the first time. It is evident that at a minimum the figure is equal to the net annual increase of 350,000. This increase of 350,000 members is seven times greater than any previous annual increase registered and is, in fact, greater than the sum total of all increases recorded by the Union for the twelve years prior to the passing of the new Act of 1946.

This fantastic increase is startling but undeniable evidence of apathy within the ranks of the T.G.W.U. This holds true even if one considers the fact that 40 per cent (513,000) of the membership took the initiative to contract out in 1947, while only 35 per cent (450,000) contracted in during 1946. Mass affiliation on such an enormous scale is a danger signal which the Labour Party and the T.G.W.U. would be unwise to overlook[1].

It is a warning to those in the Labour Party who complacently accept the following statement written in 1937 by Clement Attlee, in *The Labour Party in Perspective:*

> In the Labour Party, the Trade Union element serves as the solid core of disciplined membership. The loyalty to majority decisions, which is the foundation of industrial action, takes the

[1] It is interesting to note the satisfaction with which the *Daily Herald*, the official Labour Party paper, on August 12, 1948, printed excerpts of a report to the Annual Conference of the National Union of Seamen by Mr. Percy Knight, National Organiser of the Union (he too was satisfied), to the effect that 'only 221 out of the 60,000 members of the National Union of Seamen have "contracted out" and refused to subscribe to its political fund', for in the previous year (1946) only 7,000 members affiliated to the Labour Party. The paper and Mr Knight would have been wise to point out that whereas only 221 out of 60,000 members refused to affiliate to the Labour Party in 1947, 48,000 out of the 55,000 members in 1946 refused to affiliate.

place of what is called among Conservatives the team spirit, while long training in the responsibilities of Trade Union work has induced a habit of mind which realises the practical necessity for compromise in non-essentials.[1] Members of the T.G.W.U. responsible for the enormous increase in the rise of Union membership contributing to the Political Fund and thus affiliating to the Labour Party were, in all likelihood, the least politically aware and active of the Union's entire membership. To suggest that these men represent the 'solid core of disciplined membership' is to disregard the fact that they represent a large body of apathetic members passing through the Transport and General Workers Union, seldom stopping to take up membership for a sufficiently long period of time to develop a 'loyalty to majority decisions' or 'a habit of mind which realises the practical necessity for compromise in non-essentials.'

The increase registered by all Trade Unions in the size of their respective memberships affiliating to the Labour Party was 53 per cent (1,396,088) over the total Trade Union affiliation of 1946, when a 5 per cent (124,977) increase over 1945 was registered[2]. It would be difficult, in the light of the above information, to argue that this great automatic increase in the Labour Party's Trade Union membership is a direct result of Labour's winning 'more trade union members by convincing them that the Labour Party is worthy of their support.'[3] This dilution of Labour Party membership automatically increases the power position of Unions whose membership is charac-

[1] C. R. Attlee: *The Labour Party in Perspective*. (Gollancz, 1937), p. 127.

[2] Based on figures in the Report of the National Executive Committee to the Forty-seventh Annual Conference of the Labour Party (Scarborough, May 21, 1948), p. 28.

[3] 'Labour hopes that an increasing number of trade unionists will join the Labour Party, and the repeal of the 1927 Act's vexatious requirements will doubtless give them encouragement to do so. But there will be no great automatic increase in the Party's trade union membership, or in trade union financial aid as the Tories suggest. Labour will win more trade union members by convincing them that the Labour Party is worthy of their support.' Labour Discussion Series, No. 5, 'Repeal of the Trade Disputes Act', issued by the Research Department of the Labour Party after the passage of the Act of 1946, p. 11.

terized by a high degree of human inertia and whose representation in the Labour Party could be most easily captured by any highly unrepresentative though politically active body within the Union.

To the T.G.W.U. this automatic increase of 77·5 per cent (350,000) in the size of its membership affiliated to the Labour Party in 1947 is but additional evidence of apathy in the organization. This sudden increase is not the result of a mass conversion. It cannot be attributed to the fact that 350,000 additional members of the T.G.W.U. saw the light between 1946 and 1947 and changed from non-participants to active participants in the political activities of the T.G.W.U. and the Labour Party. This startling increase is but another symptom of a diseased body-politic. It means, among other things, that large numbers of T.G.W.U. members know little and apparently care less about their Union's political power or policy.

To both the Labour Party and the Union—in fact, to the Trade Union Movement as a whole—this information should be justification for an inquiry into the degree of member participation in organizations responsible for this enormous increase. This apathetic mass within the Labour Party must be made aware of its membership and of the reasons for affiliation. Otherwise it would be well to reconsider the advantages of 'contracting-in' as a safeguard against dilution by an unknowing and undisciplined group unlikely to be an asset in time of crisis.

It is evident from the analysis thus far of data on the membership's size, rate of turnover and arrears, degree of participation in elections and in the Union's Educational Scheme, and affiliation to the Labour Party that the term 'apathetic' can, without hesitation, be applied to a very large proportion of the members of the Transport and General Workers Union.

It must not be forgotten that though we have been

dealing with statistics, we have, in fact, been talking about many thousands of individuals who think and feel and wonder. It is to the individual in his Branch, and to the large number of individuals alien to the life of their Branch, that we must turn for further clarification of the problem of apathy and the democratic process in the government of the T.G.W.U.

PART THREE

Where every man is a sharer in the direction of his ward-republic, or of some of the higher ones, and feels that he is a participator in the government of affairs, not merely at an election one day in the year, but every day; when there shall not be a man in the State who will not be a member of some one of its councils, great or small, he will let the heart be torn out of his body sooner than his power be wrested from him by a Caesar or a Bonaparte.

(*Writings of Thomas Jefferson*—20 Vols., Washington, 1904, Vol. XIV, p. 422.)

Chapter 10

MEMBER PARTICIPATION AT BRANCH LEVEL

THE PROBLEM, SOURCES OF INFORMATION AND THE METHOD OF INQUIRY

Where every member is a sharer in the direction of his Branch, or of some of the higher constitutional bodies and feels that he is a participator in the government of the Union, not merely at an election one day in the year, but every day; when there shall not be a man in the Union who will not be a member of some one of its councils, great or small, he will endure untold hardships sooner than let his power be wrested from him by a Labour czar or a proletarian Bonaparte[1].

These requisites of representative democracy originally written to apply to a nation state may appear to be too exacting for a Trade Union—a state within the state. But as has already been pointed out, apathy in a state may be less serious than in a Union, primarily because there are not within Unions two or more recognized and organized parties competing for power and acting as a check on the activities of incumbent officers, both elected and appointed. Furthermore, these requisites of representative democracy are goals the T.G.W.U. and British Trade Unions in general have set for themselves and occasionally claim to have achieved. (See Appendix No. 6.)

Rank and file participation at Branch level is the secret of democracy in the Trade Unions. The analysis of the T.G.W.U.'s Constitution clearly reveals that the Branch is the base upon which the entire structure of Union organization is built. The extent to which the

[1] A paraphrase of a sentence from the *Writings of Thomas Jefferson*—20 Vols. (Washington 1904), Vol. XIV, p. 422.

Union can proclaim that it is a representative democracy is dependent upon the amount and degree of participation by rank and file members at Branch level. Without participation there can be no democracy. Without democracy the control of this powerful state within a state can rest in the hands of an irresponsible few.

It is with this in mind that we turn to the Branch, to the individual member in his Branch, and to the rank and file member alien to Branch life to investigate the manifestations and, where possible, the causes of apathy at this fundamental level of Union organization. The evidence of apathy of a national character already submitted is but a collective image of member participation in approximately 4,000 T.G.W.U. Branches as reflected annually in the mirror of statistical analysis. The Branch itself, however, remains the most obscure of all levels of Trade Union structure. Though the Branch is the unit of organization to one of which all members are attached, its membership, operation and activities have been the subject most neglected both by Trade Unions and in studies of Trade Unionism. A recent survey of British Trade Unions, for example, characterised the rank and file member as 'a great question mark in Union structure'.[1] Unfortunately, to a large extent, the same punctuation is a distinguishing mark of studies on American Labour Unions[2].

In general, official Union literature and studies of Trade Unionism have, in dealing with the Branch and the role of the rank and file member, presented only theoretical concepts. The aim of the investigation recorded in the following pages is to study member participation in Branch activities in order to help fill in the gap characterized by the 'great question mark' hovering over the rectangle designated 'Branch' in the T.G.W.U.

[1] P.E.P. (Political and Economic Planning), *British Trade Unionism* (London, 1948), p. 31.
[2] C. Wright Mills, *The New Men of Power*. (Harcourt Brace & Co., New York, 1948), p. 38.

organizational chart. The focus of attention is on the extent of member participation and on the degree of the rank and file's awareness of and identification with the activities, policy and leadership of both the Branch and the Union.

After determining the extent of rank and file participation, one of the fundamental problems that remain is to locate the apathetic members, the non-participants, to ascertain who they are, why and under what circumstances they fail to exercise their rights of membership. The reverse side of this problem is to determine who of the rank and file exercise the rights of membership, why and under what circumstances. A complete inquiry, therefore, would involve a study of both the active and inactive members. Though the emphasis throughout this research is on the evidences of apathy in relation to the inactive member, the role of the active member is discussed where relevant, and, for purposes of comparison, the active membership is used where possible as a control group.

Before turning to the case study of the Branch the main sources of information—including the Branch selected—and the method of investigation will be considered.

I INTERVIEWS WITH T.G.W.U. OFFICIALS

Interviews with full-time paid officials of the T.G.W.U. varied from informal and frank discussions lasting several hours, to formal, rather cryptic conversations of fifteen or twenty minutes duration. Some officials were interviewed but once; others, with whom I was continually in contact either in Area 1 Office or in Transport House, were frequently willing to discuss Union matters.

For the most part these interviews were concerned with the respondent's views on rank and file participation in the Union and Branch, the effects of national wage negotiations on Branch life, the sharing of responsibility, serving on committees, the success or failure of the channels of communication between leaders and rank and file, and Communist infiltration.

Among those interviewed were: the General Secretary, the Minute Secretary, the Secretary and members of the staff of the Political, Research, Education and International Department, as well as an Area Secretary, an Area Financial Secretary and some Area and District Trade Group Organizers.

The response of these officers, particularly on those phases of Union administration on which they were considered expert, provided background material essential to an understanding of the problem of apathy in relation to the democratic process in the government of the Union. Through their co-operation I was given access to important sources of information not otherwise available and invaluable in carrying out this inquiry at Branch level.

II   RECORDS AND DOCUMENTS

Certain records and documents utilized in this study will be discussed briefly to give some indication of the adequacy and reliability of the material that became available.

Of a general character but of considerable value and significance as background for this investigation are both the essays written by T.G.W.U. members and the verbatim, though unpublished, reports of T.G.W.U. Biennial Delegate Conferences. 'The Importance of Well Attended Branch Meetings' was the essay subject chosen by sixty-seven (75 per cent) of eighty-nine applicants for college scholarships under the Union's Educational Scheme for the academic years 1946 and 1947. Included among the essayists were forty-eight Branch Officials who wrote, with considerable skill, from personal experience of Branches representing members from at least ten of the twelve active Trade Groups located in twelve of the thirteen Territorial Areas of the T.G.W.U.[1]

The unpublished verbatim reports of the Biennial Delegate Conferences, particularly in closed session, were reliable aids in determining the awareness of T.G.W.U. leaders of this problem of member participation at Branch level.

Of a more specific character are the Minutes of Branch meetings and the Branch Membership Records compiled in Area 1's Central Office. Both these documents were essential to this investigation of the 1/AAA, the Branch selected. The names of places, persons, and firms used in this study, except for the names of Union officials above Area level, are fictitious.

The Minutes of all Branch meetings recorded since the first meeting held on May 20, 1942, until December, 1948 (except for the year 1944 for which the records are incomplete) were used in this study. The Minutes for this period are of varying degrees of statistical adequacy and accuracy. Being the work of three Branch Secretaries, the records differ according to their ability and interests in both style and detail. However, it can be said that as all Minutes are read and corrections made before the Branch, these documents are in general reliable. Early records are less exact than those kept since 1946. All Minutes contain the date, time and place of the meeting, the business carried out, including the wording of resolutions, who proposed and seconded them and their fate, the names of those members giving reports and, to a somewhat lesser extent, of those initiating discussion. Prior to 1947 the number of members attending was not regularly recorded. Discussions with Branch Secretaries indicated that absence of an attend-

---

[1] From the analysis of all applications made in 1945 and 1946.

(a) Note an applicant may hold more than one position but here only the most important position for each is recorded: Branch Chairmen, 15; Branch Secretaries, 8; Shop Stewards, 17; Branch Committees, 7; Collectors, 1.

(b) Area 11, Ireland, was not represented.

ance record signified poor attendance. As a member-participant, I took notes to supplement the Minutes of meetings held during the course of the survey.

The Membership Record of the 1/AAA Branch compiled by Area 1 Office is in two sections. The first section is entitled 'Record of Quarterly Changes in Size of 1/AAA Branch Membership'. This section contains the data required for calculating the rate of membership turnover and arrears. This material is used in the discussion of the size of and fluctuations in 1/AAA membership in relation to the opportunities for member participation. The second section contains a complete list of names and addresses of all 1/AAA members, entered according to the shop within Colins' Electroparts Ltd., in which most members work, and within these divisions in order of their joining the Union[1]. In addition, the age and date of entry of each member are recorded. Failure of members to give their right ages or any age at all on application blanks, or to notify the Union of change of address, limits to a certain extent the reliability of the membership list in this section[2]. Except for these limitations both sections of the Record are accurate. This material was used as a basis for stratification of the sample of inactive members and in part for that of active members.

In addition to this raw source material miscellaneous documents were collected. These include, *inter alia*, a Memorandum of Agreement (1946) between Colins' Electroparts Ltd. and eight Unions, including the T.G.W.U.; essays on the 1/AAA Branch written by active members; printed notices of Branch meetings; and ballot papers. It is hoped that by combining these various types of records and documents with the data

[1] Strictly speaking it would be more accurate to say that the members were listed under the Collectors responsible for them, as about 1 per cent of the membership in 1947 did not work at Colins' Electroparts Ltd.

[2] The ages of 35 of the 1,059 members of the 1/AAA were not recorded and approximately 10 per cent of the addresses selected for the sample were incorrect.

collected as a member-participant and through personal interviews, an integrated picture of the extent of member participation in Branch life will have emerged. Every effort has been made throughout to warn wherever data presented are based on inadequate or doubtful sources.

III THE BRANCH SELECTED

For a full study of member participation at Branch level both as a political and sociological phenomenon a very elaborate apparatus would be required. There would need to be an intensive examination by a large staff of a wide variety of Trade Union Branches of different sizes, with members both skilled and unskilled, representing all major Trade Groups located in both urban and rural areas throughout all of Great Britain. This being the work of a single person and because of the scarcity and inadequacy of relevant data, this section must of necessity be devoted primarily to one Branch. In limiting this investigation to a single Branch it has been possible, I believe, to make a more detailed analysis of the problem of apathy than could otherwise have taken place under these circumstances.

For this study of member participation in Branch life, chance rather than careful selection dictated the choice of this T.G.W.U. Branch which we have called the 1/AAA. I do not submit that this Branch is representative of Trade Union Branches, for strictly speaking, a typical Trade Union Branch or even a typical T.G.W.U. Branch does not exist. Even if one does exist, it must go unrecognized, so inadequate are the records and materials available for setting up any criteria by which to judge. I do suggest, however, that there is much which recommends chance's selection for this investigation. A few comments will serve to throw some light on the 1/AAA as a Branch in comparison with other T.G.W.U. Branches[1].

[1] Where comparisons will of necessity be vague because of the absence of data required, words such as 'like many', 'most', 'some' and 'few' will be employed.

A. *The Community of which the 1/AAA is a part*

Like many T.G.W.U. Branches the 1/AAA is located in an urban area—a section of London which, for the purposes of this study, will be known as Southboro. Southboro, in contrast to its proud neighbour Northboro, is in the main a working-class borough of 2,000 acres, with an estimated population (1947) of 116,000. Most prominent landmarks in Southboro are the towering chimneys (each over 200 ft. high) of the Metropolitan power station, and the solitary chimney of the Southboro works of Colins', making dwarf-like the myriad of chimneys atop the houses for workers in the factories.

Southboro people are well acquainted with the housing problem. In 1921, 19 per cent of Southboro's population of 168,000, compared with 18 per cent of London's 4,484,523 people, were living in overcrowded conditions of more than two persons per room. Approximately 50 per cent of Southboro's 43,000 families lived in structurally undivided houses occupied by two or more families. Compared with 44 per cent for Northboro and 50 per cent for all London, 55 per cent of the undivided houses of Southboro were occupied by two or more families. Though strictly comparable figures are not available, housing conditions have improved. By 1938 only 4 per cent of the Borough's reduced population of 141,700 were living in overcrowded dwelling places. Up to 1945 the Borough Council had erected 1,000 dwellings and by the close of 1947 this figure was approximately 1,500, including prefabricated bungalows. By 1948 its official guide claimed 'that in no other borough is better housing accommodation provided for the working class population than in Southboro'.

There is no doubt that much effort, with fine results, has gone into the Borough's work of providing suitable housing accommodation for its people. Southboro remains, however, an unattractive factory town with flats, houses and tenements originally built for workers be-

tween 1839 and 1898 dominating the scene. The clean,
green, open spaces of the Borough—Southboro Park
and Gardens—set out in bold relief the drab atmosphere
of street after street of smoke-covered brick and mortar
which are the work places and dwelling places of its
inhabitants.

Though the majority of Southboro's approximately
40,000 insured workers (working population approximately 60,000) travel to other areas for their work there are
in the Borough sixty firms employing 100–500 workers;
eight firms employing 500–1,000 workers; and seven
firms employing 1,000 or more workers; producing electrical components and canisters, paints, polishes and
publications, as well as metal goods and machines; and
providing services of gas, electricity and transport. The
average rate of pay (1947–1948) for skilled workers at
these firms is 3s. per hour; for the unskilled men and
women it is 2s. 4d. and 1s. 10d. per hour respectively.

Of these firms the largest is Colins' Electroparts Ltd.,
employing, at better than average wages, 2,800 persons
of whom just over 1,000 are members of the 1/AAA
Branch. Many of the 1,800 employees not in the 1/AAA
are members of one of the seven Unions, who, with the
T.G.W.U., are signatories to a Memorandum of Agreement (1946) with Colins'. This culminated many years
of Union activity in what was generally known to be an
anti-Union factory. Though no reliable figure is available, an indication of the extent of unionization in this
firm is to be found in a clause of the Memorandum of
Agreement, which limits workers' representatives on
Joint Production Advisory Committees and the Works
Council to Trade Union members. The Personnel
Manager of Colins' is under the impression that 86 per
cent of the firm had been organized by 1946. The 1/AAA
has the largest number of members of all the Union-
signatories to the agreement.

Periods of unemployment in Southboro are within the

memories of most of the 1/AAA's members. In 1931 there was a daily average of approximately 10,000 on the live register for unemployed at the Labour Exchange. At this time placements averaged about 160 a week. By 1937, when there was an insured population of about 54,000, the daily average of unemployed on the register was down to between 3,500 and 4,000. Southboro now (1947–1948) enjoys full employment. Of the 40,000 insured workers (29,000 men and 11,000 women) an average of only 700 are on the register each *week* and placements average about 1,300 a *month*.

There is a rather common belief among T.G.W.U. officials that Branches located in the North of England, because of their long Labour tradition, are more alert and active than Branches of the South, particularly London[1]. Though it has not been possible to verify that this is the case and the explanation, it is worth noting Southboro's pride in its long-standing Labour tradition. This borough in which 1/AAA members live and work, and, in many cases, grew up, was in the early 'eighties 'the nursery and the cradle of the modern Labour movement and the district to send one of the first really independent Labour M.P.s to Parliament'. He was a Southboro product by birth, by breeding, by schooling and by trade, who entered Parliament as a Socialist toward the close of the nineteenth century.

The Southboro electorate has a better-than-average record in comparison with all London of participation in each of the five General Elections from 1924 to 1945 (Southboro 70 per cent, London 66 per cent); as well as in each of the last four Triennial London County Council and Borough Council elections from 1931 to 1946 (Southboro 36 per cent, London 34 per cent). At the General Election of 1945 Southboro maintained its reputation as a Labour Borough by sending its two

[1] Interview with Miss E. McCullough of the T.G.W.U. Education Department, October 27, 1949.

Labour candidates to Parliament. Compared with a London average of 68 per cent and a national average of 73 per cent, 72 per cent of the Southboro electorate of 70,000 participated in this General Election.

This, by way of background, is something about the community of which the 1/AAA is a part.

B. *Certain Characteristics of the 1/AAA's Membership*

In size the 1/AAA is not unlike Branches to which approximately 35 per cent of the T.G.W.U.'s membership are attached, though only 5 per cent of all T.G.W.U. Branches are in a similar size category. In 1942, at its inception, it was a General Workers Branch with approximately 300 members, rather evenly divided between men and women. By 1945 it had become a composite Branch of General, Engineering and Building Workers and had doubled its membership which had already passed the 600 mark. During the course of the survey (1947–1948) the size of membership fluctuated within closely confined limits above and below 1,000 men (65 per cent) and women (35 per cent) members of whom 56 per cent were General Workers, 38 per cent Engineering Workers and 5 per cent Building Workers[1]. The growth of membership over this seven-year period has placed the Branch at some time during its history in four different size-of-Branch categories, already discussed, in which over 70 per cent of the membership in 1945 were found. (See Table I.) To some extent, therefore, it will be possible to examine the relationship between member participation and the size of the Branch.

The 1/AAA has been confronted with problems of administration and organization associated with both a single Trade Group Branch and a composite Branch—

[1] Note: Of the 1,059 Branch members (1947) 99 per cent were classified as members of one of these three Trade Groups. Less than 1 per cent (not specifically considered in this study) were classified either as Administrative, Clerical and Supervisory Workers or Road Transport Workers.

for intervals of four and three years respectively. In
1947, 43 per cent of the Union's membership belonged to
one of the three Trade Groups of which the Branch is
now composed. (See Table III.) Like many composite
Branches, moreover, the 1/AAA is organized around a
single place of employment—Colins' Electroparts Ltd.
The disadvantages created by not having a membership
with a single Trade entity are counteracted by the common problems and experiences connected with similar
employment under a single employer. This situation, in
addition to the fact that more than 90 per cent of the
Branch's membership live as well as work within walking
distance (a 1½d. bus ride) of the Branch meeting place,
tends to strengthen the Branch as a local organization.

Like some T.G.W.U. Branches, being composed of
both men and women members, the 1/AAA provides an
opportunity for examining the differences in degree of
participation and reasons for non-participation of these
two groups. Approximately 89 per cent of the Union's
membership and only 65 per cent of the Branch's
membership are men[1].

The average annual rate of membership turnover for
the Branch (1942–1947) has been considerably higher
than that for the entire Union over the same period.
This is explained, in part, by the growing pains and
lack of stability characteristic of a relatively young
organization, and in part by the relatively high rate of
turnover characteristic of the three Trade Groups to
which the 1/AAA members are attached. By 1947, however, these fluctuations began to level off. During that
year the Branch registered 46·4 per cent lapses in
membership compared with a national rate of 34·4 per
cent, and a rate of approximately 42 per cent for the
three National Trade Groups combined. The Branch
turnover, based on size of new membership, was 39·1 per

[1] 'T.G.W.U.'s Report and Balance Sheet for the year ended December 1947',
p. 5. Total membership, 1,317,842. Female membership, 144,069.

cent, compared with a national rate of 36·6 per cent and a rate of approximately 41 per cent for the three National Trade Groups combined. (See Tables II, III, and XVIII.) As expected, the discrepancies between the Branch figures and the figures for the three Trade Groups combined in proportion to their relative strength in the Branch, are much smaller than those between the Branch and national figures. The rate of falling into arrears for 1/AAA membership has been strikingly similar to the national rate. (See Tables IV and XX.)

Though the implications of these comparisons are by no means definite they do suggest that the 1/AAA is not a unique Branch. It is not to be found in any extreme categories; rather it tends to be located centrally among all T.G.W.U. Branches whose respective size, composition, rates of membership turnover and arrears have influenced these national and Trade Group averages. It can be said with some assurance that the problems of member participation confronting the 1/AAA that are in any way the result of these fluctuations are not uncommon to many T.G.W.U. Branches. Thus, in relation to these factors, chance has selected a suitable Branch as subject for the study of apathy.

C.   *The 1/AAA's Participation in T.G.W.U. Government, the Educational Scheme, and Outside Trade Union Bodies*

One of the most important factors to be considered in determining the suitability of a particular Branch as the subject for such a study is the extent of its participation as a Branch in the government of the Union. It was first thought that an active Branch, maintaining constant, direct and close contact with the most important constitutional bodies in the T.G.W.U. would, because of its very activity, be an unsatisfactory subject for a study of apathy. On further consideration, however, it became obvious in the light of the analysis of the national organization that a Branch's activity, like a Trade Union's activity, was not an indication of the extent of member participation. Furthermore, in order to determine the effectiveness of the constitutional provisions for member participation at Branch level, it is necessary that the Branch selected be functioning in its relation with other units of the T.G.W.U.'s body politic in accordance with the rules of the Constitution.

As a Branch the 1/AAA has been and is in close and direct contact, via constitutional channels of communication and administration, with the highest and intervening governmental bodies of the Union's organization. The 1/AAA is not an isolated Branch. In fact, if one were searching for a Branch which could be classified among the more active T.G.W.U. Branches, in relation to its own internal operation, its contact with units of organization above Branch level, its participation in the Union's Educational Scheme and its contacts with outside bodies in the Trade Union world, the 1/AAA would be an appropriate choice.

While the rules of the Union require the holding of one Branch meeting monthly, the 1/AAA meets regularly twice each month. Of the seventy-two Branch meetings held during the years 1946, 1947 and 1948 there were twenty-two (30 per cent) at which one or more full-time paid officials were present. In its operation, therefore, it appears on the surface that the 1/AAA provides considerable opportunity for maintaining contact between rank and file, Branch officials and full-time paid Union officials.

Unlike many Branches the 1/AAA has direct contact with all but one of the most important constitutional bodies in the T.G.W.U. At both the 1947 and 1949 Biennial Delegate Conferences of the Union there were two 1/AAA members acting as delegates, while no more than one out of every six or seven T.G.W.U. Branches could possibly have had a representative attending these important policy-making conventions[1]. The number of Branches that could possibly have direct representation on National Trade Group Committees is even smaller (about one Branch in every eighteen). Yet during the 1946-1947 electoral period there were two members of this Branch serving on National Trade Group Committees, as well as, of course, on the corresponding Area Trade Group Committees. In the 1948-1949 electoral period the Branch has only one representative on Area and National Trade Group Committees[2]. Though no member of the 1/AAA sits on the General Executive Council, the Branch's members on the National Trade Group Committee have direct contact with at least one General Executive Council member. With these facts in mind, a glance at the organizational chart on page 44 reveals clearly that the 1/AAA as a Branch is directly linked with the main constitutional bodies of the Union.

Other indications of the Branch's close ties with the Union and its full-time paid officials are to be found in the 1/AAA's sending one of the 121 delegates to the Second National Delegate Conference of Women Members of the T.G.W.U. in 1947[3] and in its sending a delegate to a Conference of Area 1's Women Members in January of 1948, to which only twelve of the 100 Branches invited by Miss F. Hancock, National Woman Officer, to send delegates did so.

As for participation in the Union's Educational

[1] Number of Branches in T.G.W.U. in 1947: 4,642, according to Mr. Edwards, Assistant to the T.G.W.U.'s Minute Secretary. Number of delegates at B.D.C. approximately 700 in 1947 and 1949—Minutes and Record of the Proceedings of the Twelfth (and the Thirteenth) Biennial Delegate Conference—Appendix II, pp. 54-59 (Appendix II, pp. 54-60).

[2] About 225 members serve on the various National Trade Group and Trade Committees—T.G.W.U.'s Report and Balance Sheet for the Years 1945-1948.

[3] T.G.W.U. Minutes and Record of the Proceedings of the National Delegate Conference of Women Members, held on April 25, 1947, London, Appendix III, pp. 19-21. There is no constitutional provision for conferences of this character. The first such conference was held in 1943.

Scheme, the 1/AAA appears to be above average. Of the 151 applications from Union members for University scholarships since this programme began in 1945 (1945–1947) two were received from members of this Branch. Both of these applications were among the 28 accepted[1]. Under the highly unlikely assumption that each of approximately 3,500 enrolments for the correspondence course 'The Union, Its Work and Problems' came from a different Branch, a maximum of 85 per cent of the Union's more than 4,000 Branches could have had but one member enrolled for this course. During this period (1942–1947) four members of the 1/AAA Branch enrolled in the course. In 1947 the General Executive of the T.U.C. inaugurated a series of four-week training courses for active Trade Unionists. Of the forty-one students sent from the T.G.W.U. during the 1947–1948 period three were from this Branch. Thus it can be said that as a Branch the 1/AAA has taken advantage of the facilities provided by the Union's Education Scheme to a greater extent than most T.G.W.U. Branches.

The 1/AAA's most important affiliations outside the T.G.W.U. but within the Trade Union and Labour Movements are with the Labour Party to which its entire membership—both before and since the repeal of the Trade Disputes and Trade Union Act of 1927—has been affiliated. This may be compared with a national affiliation in 1947 of 60 per cent of the membership. (See Table XIII.) This Branch has maintained direct contact with other Trade Union Branches in the area and with the local Labour Party by affiliating to the Southboro Trades Council and Borough Labour Party. In this respect the 1/AAA is like approximately two out of three T.G.W.U. Branches located in Areas outside of Scotland

[1] Both 1/AAA members attended a University for an academic year. Only 27 were officially accepted, for one of the 1/AAA's applicants attended under the auspices of the T.U.C., which awarded her a scholarship at this time as well. (From the files of the T.G.W.U.'s Education Department.)

and Ireland[1]. A 1/AAA member is a delegate from the Southboro Trades Council to the London Trades Council.

Thus chance has to a certain extent biased the selection of a Branch in the direction of more than average activity and more than average direct representation on and contact with the higher and highest levels of the Union's governmental structure. These very features, as has already been suggested, recommend this Branch as a suitable subject for investigating the problem of lack of member participation and interest at Branch level.

If it can be shown that the process of member-participation in the government of this Branch has broken down in spite of the active part it plays in the government of the Union, there would be some justification for the belief that apathy has also infected many of the less active Branches. Certainly many of the problems of member participation confronting the 1/AAA are not uncommon to T.G.W.U. Branches in general. As to its location in the community, the nature of its membership, its location in the T.G.W.U. hierarchy and its affiliations with Labour groups outside the Union, the 1/AAA appears therefore to be a happy choice for chance to make.

IV MEMBER-PARTICIPANT-OBSERVER

One of the real barriers to an understanding of Branch life by an outsider is that normally only members are allowed to attend Branch meetings. To overcome this barrier and thereby to increase the range, reliability and relevance of the material available and the material to be collected, I decided it was essential to join a Trade

[1] 'In 1947, 14,041 branches were affiliated to 485 Trades Councils, which were then registered. . . . The largest union (T.G.W.U.) affiliated to the T.U.C. also has the largest number of branches affiliated to Trades Councils.' (From a letter addressed to me from R. Boyfield, Secretary, Organization Department of the T.U.C., dated October 24, 1949.) In a telephone conversation with Mr. Boyfield on October 25, 1949, I was told that, excluding Scotland and Ireland, on which the T.U.C. has no information, over half of all T.G.W.U. Branches are affiliated to Trades Councils.

Union and participate as a regular member in its Branch life. This method of investigation is in the field of sociology called the participant-observer technique. The key to the success of this technique is to be regarded by members of a community, here the active members of a Branch, as a participant in their activities and interests. The method of observation was a conscious, and where possible, systematic sharing in Branch activities, in order to reduce to a minimum, by direct contact with a Branch in action, the distortion that results from investigations by an outside agent[1].

Briefly, these are the circumstances under which I became a member of the T.G.W.U., with some comments on the extent to which I was accepted as a member of the 1/AAA Branch: In 1947 I enrolled as a student in a four-week training course sponsored by the T.U.C. to provide intensive instruction for active Trade Unionists on specialized Trade Union subjects. The class, which met at Maritime House, Clapham, was made up of twelve Trade Unionists, representing among others the Electrical Trades Union, the National Union of Mineworkers and the Transport and General Workers Union. During this period, over a cup of tea at a corner cafe or in discussion outside of class, I became quite friendly with most of the student-Trade Unionists. Toward the end of the course I was invited by several class mates to attend their Branch meetings and by one, a shop steward in the T.G.W.U., I was invited to join his Branch. Thus, in November 1947, on payment of my first 7d. weekly contribution, I was issued my T.G.W.U. card and attached to the 1/AAA Branch.

I was somewhat concerned as to what type of reception I should be given by the members of the Branch at my first meeting. To my relief, but to my surprise, new

1 See Florence R. Kluckhohn, 'The Participant-Observer Technique in Small Communities' in *American Journal of Sociology*, Vol. XLVI, 1940, pp. 331–343— for an interesting discussion of the advantages and disadvantages of the participant-observer technique.

members were given no special attention or welcome at their first meeting. Thus, with card and with the obviously apparent friendship of a respected shop steward, I found myself accepted by Branch members without their becoming aware of my peculiar interests in their activities. With the shop steward who befriended me, I had already achieved the status of a fellow Trade Union student whom he was able to instruct.

Through regular and punctual attendance I gradually became recognized by active Branch members as an interested member of the Branch. I never played the Branch member perfectly, but there were several indications that I had gained the confidence of the active Branch members. As was customary among members, I was addressed or referred to as 'Brother', or often, in conversation, by my first name. Other indications of acceptance were my nomination as Branch delegate to a meeting to which the Branch was invited to send representatives, and my invitations to attend a meeting of shop stewards on the firm's premises, as well as a meeting of the Southboro Trades Council. The atmosphere of friendliness which surrounded my membership and association with Branch members was the best indication of my being accepted as one of them.

On informing some of the leading members of the Branch, once I had gained their confidence, of the proposed survey and its purpose, I sought their advice and assistance. Of the Branch officials first consulted, only the Branch Secretary, I believe, became suspicious of me, or at least of the proposed survey. She sought advice on this matter from the Secretary of Area 1 and the Union's Education Officer, in order to cover herself in the event of repercussions which might hinder her Trade Union career. It was her fear, which proved to be unwarranted, that members would hold her responsible for giving me their addresses (though names were obtained elsewhere) and that she in turn would lose the confidence not only of her membership but also, and more particularly, of those higher up. Apparently, the Secretary was advised to co-operate with me, for ready access was given to the Minutes of all meetings held by the Branch since its formation in 1942. Frank and open discussion on many Branch problems took place with Branch leaders. Finally, their assistance was sought in the preparation of the schedule of questions for the proposed survey of inactive members. Questions they wanted answered were submitted to me and after several weeks of discussion with a few active members who were convinced of the value of such a survey, the co-operation of the Branch was pledged unanimously at a meeting held on Feburary 23, 1948[1].

As a member-participant I was able to observe who were the regular attenders and how a meeting was actually operated; become conversant with the problems and situations facing the members; and see how paid officials behaved at Branch meetings and how members attending responded to them. My understanding and 'feel' for Branch life and the problems of organization increased through this method and it is hoped thereby that greater accuracy and objectivity than might otherwise have been achieved, have resulted.

V   INTERVIEW SCHEDULE AND INTERVIEW TECHNIQUE[2]

After a short period of regular attendance at Branch meetings, and after an analysis of Branch Minutes and Records of Attendance, it became obvious that these sources, though essential to the success of the study, would not provide a great deal of information about the

[1] Unanimous support of the Branch of 1,059 members was achieved through the vote of 19 members in attendance.

[2] Those who are interested primarily in the results of the survey and are not concerned with how these results were obtained, or with the tests of the samples' reliability, may wish to pass over this section of the study. 'The importance of fully describing the sample and how it was drawn cannot be over-emphasized. Without such information it is impossible to evaluate a given research.' (Quinn McNemar, 'Sampling in Psychological Research' in the *Psychological Bulletin*, Vol. 37, No. 6, p. 349.)

rank and file and their concepts of and familiarity with the Union, the Branch and the officials of both. Attendance at Branch meetings being low, there was no opportunity for making contact with the majority, or even a representative cross section of the total Branch membership. Though it was possible to ascertain the extent of member participation at Branch level, specifically at Branch meetings, there remained a host of questions the answers to which, it was believed, would throw some light on the problem of apathy and could only be found by questioning a cross section of the inactive population. It was decided, therefore, to interview a representative sample of the inactive population (the non-participants) of the 1/AAA and for purposes of comparison to make a similar inquiry of a cross section of the active population (the participants). A discussion of the method of sampling employed will follow the comments on the interview schedule and the technique employed in holding interviews.

The schedule of questions for interviewing is in Appendix No. 9. It was designed to obtain information that would presumably be useful in an analysis of member participation at Branch level. More specifically, these are some of the major questions, the answers to which the interview schedule was devised to find: Why do people join the Union? Do members realize that the structure of the Union provides for their participation in Union activities if they so desire? How effective are the channels of communication relied upon by the Union? What do members know about their Branch, its leaders and their activities? Do they identify themselves with the Union, the Branch and the policy and leaders of both? What are members' reasons for not attending Branch meetings? Do members consider the Branch a unit of a large national organization or do they associate it only with the factory in which they work?

Because the picture of apathy among the rank and file

is so vague, it is with the overall results of the survey that this study is primarily concerned. However, where it is considered relevant and of value, an attempt is made to determine whether or not the response to these questions is significantly different for the active and inactive, and within the inactive population, for married and single, for men and women, for those under 40 and those 40 and over, for those who voted in the General Election of 1945 and those who did not, for those who have been unemployed as much as six months and those who have not, for those whose fathers were Trade Unionists and those whose fathers were not, for those who have attended Branch meetings and read the Union's Rule Book and those who have not. These are some of the major problems on which the questions and sets of questions under the headings YOU, YOU AND THE UNION, and YOU AND THE BRANCH in the interview schedule are designed to throw some light.

All questions were formulated and revised after consultation with Union officials and Branch leaders, and pre-tested in preliminary interviews with members of the 1/AAA Branch. It is believed that all questions asked, with the exception of a set of three (YOU AND THE UNION, Questions 11, 12, 13), concerning 'Union policy' were in language understandable to respondents. To some the term 'Union policy' had one meaning, to others another. Though the interview schedule did not provide for their distinctions, respondents' qualifications on the phrase 'Union policy' were noted during the course of each interview. The response to this series of questions, in spite of these limitations, proved useful in the analysis of the problem.

Another limitation on the adequacy of some questions employed should be noted. Though most questions were designed to be answered by YES, NO, I DON'T KNOW, NEVER HEARD OF IT, or NEVER THOUGHT ABOUT IT, some questions required the respondent to analyse his or her own behaviour or reasoning. Specifically, these questions asked the respondent to give his reasons for joining a Union, or for not attending Branch meetings regularly. Among statisticians this type of question is considered a weak tool of analysis[1]. Since it was decided to include questions of this character, because they lead the respondent rather than the interviewer to determine on what reasons the focus of attention will be placed, a comment on two possible qualifications on their reliability is in order. In the first place, a respondent may not be able accurately to analyse his behaviour. Secondly, a respondent, though able to analyse his behaviour, may not report his reasons accurately, because certain answers may be considered more or less acceptable or embarrassing than others. No doubt, the first qualification applies to several interviews; it remains of interest, however, to know what people think are their reasons for certain behaviour. The second qualification applies to but a few cases and, I believe, seldom went undetected. One example of this will suffice. During the course of an interview a respondent seemed somewhat ill-at-ease in answering the question on his reasons for not attending Branch meetings regularly. Before the end of the interview, the respondent's wife, who had been present all the time, said: 'John, why don't you tell him I won't let you go.' Then the story was divulged of how the wife's brother-in-law ruined his home life by spending all his spare time on Union duties as a shop steward. The value of the data obtained varies greatly, but may be used when these qualifications are borne in mind.

All but one of the questions asked were the same for both the active and inactive samples. Active members were asked what reasons they attributed to inactive members for not attending Branch meetings regularly.

The interview schedule contains a check list of possible replies. These lists were devised after consultation with

[1] Hans Zeisel, *Say It with Figures* (Harper Bros. N.Y., 1947), p. 4.

Union officials and Branch leaders and were used merely as an aid to record responses. The check lists were by no means complete and pre-testing did not reveal many of their inadequacies. The interview schedule in Appendix No. 9 contains the questions as they appeared on the schedule employed, but includes check lists of possible responses containing some revisions based on the experience of the survey itself. Space was provided on the schedule for additional comments about respondents.

The survey of the inactive population was initiated on March 17, 1948, and completed on May 31, 1948. The survey of the active population commenced in February 1948, and sixteen of the nineteen respondents had been interviewed by June 1948. In order to get a representative proportion of active men and women in this sample, three interviews were taken in September 1949. All the interviews took place during a period when both the Union officials and Journal, as well as the national Press, were arousing a great deal of interest in Communist infiltration in the Trade Unions via the Branch. It can be assumed that some replies were coloured by this increased interest in Branch activities.

A local issue, which occurred midway in the course of the interview period, may have resulted in an increase in the number of respondents who expressed some familiarity with Branch and Union activities as well as leaders. After the decision of Colins' Electroparts Ltd.—the employers—to revert to a basic work week of forty-four hours from the forty-hour basic week which the company had adopted in 1937, meetings were held throughout the factory, and a meeting with the largest attendance (sixty-seven of 1,015 members) of any Branch meeting held in 1947 and 1948 took place, with three paid officials present. No attempt has been made to ascertain the effect of this event on the sample, for such occurrences are not to be considered unique in the history of a Branch.

Concurrently with the pre-test of the questions to be included in the interview schedule a pre-test of the approach and technique of holding an interview took place. As a result of this preliminary survey it was decided that interviews with all inactive respondents were to be without advance notice and that all calls were to be made after working hours in the evenings, any day of the week other than pay-days and during week-ends. With the exception of those few who were not at home on a first call—which included mainly shift workers—all interviews took place without prior notice. Where on shift work, arrangements were made to call the following day at a time convenient for the respondent. The decision not to inform members of an impending interview was reached after it was found that those who had been notified tended to consult the Union Rule Book or Handbook to find out about their Union before my arrival. Each interview lasted approximately three-quarters of an hour to an hour-and-a-half.

All interviews were carried out by me. I introduced myself as an American interested in British Trade Unions, who desired their help in gathering material on this subject. I explained that I had some questions I would like answered, that all answers would be considered confidential and that if the respondent preferred not to answer certain questions he should feel free so to indicate. I also expressed a willingness to answer any questions they might have. Of the very few who asked how I obtained their names, all were satisfied by my reply—that a person previously interviewed had mentioned their name. I did not keep the names of those interviewed on the interview schedules, as all was considered confidential; consequently I was not expected to reveal the name of my informant. During the pre-test I found that when introducing myself as an American I was given a more cordial reception than when I omitted the word 'American.' Respondents appeared to be flattered by the interest of a foreigner in their activities, and at the same, time were relieved of any suspicion they might have attached to such an inquiry by an Englishman. There was no possibility of members of the inactive population associating me with the management or the Union.

All but two showed a genuine desire to help me out. I was refused interviews once by a young fellow who went out every evening as soon as he had washed and changed after work, and the second time by the guardian of a prospective female respondent: he, with the assistance of a large dog, was able to convince strange men not to pay calls on his charge. These were the only exceptions. In all other cases I was welcomed into the respondent's home where the interview took place over a cup of tea, or often, weather permitting, we sat on the front steps together, going over the questions.

Questions found under the heading YOU AND THE UNION and YOU AND THE BRANCH were asked in the order in which they appeared on the schedule, unless the respondent in the course of his comments answered questions yet unasked. Questions under the heading YOU on the interview schedule were usually answered haphazardly during the preliminary discussion when we were getting to know each other. Most of the interviews were carried out in the presence of members of the family—wife or husband—a fact which may have influenced the respondent to give answers that placed him or her in the most favourable light. On the other hand, the presence of members of the family made unlikely exaggerations of high degree. In addition to some internal checks of consistency, age, a fact available prior to the interview, was used in checking the veracity of the respondent's answers.

In the case of the active population, many of the respondents were apprised of my Branch membership and of the proposed survey. Because of the relationship that had developed between myself as member-participant and these regular attenders of Branch meetings, interviews by appointment replaced unannounced visits. With these modifications the technique of holding interviews with the active sample was the same as that with the inactive sample.

A possible source of bias is the interviewer himself. As interviewer I made every effort to observe the method decided upon after the pre-test and interviewed only those members selected in accordance with the stratified samples. It is left to the reader to determine the bias of the interviewer, who, as writer, finds difficulty in pointing out his own prejudices.

We now turn to the method of selecting the two samples to determine whether or not the cross sections obtained are fairly representative of the populations from which they were drawn.

VI INTERVIEWS WITH A REPRESENTATIVE SAMPLE OF THE INACTIVE AND ACTIVE POPULATIONS OF THE I/AAA BRANCH
It is necessary, before discussing the method used in selecting the samples, to define for purposes of this investigation the active and inactive populations (or universes) from which the samples were drawn.

The *active population* is made up of the Branch Chairman, Branch Secretary, the Convener of Shop Stewards and all Shop Stewards, Shop Steward-Collectors and Collectors of the 1/AAA Branch as of December, 1947. At the start of this investigation this population was tentatively defined as all those members attending Branch meetings regularly. As a member I soon became aware of the fact that regular attenders could generally be placed in one of the above six categories[1]. Though it

[1] One member, a regular attender not falling in one of these six categories, was excluded from the active population because she never took part and because of rather unusual circumstances surrounding her attendance. It is not suggested that this definition of the active population would apply to all Branches of the T.G.W.U., though some T.G.W.U. officials are of the opinion that such a definition is applicable to many Branches. (Discussion with Miss E. McCullough, of the T.G.W.U. Education Department, October 29, 1949.)

would not be valid to imply that all within these six categories attended Branch meetings regularly, all have been included in the active population on the assumption that being an incumbent officer is an indication of more than average member interest or participation. Of the 1,059 members as of December 31, 1947, thirty men and nine women (about 4 per cent of the total Branch universe) comprised the active population[1].

The *inactive population* includes all members of the 1/AAA Branch as of December 31, 1947, with the exception of all those who joined the Union during the last quarter of 1947 and, of course, the active population. The exclusion of members joining during the last quarter of 1947 was for reasons of convenience and was based on the assumption that these members would have had little opportunity to take part in meetings or become familiar with the Union or the Branch, and also on the fact that all were ineligible to participate in the vote by ballot for Area Representatives to the General Executive Council, held in December 1947. Since questions on the interview schedule concern such matters as regularity of attendance at Branch meetings, familiarity with Union rules and structure, as well as participation in ballot voting, and since it was not practical to determine and thus exclude for example all those who had been in the Union one day, one week or one month, it was decided to exclude all who joined during the last quarter of 1947. About 10 per cent (103 members) of the total Branch universe were excluded with this group. Thus, with the exclusion of the active population of thirty-nine and of the 103 members who joined during the last quarter of

---

[1] In determining the names of the 39 members of the active population it was necessary to include those holding one or more of these positions for the major part of 1947 though in two or three cases the individual concerned either no longer held the position as of December 31, 1947, or was a recent appointee. The number 39, therefore, slightly overestimates the size of the active population at any given time. The list of names of those comprising the active population was obtained primarily from the Branch Secretary and supplemented by data available in the Membership Records of the 1/AAA.

1947, there remained an inactive population or universe of 917 members from which to draw a sample.

A. *The Inactive Sample*

The sample of the inactive population was controlled in two ways—by sex and age groups. This sample of ninety-two respondents was so selected that the proportions of each sex from each age group were similar to those of the total inactive population of the Branch. Table XIV shows the distribution according to sex and age groups of the stratified sample and the inactive population from which it was drawn.

Table XIV
AGE AND SEX DISTRIBUTION OF THE INACTIVE POPU-
LATION AND SAMPLE OF THE 1/AAA BRANCH AS OF
DECEMBER 31, 1947 (a)

| | Inactive Population | | Sample | |
Age	Number of Members	% Distribution	% Distribution	Number Interviewed
TOTAL	917	100	100	92
Men				
15–24	65	7·0	6·5	6
25–34	199	21·6	21·7	20
35–44	197	21·0	21·7	20
45–54	98	11·0	10·9	10
55 and over	40	4·4	4·4	4
TOTAL FOR MEN	599	65·0	65·2	60
Women				
15–24	50	5·5	5·4	5
25–34	75	8·2	8·7	8
35–44	108	12·0	12·0	11
45–54	71	7·8	7·6	7
55 and over	14	1·5	1·1	1
TOTAL FOR WOMEN	318	35·0	34·8	32

(a) Source: Based on information in the Membership Records of the 1/AAA Branch, compiled by a staff clerk and filed in T.G.W.U. Area 1 Office.

Within each of these groups, the sample was drawn at random from the list of 1/AAA members in the Membership Record. The names and addresses on approximately 100 pages of the Record were listed according to the Collector in charge of the shop or shops in which members work, and therein in the order of their joining the Union. To ensure that members of the various Trade Groups represented by various Shop Stewards and/or Shop Steward-Collectors were included within the sample, one name was drawn from almost every page of the Membership Record[1]. It was considered desirable that the sample should resemble the inactive population in this respect, for it was assumed that a respondent's concept of the Union, of the Branch and of his or her responsibilities as a member might be influenced by that member of the active population with whom he or she has most contact.

Unfortunately it has not been possible to obtain all the data required for constructing a table to compare the sample with the inactive population in relation to this variable. An imperfect check of the sample's representativeness has been effected, however, by comparing the percentage of the Branch population (1,020) for which each Shop Steward interviewed claimed to be responsible with the percentage distribution of the inactive sample by each of these Shop Stewards. This check is both imperfect and partial because, firstly, not all Shop Stewards were interviewed; secondly, not all Shop Stewards interviewed revealed the size of their respective 'constituencies'; thirdly, the size of each 'constituency', unlike that of the inactive population, included members who joined in the last quarter of 1947; and fourthly, it was not possible in every case to ascertain who an inactive respondent's Shop Steward was. As a result of

[1] More than one hundred names were drawn in the event that respondents had moved or that for some reason interviews had to be discarded. Of one hundred persons interviewed ninety-two (10 per cent of the inactive population) were included in the sample.

these limitations, Table XV only covers 70 per cent of the inactive sample and 75 per cent of the Branch population of 1,020, 90 per cent of which comprise the inactive population. Table XV indicates that there is

Table XV

A PARTIAL COMPARISON OF THE INACTIVE SAMPLE WITH THE BRANCH POPULATION OF 1,020 ACCORDING TO THE DISTRIBUTION OF MEMBERSHIP BY SHOP STEWARDS RESPONSIBLE, AS OF DECEMBER 1947 (a)

Shop Stewards Responsible (b)	% of Branch Population (c) (1,020)	% of Inactive Sample (d) (92)
A-1	9	7
A-2	3	3
A-3	12	10
A-4	5	5
A-6	3	5
A-7	6	5
A-9	3	1
A-10	5	7
A-11	3	1
A-13	4	7
A-15	6	5
A-19	16	14
TOTAL %	75	70

(a) Source: Based on data collected during the survey of the active and inactive populations, and on information from the Membership Records of the 1/AÅA, compiled by a staff clerk, and filed in Area 1 Office.

(b) 'A-1', etc., are the code numbers used in filing the interview schedule of active members.

(c) Note: (i) Percentages are of the Branch population of 1,020 and not of the inactive population of 917.

(ii) The possibility of a Shop Steward respondent's inflating the size of his 'constituency' to give the impression of greater responsibility than actually possessed is not to be ignored.

(d) The percentages are of a sample of ninety-two drawn from an inactive population of 917. Thus the corresponding figures in the '% OF BRANCH POPULATION' column are not strictly comparable.

L

some justification for concluding, after taking these limitations into consideration, that the distribution of the inactive sample by Shop Stewards responsible does not differ materially in this respect from the actual distribution of the inactive population from which it was drawn.

A check of the method of random selection within the stratified sample in relation to the length of membership (based upon the year of entry) of the inactive population with that of the sample has been possible. Length of membership is another variable factor which might influence a member's response to queries relating to his familiarity with and concept of the Union and Branch. By comparing the observed characteristics of the length of membership of the respondent interviewed with the expected characteristics, the 'goodness of the fit', or the reliability of the sample can be judged. The expected characteristics are those which the sample would have had if it were stratified, according to length of membership, as was the case for sex and age groups. The observed characteristics are those that actually resulted in the sample taken. In using a chi square (x^2) formula to test the goodness of the fit, if P is found to be between ·05 and ·95 the fit is said to be satisfactory[1]. That a fairly representative sample was obtained is indicated by Table XVI. P is approximately ·50 which means that as great a discrepancy between the observed and the expected characteristics in relation to length of Union membership of a sample would be found in one out of every two such samples. There appears to be no significant bias as to this variable, which might be reflected in the sample of the inactive population. The sample's representativeness is therefore satisfactory.

Marital status of members of the inactive population is another characteristic by which the sample would have

[1] For a detailed discussion of the use of *chi* square (x^2) for testing 'the goodness of fit' see Quinn McNemar, *Psychological Statistics* (John Wiley & Sons Inc., N.Y., 1949), Chapter 11, particularly pp. 211–215. $x^2 = \Sigma[(O-E)^2/E]$, id. at p. 186.

Table XVI

OBSERVED AND EXPECTED FREQUENCY DISTRIBU-
TION OF THE INACTIVE SAMPLE OF THE 1/AAA BRANCH
ACCORDING TO LENGTH OF MEMBERSHIP IN THE
T.G.W.U. AS OF DECEMBER 31, 1947 (a)

Length of Membership Years (b)	Actual Number Observed in Sample O	Number Expected in Sample E	$O-E$	$(O-E)^2$	$(O-E)^2/E$ (c)
One	15	17	−2	4	·24
Two	50	44	+6	36	·82
Three	17	19	−2	4	·21
Four	7 ⎫	6 ⎫			
Five	1 ⎬ 10	2 ⎬ 12			
Six	2 ⎪	3 ⎪	−2	4	·33
Seven	0 ⎭	1 ⎭			
TOTAL	92	92	0		$1·60 = x^2$

$$df = 3$$
$$x^2 = 1·60$$
$$P = ·50$$

(a) Source: Based on information in the Membership Records of the 1/AAA Branch, compiled by a staff clerk and filed in T.G.W.U. Area 1 Office.

(b) Any fraction of one year is counted as a full year, i.e., all members counted in the two-year length-of-membership category joined sometime in 1946.

(c) See note 1, p. 162.

been stratified, if possible. This information was not available on the male membership of the Branch. It was possible, however, to estimate the marital status of the female membership by counting those whose names were prefixed by 'Mrs.' in the Record of Membership.

'Mrs.' sometimes indicated divorced, separated or widowed members, and it was found during the course of the survey that some married women members failed to indicate their marital status on application blanks. This method of determining marital status, therefore, results in at best a rough estimate. Of the Branch popu-

lation of 1,020 which excludes the active population, 25
per cent (251) were married women (i.e., listed as 'Mrs.'),
while 24 per cent (22) of the sample of the inactive population were married women. The sample, therefore, based
on this rough estimate in relation to marital status,
appears to be fairly typical of the inactive universe.

One other variable which might have been controlled
if it had not been considered both impracticable and
unnecessary for the purpose of this survey was the distance between home and Branch meeting place. Certainly
this factor could, particularly in rural areas, affect member participation in Branch activities. An estimate prior
to making the survey indicated that more than 90 per
cent of the total Branch membership of 1,059 lived
within a short distance, i.e., a 1½d. bus ride—or a maximum of one mile—from the meeting place. While about
5 per cent of the total Branch membership lived more
than three miles—or at least a 4d. bus ride—from the
Branch, four (4·4 per cent of the sample) inactive
respondents of the ninety-two interviewed lived as much
as or more than a 4d. bus ride from Southboro Trades
Hall, the Branch meeting place[1]. There appears to be
no significant bias, therefore, in relation to this at-
random characteristic of the sample.

This information on the basis of stratification, the proportion of certain at-random variables in relation to
estimates of these variables in the inactive and total
Branch populations, and the comparisons of expected
and observed characteristics of various at-random features of the sample tend to establish that the sample is
typical of the population from which it was drawn. It is
safe to assume, therefore, that this sample is a representative cross section of the inactive population of the
1/AAA Branch.

[1] Average distance covered by each fare-stage of London Bus Routes is one mile.
For example, 1½d.=1 mile, 2½d.=2 miles, 4d.=3 miles, etc. (Public Relations
Department, London Transport Executive); and the A1 *Atlas of London and Outer
Suburbs* (Geographia Ltd.).

B. *The Active Sample*

It was not practicable in drawing the sample of the active population to apply the same method of stratification employed for the inactive sample. Nor was it possible to obtain a sample that was completely at random outside the only stratified variable—sex. A large proportion (50 per cent) of the active population of thirty-nine were interviewed. Of these nineteen respondents, 79 per cent (15) were male, in comparison with the 77 per cent of the active population who fell in this category.

Table XVII

DISTRIBUTION BY SEX OF BOTH THE SAMPLE AND THE ACTIVE POPULATION OF THE 1/AAA AS OF DECEMBER 31, 1947

(Showing actual size in parentheses)

	Sample %	Population %
Male	79 (15)	77 (30)
Female	21 (4)	23 (9)
TOTAL	100 (19)	100 (39)

Though it was intended that the sample be at random for all other characteristics, the circumstances surrounding the arrangements for interviews prevented this and resulted in a definite bias in favour of the most active and influential members of this universe. This was due to the fact that interviews with active members, unlike those with the inactive, were by appointment only. Many who were approached either expressed an unwillingness to be interviewed or claimed to be too busy whenever asked. This was the case particularly among active members who did not attend Branch meetings regularly and who, being unfamiliar with the Branch's approval of the survey, were reluctant to take part. Most of those interviewed, therefore, were members with whom I became well acquainted at Branch meetings. These respondents included the Branch Chairman, the Branch Secretary, the Convener of Shop Stewards and the leading Shop Stewards and Shop Steward-Collectors representing more than 70 per cent of the Branch membership. (See Table XV.) The fact that the response was greatest from the most active and influential members of the active population may be reflected in the results obtained by indicating a more significant difference between the active and inactive population than does in fact exist.

It has been possible, however, to ascertain the representativeness of this sample in relation to age groups (under forty and forty and over) as well as in relation to length of membership in the Union. The application of the chi-square test revealed that a cross section fairly typical of the active population in relation to these variables was obtained. Though there tends to be a bias in the sample of active women in the direction of those forty years of age and over, P is approximately ·30 which indicates that the discrepancies between the observed and expected frequencies of these age groups are not significant. In relation to length of membership, the value of P is approximately ·70. The fit is satisfactory for in seventy out of a hundred such samples it is probable that similar results would obtain,

Thus, in spite of the bias already noted, the sample appears to be typical of the active population in several variables. The fact that the most influential members of the active population appear to dominate the sample does not, I believe, impugn its value for purposes of comparison with the inactive population in this study of apathy.

In summary, the purpose of this discussion of the problem, the sources of information—including the Branch selected—and the method of inquiry, has been to point out the areas of possible bias and error as well as the degree of reliability of the data collected and the representative nature of the samples and of certain characteristics of the Branch from which they were drawn. Though there is considerable evidence for concluding that the samples and the Branch selected are significant objects for this investigation, it cannot be overemphasized that this section is devoted primarily to a study of one Branch and its membership. Therefore, the general applicability of the findings and certainly the conclusions, where based solely upon this Branch, are but tentative and must await the substantiation, refinement or contradiction of future surveys.

Chapter 11

THE IMAGE OF THE BRANCH IN THEORY

> 'It is in the Branch that Union policy is hammered out, and it
> is in the Branch that the individual member can begin to play
> his or her part in Union affairs. A healthy Branch life is therefore
> essential. No voluntary organisation, such as our Union, can
> progress without a virile membership, experienced in debate and
> accustomed to giving and receiving constructive criticism.'
> (*T.G.W.U. Members Handbook*, p. 11.)

The constitutional provisions relating to member participation in the government of the Branch and the function
of the Branch in the government of the Union have
already been analysed in some detail. A review of the
theoretical image of the Branch disclosed in this analysis
will serve as a frame of reference for the image of the
Branch in action as it emerges from the study of the
1/AAA.

The Branch is the only organ of the Union's body
politic of which all members are always a part. Unlike
the other constitutional units of Union organization, the
Branch is not a representative body. It is rather the
membership itself. The Branch system is a device whereby the Union's membership is divided according to trade,
place of work, or both, into effective governmental units
of which all other levels of organization are representative.

The Branch is the meeting place of the members. It is
the only level of organization on which every member
is entitled to participate in the government of the Union.
Branch officials—the Branch Chairman, the Branch
Secretary and Branch Committee men—are nominated
and elected by and from its membership for two-year
terms. It is in the Branch that candidates are nominated

to stand election to the various Trade Group, Area and National bodies, and it is through the Branch that the distribution of ballot papers is effected. The Branch is more than the local government of a nation-wide organization, for it concerns itself with matters of national as well as local character. It is required to convene at least once a month in order to provide all members with the opportunity to share the power of initiating policy as well as the responsibility of carrying it out. The Branch is the members' forum. 'It is there that he can express his opinion, record his vote, make known his objection (and) air his grievances in a truly democratic manner, because the formation of that policy . . . is in his own hands.'[1]

The Branch is the primary channel of two-way communication between the individual member and those serving on all higher levels of Union organization. It is from the Branch that resolutions, prepared and approved there, are sent to the Biennial Delegate Conference, the General Executive Council and all bodies at intervening levels of organization. It is to the Branch that the Union Organizer and other full-time paid officials address their communications. It is to the Branch meeting place that these officials go in order to maintain contact with the rank and file for whom and to whom they are, in the final analysis, responsible. In like manner, the rank and file members attend Branch meetings in order to maintain contact and thus communicate with their paid officials as well as their fellow Branch members.

The Branch, therefore, is the democratic foundation upon which the Union's structure rests. Though the Branch is not, strictly speaking, the Union's local authority, like local government it serves as an object—smaller and less remote than the National Union or even

[1] From an essay on 'The Importance of Well-Attended Branch Meetings', by a T.G.W.U. member from Area 2, applying for a scholarship under the Union's Educational Scheme.

the Territorial bodies—with which members are able to identify themselves and thus experience a sense of belonging. In his reply to Press criticism following the Dock Strike of 1948, the General Secretary expressed this concept concisely when he said: 'Above all, there is a place for every member in his branch, from which all Union activity springs.' (See Appendix No. 6.)

The analysis of the Union's Rules and Constitution disclosed that the body politic of the T.G.W.U. in theory provides ample opportunity for all members to participate in its activities, and that the success or failure of this system of representative government depends upon the degree of member participation at Branch level, i.e., the extent of Branch life or lifelessness. The Branch, in providing the means for sharing information, power and responsibility with the broad base of Union membership, is the fundamental unit underlying the hierarchy of policy-making and executive bodies which constitute the government of the Union.

The operation of the Union's organization as a democratic association obviously rests on the assumption that there is a high degree of member participation in Union activities at Branch level. We must examine, therefore, the Branch in action to determine how valid is this assumption or, in other words, how close is the resemblance between the theoretical image of the Branch and the image of the Branch in practice about to be disclosed.

Chapter 12

THE IMAGE OF THE BRANCH IN ACTION

AN INTRODUCTION

'. . . The members of our early formed Branches fought because every single issue was a live, personal and intimate one. They knew what was happening and why it was happening, and the importance of the Branch was clear. . . . (They) followed with anxiety the every turn and twist in the local negotiations and eventually felt the pangs of disappointment or the joy of success. . .

'. . . That such (national) machinery is both necessary and essential would be foolish to deny, but I cannot but feel that it does tend to make the fight a less personal one for the average member. Not being an actual eye witness to all that the struggle entails he too often simply sits back contented that his sole obligation is that of paying subscription.'

(From an essay by a T.G.W.U. Branch Chairman of Area 3.)

The centralization of Union administration has been an inevitable concomitant of the trend toward national wage agreements[1]. This marked trend, in addition to an apparent trend toward an official T.U.C. national wages policy, has removed an immediate bread-and-butter

---

[1] (a) *The Union, Its Work and Problems*, Part III.

(b) An Area Secretary of the T.G.W.U., in a personal interview in February 1948, gave another interesting illustration of this trend: 'We've often negotiated pay increases or holiday pay without the knowledge or the suggestion of the rank and file. The first time they realize that there has been a wage increase is when they receive their pay packet.'

(c) 'Because negotiations in many major fields are on a national level the interest in the Branch is dropping.' (From my notes of remarks by Vincent Tewson, General Secretary of the T.U.C., Transport House, October 30, 1947.)

(d) For an excellent discussion of this trend towards national wage agreements and their effects on U.S. Labour Unions see Joseph Shister, 'Trade Union Government: A Formal Analysis', in *Quarterly Journal of Economics*, Vol. LX, November 1945, No. 1.

incentive to member participation at Branch level[1]. The establishment of national wage agreements by no means eliminates the function of the Branch in its relations with management and the factory. Wage agreements must be enforced. Piece rates are determined by local negotiations. The settlement of grievances is an important item of business at most Branch meetings and a major activity of shop stewards. Hours of work, grievance procedure, safety requirements, canteen facilities, order of layoffs during periods of redundancy, and other matters of every-day interest to workers in a plant are subjects of local Branch-management negotiation.

The importance of such participation to the democratic process in Union organization has increased rather than, as might be argued by the efficiency expert, decreased, for it cannot be overemphasized that a Trade Union is more than a service organization or an economic institution. It is a powerful political creature whose decisions to act or restrain action and whose ability to enforce its decisions have wide socio-political as well as economic implications—not only for its members but also for the nation of which it is a part[2].

The democratic determination of Union policy, however, is endangered for the very reason that the efficient administration of the Union's service functions requires

---

[1] (a) '. . . Congress pledges its continued support of the policy aimed at securing the greatest possible measure of restraint in seeking to increase personal incomes and expenditure unrelated to increased productivity.' (Part of a motion approved by a 6 to 1 majority—The Report of the 81st Annual Trades Union Congress, Bridlington, 1949, pp. 435–460.)

(b) 'The General Council are emphatic that while it is the responsibility of the Unions themselves to operate wages policy, Unions nevertheless must pay regard to the realities of the economic situation in framing their policy and act loyally in conformity with the policy now recommended by the General Council.' (From a circular letter sent by Mr Vincent Tewson, General Secretary of the T.U.C., to all affiliated Unions and quoted in *Labour—The T.U.C. Magazine*, December 1949, p. 544.)

[2] As a result of the Unofficial Dock Strike, for example, which occurred in 1949, over 400,000 working days were lost in the Port Transport Industry. ('Review of the British Dock Strikes 1949', presented by the Minister of Labour, December 14, 1949, H.M. Stationery Office, Cmd. 7851.)

a highly-skilled bureaucracy. In the absence of an active rank and file the members of this bureaucracy, permanent paid officials whose power and authority are enhanced by the very nature of their activities, may assume the function of policy makers[1]. The Branch, as has already been noted, remains the only unit of Union structure available to all members at all times for that continuous participation virtually indispensable to democratic control, if bureaucracy's bent for omnipotence is to be checked.

Therefore, because of the increasing need for Union 'civil servants' and in spite of the fact that a powerful incentive to participation at Branch level has been removed, a high degree of member interest is vital not only to the success of the democratic process in the government of the T.G.W.U., but also to the economic life of the nation which benefits or suffers from the Union's success or failure in carrying out its decisions.

With this comment, and the image of the Branch in theory as reference, we turn to the 1/AAA Branch in motion and to other T.G.W.U. Branches on which information is available, to determine how successful the Branch is in fulfilling its function of eliciting member participation in the government of the Union.

[1] An interesting analysis of this problem in relation to American Labour Unions has been made by Will Herberg, Research and Educational Director, New York Dress Makers' Union of the International Ladies' Garment Workers Union (A.F.L.) in 'Bureaucracy and Democracy in Labor Unions', in *The Antioch Review* (Fall 1943).

Chapter 13

THE SIZE, TURNOVER AND ARREARS POSITION OF THE 1/AAA BRANCH MEMBERSHIP

In the chapters devoted to some causes and evidence of lack of member participation in the T.G.W.U., statistics on the size of membership and its turnover and arrears position served as useful indices of apathy. This same method of analysis is applied at Branch level in an examination of the 1/AAA membership.

1 SIZE

The size of a Branch is an interesting index of its external strength within the factory in which it operates, within the Union of which it is a part and within the Trades and Labour Councils to which it may be affiliated.

Unlike corresponding figures for the Union, the actual size of a Branch's membership and the record of its growth and decline are, as a rule, not made public. It is assumed that by creating a myth of membership greater than does exist, the power and prestige of a particular Branch in its negotiations with management and its relationship with the workers themselves, are enhanced. Within the government of the Union, size, in spite of constitutional checks, may to a large extent determine the weight of a Branch's authority.

Between 1942 and 1948 this Branch has registered an average net annual increase of 29·6 per cent. (See Table XVIII.) At the time of the survey (1947) the Branch's membership of 1,059 men and women represented an increase in size of approximately 260 per cent over its original 1942 membership of 292. In the years 1945 and 1946 the membership increased by 133 per cent (394 members) and 71·4 per cent (493) members respectively. Though these figures were not made public, this enormous growth, in conjunction with successful organizing campaigns by seven other Unions, resulted in recognition by and a works agreement with the traditionally anti-Union Colins' Electroparts Ltd. in 1946. As the Branch is the basic unit of Union organization, its size and the changes in its size, unlike corresponding data on the Union as a whole, disclose substantial information on its ability to provide an opportunity for member participation. Branch size alone has deprived most 1/AAA members of the opportunity of taking an active part in Branch activities. Very little imagination is required to visualize how unwieldy and inefficient the administration of the 1/AAA's twice monthly meetings would be if even its mimimum membership of 292 ever decided to attend regularly. The physical impossibility of the 1,059 members becoming 'experienced in debate and accustomed to giving and receiving constructive criticism' by regularly attending 1/AAA Branch meetings is patently obvious. As has already been disclosed in Chapter 5, Branches within this size-of-membership range are common to the T.G.W.U. More than 75 per cent of the Union's 1,019,069 members in 1945 were in Branches with memberships of 200 or more workers. (See Table I.)

The huge net increases in size registered in 1945 and 1946 give some indication of how enormous is the problem confronting the Branch of establishing communication with new members and thereby orienting them to the responsibilities of citizenship in Union government. A more comprehensive picture of this problem can be had by an examination of the real ebb and flow of membership as revealed in member turnover figures.

II TURNOVER

Essential to an understanding of a Branch's internal strength and of the extent of rank and file participation that can take place in its activities is an analysis of the real gains and losses in membership as expressed in the size of a Branch's turnover[1].

Evidence of apathy is to be found in membership turnover as expressed in the rate and number of annual lapses in membership. A fundamental reason for lapses in membership is the failure of the member to identify himself with the Branch and through the Branch with the Union to which he belongs.

Large turnover as expressed in both the size of new membership and lapsed membership is a principal cause of apathy within a Branch. A high rate of turnover automatically limits the number of Branch members entitled to hold office. At the same time it makes continuous two-way communication between Branch leader and rank and file and in turn, between Union leader and rank and file, extremely difficult. It is high turnover at Branch level which should serve as a danger signal to both Branch leaders and Union officials of a breakdown in the system of participation which is a requisite of its democratic government.

It is with these factors in mind, in addition to those already discussed in Chapter 5, that the statistics in Table XVIII on the Annual Changes in Size of Membership of the 1/AAA Branch, showing new and lapsed membership for the years 1942–1948 are to be analysed. The footnotes to this Table set out certain qualifications which must be taken into consideration in using the data presented.

During the 1942–1948 period covered in Table XVIII turnover, as expressed in terms of lapsed membership, has been on an average 69·0 per cent of the total Branch membership. During the war, when many families were

[1] Formula: (a) $\text{Turnover} = \dfrac{\text{lapsed membership of current year}}{\text{total membership of previous year}}$

(b) $\text{Turnover} = \dfrac{\text{new membership of current year}}{\text{total membership of current year}}$

being evacuated from Southboro and when the Branch was struggling, as young organizations must, to establish itself, lapses were extremely high. In 1943 a maximum of 94·7 (284 members) of the Branch membership of 300 lapsed. Since that year the rate of lapses has steadily declined. A minimum of 46·4 per cent which appears to be a levelling-off point was reached in 1947. It is interesting to note, however, that during that year the largest number of lapses (550 of 1,184 members) took place.

Table XVIII
T.G.W.U.'S I/AAA BRANCH ANNUAL CHANGES IN SIZE OF MEMBERSHIP
DECEMBER 31, 1942—DECEMBER 31, 1948 (a)
(Showing Gains and Losses in Membership and the proportion of previously Lapsed Membership which rejoins the Union in relation to New Membership)

Year	Total Branch Membership	Lapsed Membership (b)	Lapsed Membership as % of Last Year's Total	New Membership (c)	New Membership as % of Current Year's Total	Rejoined Membership as % of New Membership (d)	Net Increase or Decrease (−)	Net Increase or Decrease (−) as % of Last Year's Total
1942(e)	300	151	—	—	—	—	—	—
1943	265	284	94·7	247	93·2	4·9	−35	−11·7
1944	297	226	85·2	260	87·5	0·8	32	12·1
1945	691	217	73·1	613	88·8	0·8	394	133·0
1946	1,184	473	68·5	963	81·2	5·0	493	71·4
1947	1,059	550	46·4	414	39·1	18·6	−125	−10·5
1948	881	492	46·5	322	36·5	29·5	−178	−16·8
Average %			69·0		71·3	9·9		29·6

(a) Source: Compiled on the basis of information in the Record of Quarterly Changes in Size of I/AAA Branch Membership, compiled by a staff clerk and filed in T.G.W.U. Area I Office.
(b) Lapsed membership: (i) Excludes lapses through death. During period 1942–1948 only two Branch members lapsed through death. (ii) Excludes members transferring out of the Branch but remaining in the T.G.W.U.
(c) New membership: (i) Includes previously lapsed members who have rejoined the Union. (ii) Excludes members transferring from another T.G.W.U. Branch.
(d) Rejoined membership means: Members previously lapsed who have rejoined the Union.
(e) Membership was first recorded in the I/AAA Branch on May 20, 1942.

To attribute this high rate at which 1/AAA members drop out of the Union to a high labour turnover at Colins' is, on the basis of the incomplete evidence available, without justification. It is generally accepted by workers at Colins' that long service and low turnover are characteristic of the employment situation there[1]. Lapses are in part explained by the failure of Collectors energetically to pursue their 'constituents' for dues each week. This is, however, but another indication of the individual member's lack of interest. As these lapse figures exclude all those transferring out of the Branch though choosing to remain in the Union, they clearly indicate how widespread is the indifference of the individual member to his Union. This indifference is further reflected in the large percentages (18·6 and 29·5) of new members who had previously lapsed and who in 1947 and 1948 rejoined the Branch. These enormous fluctuations expressed in terms of lapsed membership give evidence of the failure of the 1/AAA Branch to elicit the active participation of those it represents.

Though an average net annual increase of 29·6 per cent was recorded for this period (1942–1948) an average of 71·3 per cent of each year's membership was comprised of new members. Turnover expressed in new members was at a maximum in 1943 when 92·2 per cent of the 265 members had joined within the year. The fact that the proportion of new membership to Branch membership remained well above 85 per cent between 1943 and 1946 is to be explained in part by the Branch's organizational drive which was given real impetus by the arrival of Sister Johnson and Sister Brown in 1945, and in part by the high rate of lapses concurrently re-

[1] The firm refused to divulge labour turnover figures. The Convener of Shop Stewards believes that labour turnover has always been considerably below 20 per cent. Some other indications that there is not a close correlation between lapses and labour turnover are that of five lapsed members met by chance during the survey all were still Colins' employees, and of seven replies to an unsuccessful postal survey in which fifty lapsed members were sent questionnaires, five (71 per cent of the respondents) were still working at Colins'.

corded. More will be said of Sisters Johnson and Brown, energetic Communist Party members, at a later stage of this survey. In 1947, 414 new members (39·1 per cent of the total membership) joined the Branch. This percentage was the lowest recorded up to that time and is considerably below the 71·3 per cent average for the entire period.

The effect of these high rates of turnover on the distribution of the Branch's membership according to length of membership as of 1947 is presented in Table XIX.

Table XIX
THE DISTRIBUTION OF T.G.W.U.'s 1/AAA BRANCH MEMBERSHIP BY YEAR OF ENTRY AS OF DECEMBER 1947

Year of Entry	Number	% of Total Branch Membership
1947	278	26
1946	454	43
1945	198	19
1944	70	6
1943	18	2
1942	29	3
1941	12	1
	1,059	100

This table reveals that in 1947 only 4 per cent of the entire membership, which is about 14 per cent of the original membership, had been in the Union since the Branch's founding in 1942. Though, from a statistical point of view, a complete turnover in membership took place during the 1946–1947 period, only 70 per cent of the membership were comprised of workers who joined the Branch during this period[1].

[1] The discrepancy between the 26 per cent figure for the membership that had joined the Branch in 1947 and remained in it and the 39.1 per cent figure for new membership (see Table XVIII) should be noted. This is to be explained in part by the fact that some members joining in 1947 lapsed in 1947 and, of more importance, by the fact that rejoined members may be listed in the Records of Membership as of the initial date of their joining.

This analysis of member turnover in relation to apathy and lack of member participation in the 1/AAA leads to the same conclusions as those reached in the analysis of the T.G.W.U.'s turnover figures which were, after all, a reflection of similar situations in many of the Union's 4,000 Branches.

III THE ARREARS POSITION AND THE PROPORTION OF MEMBERSHIP ELIGIBLE TO HOLD OFFICE

It has already been explained in some detail that to be in arrears for six consecutive weeks or more is to deprive oneself of the right to apply for any official position in the Union for a two-year period subsequent to rejoining the ranks of members in good standing. To fall into arrears for thirteen consecutive weeks is to forfeit the right to vote in Union elections by ballot.

Table XX presents the arrears position of the membership of the 1/AAA Branch for each quarter from June 1942 through December 1948. At the close of each quarter during this period an average of 84·5 per cent of the membership have been in benefit. This means that during each quarter at least one out of every seven members disqualified himself from serving the Branch and the Union in an official capacity for a period of two years. As of December 31, 1947, of the total Branch membership of 1,059 approximately 904 (85 per cent) were members in good standing and eligible to vote, though in most cases ineligible for office. In view of the high member turnover that plagues this Branch, the low percentage of membership in arrears at any one time is more a credit to the Collectors than it is evidence of a high degree of member interest. It is a generally accepted view among members of the active population that when an efficient Shop Steward-Collector resigns or leaves his department the rate of arrears and of lapses in his former 'constituency' automatically increases. This is substantiated, for example, by the overall figures for each of the

Table XX

T.G.W.U.'S 1/AAA BRANCH ARREARS POSITION OF MEMBERSHIP FOR EACH QUARTER JUNE 1942–DECEMBER 1948 (a)

Year and Quarter	Under 7 Weeks in Arrears	7–13 Weeks in Arrears	Over 13 Weeks in Arrears	Total Membership	Under 7 Weeks in Arrears as % of Total Membership	7–13 Weeks in Arrears as % of Total Membership	Over 13 Weeks in Arrears as % of Total Membership	Total %
'42 June	279	12	1	292	95·6	4·1	0·3	100·0
Sept	306	44	4	354	86·5	12·4	1·1	100·0
Dec	227	50	23	300	75·6	16·7	7·7	100·0
'43 Mar	194	31	15	240	80·9	12·9	6·2	100·0
June	236	10	16	262	90·1	3·8	6·1	100·0
Sept	234	30	24	288	81·3	10·4	8·3	100·0
Dec	210	37	18	265	79·3	13·9	6·8	100·0
'44 Mar	201	13	7	221	91·0	5·9	3·1	100·0
June	281	17	9	307	91·6	5·5	2·9	100·0
Sept	238	13	6	257	92·6	5·1	2·3	100·0
Dec	283	11	3	297	95·3	3·6	1·1	100·0
'45 Mar	283	22	3	308	91·9	7·1	1·0	100·0
June	395	29	17	441	89·8	6·4	3·8	100·0
Sept	646	35	4	685	94·3	5·1	0·6	100·0
Dec	637	47	7	691	92·2	6·7	1·1	100·0
'46 Mar	828	95	13	936	88·5	10·1	1·4	100·0
June	1,027	96	19	1,142	90·0	8·3	1·7	100·0
Sept	1,047	120	18	1,185	88·4	10·1	1·5	100·0
Dec	986	159	39	1,184	83·3	13·4	3·3	100·0
'47 Mar	906	162	51	1,119	81·0	14·5	4·5	100·0
June	811	216	56	1,083	74·9	19·9	5·2	100·0
Sept	866	137	66	1,070	81·0	12·8	6·2	100·0
Dec	904	115	40	1,059	85·3	10·9	3·8	100·0
'48 Mar	729	209	77	1,015	71·8	20·6	7·6	100·0
June	635	217	102	954	66·5	22·8	10·7	100·0
Sept	583	192	117	892	65·4	21·5	13·1	100·0
Dec	670	122	89	881	76·1	13·8	10·1	100·0
Average %					84·5	11·0	4·5	100·0

(a) Source: Compiled on the basis of information in the Record of Quarterly Changes in Size of 1/AAA Branch Membership June 1942—December 1948, compiled by a staff clerk and filed in T.G.W.U. Area 1 Office.

first three quarters of 1948 when about one-third of the membership—just twice the quarterly average—was constantly out of benefit. Just prior to this jump a change-over in Conveners took place and two of the most energetic Shop Steward-Collectors, Sisters Johnson and Brown, left the factory. This also resulted in a decrease in membership during the same period.

By combining the arrears statistics of Table XX with those on size and turnover in Table XVIII, a very rough estimate has been computed of the number of Branch members qualified to stand as candidates for all Branch offices and all higher Union positions, both elected and appointed. (Table XXI)

It was not until the Branch elections of 1947 that there were more Branch members officially eligible to hold a Branch office than there were Branch offices to hold. (The two-year financial membership requirement was not applied, however, to 1/AAA Branch members during the first few years following its formation in 1942.)[1] Moreover, it was not until 1947 that more than 1 per cent of the entire Branch membership became eligible to stand for these Union positions or to apply for University scholarships offered by the T.G.W.U. Since 1944, the number of members as well as the proportion of membership eligible to hold office has progressively increased. By 1948, 15 per cent of the membership of 881, compared with a 1947 Union figure of 19 per cent of over 1,000,000 members, could meet the membership qualifications for office.

At the time of Branch nominations described in a report, which follows, of a typical Branch meeting, only 5 per cent (46 members) of the 1,059 were qualified to run for any office in the Branch, and, inter alia, as

---

[1] Rule 9 (a) 3. There are 10 Branch offices. See Table XXVI on the election of 1/AAA Branch officials. Note that in 1945 there were 14 candidates for 10 positions. It is unlikely, though it has not been possible to prove, that the two-year qualification was applied according to Schedule I (1), p.52 of the Rules. At best the calculation of 5 eligible for office during this year is a rough estimate.

Table XXI

T.G.W.U.'s 1/AAA BRANCH SIZE OF MEMBERSHIP ELIGI-
BLE TO HOLD OFFICE IN RELATION TO TOTAL BRANCH
MEMBERSHIP FOR THE YEARS 1945, 1946, 1947, and 1948 (a)

Year	Total Branch Membership	Membership Eligible to Run or Apply (b) for Office in Branch or Union	Eligible Membership as % of Total Branch Membership
1943	265		
1944	297		
1945	691	5	1
1946	1,184	9	1
1947	1,059	46	5
1948	881	130	15
AVERAGE %			6

(a) Source: Compiled on the basis of information in the Record of Quarterly Changes in Size of 1/AAA Branch Membership, compiled by a staff clerk and filed in T.G.W.U. Area 1 Office. (See Table XVIII and Table XX.)

(b) Determined by the following formula in which E is the membership eligible to hold office in the year of election—See Appendix No. 5 for sample calculations and comments on formula: (Note: These eligibility figures do not apply to the election or appointment of shop stewards or collectors at Branch level.)

(1) $E_2 = a - b$

$x = c\%.E_2$

(2) $E_1 = E_2 - x$

$z = d\%.E_1$

(3) $E = E_1 - z$

Key: (a)   Total Branch membership as of December 31 of the base year (i.e., two years prior to date of election). See Table XVIII.

(b)   Total membership seven to thirteen weeks in arrears in the base year. See Table XX.

(c%) Total percentage rate of lapses in membership and of falling into arrears for seven to thirteen weeks in base year plus one year. See Tables XVIII and XX.

(d%) Total percentage rate of lapses in membership and of falling into arrears for seven weeks or more in base year plus two years.(i.e., the year of election). See Tables XVIII and XX,

Delegates to Area Trade Group Committees and the Biennial Delegate Conference. Of the more than 300 Branch members who had not lapsed but had remained in the Union for at least two years prior to these elections

(Table XIX), more than 250 thought and knew so little of the Branch and the right to hold office in the government of the Union that they allowed themselves to be disqualified by falling into arrears for at least six consecutive weeks between the Decembers of 1945 and 1947. In December 1947, there were only 46 Branch members eligible for Union office. (See Table XXI.)

In the light of all this it becomes difficult to avoid the conclusion that the responsibility for the continuous operation of the 1/AAA Branch must rest on a relatively small nucleus of men and women. Since its inception the Branch, as the basic unit of Union organization, has been too large to permit effective rank and file participation in its activities. The speed with which new members join and old and new members lapse prevents, almost automatically, the creation of a stable organization capable of making new members feel a sense of belonging and a desire to participate. The overwhelming majority of its members have deprived themselves of the right to stand for offices in the Branch and the Union by falling into arrears or lapsing—both expressions of indifference to as well as ignorance of the Branch, the Union and its Constitution.

The 1/AAA Branch, therefore, has at all times been composed of a large number of men and women, new to the Branch, who have had little time to identify themselves and their interests with the Branch and through the Branch with the Union; little time to establish effective channels of communication with Branch leaders in order to become acquainted with their problems and policies; and little time to become aware of the right and responsibility actively to participate in the government of the Union.

It now becomes of interest to visit a typical 1/AAA Branch meeting to describe its activities and subsequently to determine the actual extent of member participation in these activities.

Chapter 14

FIRST IMPRESSIONS AND A DESCRIPTION OF A TYPICAL 1/AAA BRANCH MEETING

First impressions and a rather detailed description of a November 1947 meeting are presented here to give some indication of what takes place at a typical 1/AAA Branch meeting. It is hoped, thereby, to make more meaningful the material presented in the chapters on 'Who Controls the Branch?'

The 1/AAA Branch meets regularly on the second and fourth Monday of each month in the back room of Trades Hall, a few minutes' walk from Colins' Electroparts Ltd. The meeting place, which accommodates approximately fifty persons, is cold, unattractive and inadequately lighted. Its walls are decorated with beautifully designed N.U.R. membership certificates and photographs of delegations to Trade Union and Labour Party Conferences of years gone by. These symbols of a heyday in Southboro's Trade Union history look down on the many empty chairs and benches which stand as mute but material witnesses at meeting after meeting to the lack of interest among the Branch's 1,000 members, as well as to the adequacy, as far as seating capacity is concerned, of this small chamber.

On November 10, 1947, I attended my first meeting of the 1/AAA which, in retrospect, emerges as not very different from the 14th meeting and all those intervening that I attended up to July 1948. Though attendance was better than average, most of the thirty-seven members I saw or met that evening were the same persons to whom I said 'Good-bye' at my last meeting in July 1948, and 'Hello' on a return visit a year later. The types of problems facing the Branch and the members' interest and approach to their solution varied little over this period. In fact, the Branch functioned from month to month at almost the same intensity. That Branch meetings were dominated by Communist members in November and by Labour Party supporters in July is a significant distinguishing characteristic which will be discussed at a later stage of this study.

At about 6.30 p.m. the meeting of the Branch Committee, which has been in progress around the table in the front of the room for the past twenty minutes, adjourns. The little groups of men and women who are sitting in overcoats waiting for their meeting to start have just come from home where they have had a chance to wash and have tea after work. At about 6.40 p.m. the Branch Chairman, Brother Strong, age 35, a Labour Party man whom C.P. members claim to have selected and elected as a front, calls the twenty members present to order. By 7.15 p.m. another ten members will have straggled in and by 8.00 p.m. the recorded attendance of thirty-eight will have been reached. Shortly thereafter members will begin to leave one by one until adjournment at 9.25 p.m. when less than twenty members will be present. It is in this atmosphere and under these circumstances that Brother Strong, an inexperienced parliamentarian, conducts the meeting with considerable skill, too much patience and without formality through the agenda which follows.

A. *The Minutes* of the previous meeting are read by the Branch's able Secretary, Sister Johnson, for confirmation and are then signed by the Chairman.

B. *Matters Arising*
1. Brother Ball, age 39, Branch Committeeman, agrees to take charge of the distribution of collection sheets for the Children's Hospital Christmas Party. Brother Ball is one of the most active and hard-working Shop Steward-Collectors in the Branch. His extreme interest in the

well-being of children and the family is motivated by a
hope that children today will not be tormented by child-
hood memories similar to his own. As a boy, after seeing
his father crippled by an industrial accident in which
both legs were amputated, and his mother go blind from
the shock, Brother Ball was separated from his ten
brothers and sisters, sent to a poor-law school and
farmed out to a lord's estate. There, for sixteen hours
labour a day, he received board and 2s. 6d. per month.
Brother Ball is a member of the Communist Party and, as a
Shop Steward, is responsible for 16 per cent of the
Branch's membership.

2. Nominations are now open for Branch officers to
be elected at the first meeting in December. A Labour
Party man, Brother Horn, and a C.P. member, Brother
Ward, join in re-nominating Brother Strong for the position of Chairman; this office is uncontested. Sister
Johnson is re-nominated unanimously without formality
for the office of Secretary. Sister Johnson entered a factory during the war and decided, like many other
women, to continue after hostilities ceased. She joined
the Communist Party in 1941 and has since been an
energetic and active Trade Unionist. She has been
characterized by her fellow workers and by organizers
as a capable leader, 'keen as mustard', a go-getter an
opportunist eager to dominate and frankly in search
of high Union office.

Brother Ball and Brother Gray are re-nominated to
the Branch Committee. Brother Gray, age 38, is a founding member of the Branch and a regular attender of
Branch meetings. Formerly Secretary of the Branch,
Brother Gray refuses to stand for that office because he
considers it no more than an exploitation of labour and
suggests that 'charity begins at home.' He is a Shop
Steward for the building workers at Colins' and a member of the Communist Party.

Two nominations are disqualified because the members proposed have not been in the Union for two years. After considerable coaxing, six members volunteer to fill the remaining vacancies for Branch Committeemen and Auditors. Thus, with ten candidates for ten offices, the December elections have become a superfluous exercise.

3. The members approve Sister Johnson's suggestion that she contact Brother Tims, the District Organizer, to find out why a member's wage claim remains unsettled. One member suggests that Tims has been neglecting the case.

4. Brother Gray's request that the Union provide Shop Stewards with notebooks and paper gives the Secretary another letter to write on behalf of the Branch to the Area's Financial Secretary for the necessary funds.

C. *Correspondence*

1. An appeal for funds from the strike committee of 'X' Co. is read. At the Secretary's suggestion the letter is referred to the Shop Stewards' Committee at the factory because the Branch, members are informed, is not authorized to use its funds for such a case.

2. Sister Johnson reads a letter from Area 1 Office inviting the Branch to nominate two candidates for Territorial Representatives to the General Executive Council for the 1948–1949 term. Brother Vinson, age 53, a founding member, elder statesman of the Branch, Convener of Shop Stewards as well as an Area 1 Representative on the General Workers National Trade Group Committee, proposes that the Branch support the sitting Territorial Representatives, Brothers Jones and Papworth[1] who, like himself, carry Communist Party cards. Brother Vinson, who is an able speaker, says a few words and is then followed by Brother Ward, Shop Steward and member of the Communist Party, who seconds the proposal. In spite of the current Union and Labour Party

[1] Mr J. W. Jones of the 1/498 Branch and Mr A. F. Papworth of the 1/382 Branch. These names are not fictitious. See Ballot Sheet, Appendix No. 8.

campaign against C.P. domination, members of the Branch unanimously endorse Brother Vinson's nominees without even a token protest from the non-Communist members present.

3. A letter announcing the opening of applications for a General Workers' Organizer is read. Members show no interest in the opening. Brother Gray's remark that an Organizer has a thankless job, a 24-hour day, no home life and all for £9 a week, appears to sum up the not uncommon attitude of the members present[1].

4. Two letters from the T.G.W.U. Legal Department, concerning progress on claims pending, are read. There are no comments.

5. Four dozen Union badges are ordered following the reading of a letter offering these symbols of membership for sale.

D. *Secretary's Report*

Sister Johnson reports that ten members left Colins' during the last fortnight and that fourteen new members joined the Branch during the same period. There appears to be no Branch interest in the new members. No questions are asked as to who they are and in which department they work. Nor are any provisions made for summoning the new member to a Branch meeting so as to make him feel welcome and to inform him of the duties of membership as well as of its advantages. The Secretary announces that forty-nine new members' cards are still outstanding from Area 1 Office. (There is very little connection between the Branch and the distribution of new cards, which takes place at the factory. The report is in terms of aggregate numbers and never in terms of the new members as individuals.) Sister Johnson continues her report by informing Convener Vinson that six of his Collectors are three weeks in arrears in the collection

[1] 'A Trade Union Official's job is extremely exacting; in fact, he has a twenty-four-hour day and a seven-day week. With current high rates of pay and shorter working hours, it is difficult to recruit these officials.' (From a personal interview with Mr. Arthur Deakin, General Secretary of the T.G.W.U., January 22, 1948.)

of dues. She concludes by announcing that two Brothers, in answer to the letter from the Education Department, have applied for the Union's correspondence course.

Some of the members have for some time been talking in little groups among themselves; the Chairman calls the meeting to order and asks the Shop Stewards to report.

E. *Shop Stewards' Reports*

1. Brother Ball is recognized. He reports that the management have thus far refused to answer his shop's request for a 2s. 6d. basic hourly wage for men when not working piece rate. Brother Strong, the Chairman, interjects that 2s. 6d. is a misleading figure, for with bonuses the basic wage would come to 3s. Someone shouts: 'Governors' man!' Brother Ball continues and acknowledges that it would be more correct to say 3s. He announces that the management have agreed to meet him on Friday. Sister Johnson suggests, and Brother Ball agrees, that the Branch approve the calling of a meeting on the shop floor on Friday to report the results of the negotiations with the management. It is the general consensus that such a meeting would show the management that the men are militant and refuse to 'take this dilly-dallying delay lying-down'. Brother Ball is to arrange the meeting.

2. Brother Horn jumps to his feet. Horn, age 40, an energetic Branch Committeeman and Shop Steward, who attributes his Trade Union interest to his desire to make the factory a better place for his children to work in, is recognized by the chair. He reports the case of an alleged non-Union worker being paid day rate rather than the higher average daily piece rate for time lost while hospitalized for treatment of pitch wart, an industrial disease. An interesting debate takes place on whether or not a non-Unionist should receive Union assistance.

The leading shop stewards, led by Brother Gray—who,

as a matter of policy refuses to report Branch decisions to his members 'for they are entitled to attend meetings if interested enough'—oppose Horn's handling of the case. Gray argues:

'(i) If the injured worker is a non-member it is his own fault, for there is a Collector in his shop. This will teach him a lesson.

'(ii) Our members would complain even more than they do now about paying their 7*d.* if this bloke can get insurance after he falls sick.

'(iii) The Company can't use this as a precedent, for they have agreed to pay Trade Union rates.'

Sister Johnson and the less sectarian members favour Horn's taking the case. She argues:

'(i) Any undercutting in wages is detrimental to the movement. We are, after all, fighting in the interests of all working men.

'(ii) By taking this case we can win another member. In 1945 when we had only 250 members (an under-estimate) we brought the workers' grievance about rotten tea to the management on everybody's behalf; by 1945 we had 1,400 members (an over-estimate).'

Brother Horn, who has been trying to get the floor, finally succeeds. He reminds the members that he is not certain but only thinks that the worker in question is a non-Union man. None of the Branch officials have records containing complete lists of all Branch members. It would be necessary to consult Area 1 Office for this information. Sister Johnson, recognizing that without this information any further discussion would be futile, proposes that the Convener investigate, follow the case through and report back. Upon the deletion of 'follow the case through' the resolution receives Branch approval and puts off until the next meeting a final decision which would have been made at this meeting had Brother Horn prepared his report[1].

3. Shop Steward Ward, militant, rabble rousing and generally disliked even by fellow Communist Party members, who consider him an unreliable factory

[1] The sectarians won the Branch to their view when it was found that the injured worker was a non-Unionist.

worker, reports the notification by the management of impending redundancy in his department. The company's excuse, he claims, is Denmark's refusal to renew orders for electrical components. Ward, suspicious of this explanation, suggests that the real reason is management's desire to sack the active Trade Unionists, put fear in the minds of the workers and thus break the Union. To confirm these suspicions a member interrupts by saying that he heard from a clerk friend that just this past week the firm received £50,000 in overseas orders. Orders for which of the company's many products is not known. A Brother who drives finished goods to the docks adds that Colins' is exporting more than ever before.

Without trying to follow up these rumours the discussion turns on the suggestion of Brother Horn that by reducing working hours to forty there would be no redundancy at least until after Christmas. This elicits the reply from a young collector that the forty-hour week is a desirable social goal but 'workers can't eat social theory'. Forty hours is just not enough to live on; some of the men are working as much as fifty-seven hours a week.

The meeting once again is out of order. The Chairman is unable to regain control. Sister Johnson, recognizing that this debate, based on rumours and inadequate information, is bound to be fruitless, seizes this opportunity to speak and bring the meeting to order. The members soon begin to listen to her saying that if this is a case of false redundancy aimed at breaking the Union or undermining the Labour Government, the Branch should consult District Organizer Tims and Southboro's Member of Parliament. Sister Johnson suggests, and the Branch expresses its agreement in a resolution, that the best way to handle the situation is to give prominence to the matter in the firm, specifically by tearing down all posters announcing redundancy in the factory as a chal-

lenge to the management; to endeavour to get their M.P.
to attend a mass meeting; to press the Regional Production Board to give them an accurate picture of
Colins' export position; and finally to enlist the assistance
of Union organizers. Once again Sister Johnson has
taken the lead and brought to the forefront the issues and
a method of approach which the Branch considers
satisfactory.

4. Sister Green, appearing somewhat impatient because the hour is late and she has not been able to make
her report, speaks up. With considerable satisfaction she
announces success in getting the management to reinstate
a Sister from her department who was discharged while
out sick. Sister Green, age 39, is accustomed to putting
up a good fight. As one of seven children who, with a
widowed mother, grew up fighting poverty on the Tyne-
side, she learned that 'the only way to beat injustice is
to work and fight against it.'

5. Convener Vinson concludes the reports by informing the Branch that unemployment benefits have already
been arranged for another Sister, recently declared
redundant.

F. *Other Business*

By this time many of the members have left and those
remaining, chilled through from sitting in the cold, are
anxious to leave. The Chairman asks if there is any other
business. As most members shake their heads Brother
Ward jumps to his feet, brandishing a daily paper containing pictures of Greek Trade Unionists being tor-
tured. With an energy which belies the hour, he reads a
prepared resolution calling on the government to end
the foreign policy now being pursued in Greece and to
stop the murder of leading Greek Trade Unionists.
Brother Vinson seconds the motion without comment.
One dissident voice proclaims that the murder of Communists is the real issue and that it is not a Branch concern. The Branch votes in favour of the resolution with

N

the proviso that it be sent to the Southboro Trades Council with a request that the London Trades Council approach members of the Government on this matter.

The meeting is adjourned. The few remaining Shop Stewards go up to the Secretary to turn in or pick up collectors' books and then either rush home or head for the local to carry on one of the evening's debates over a pint or two[1].

The image of the Branch which emerges from this description closely resembles, at least superficially, the image of the Branch in theory, except for one significant difference. Like the theoretical Branch, the 1/AAA meets regularly, provides a channel of two-way communication via correspondence, resolutions and the occasional presence of the permanent paid official with all higher levels of organization. Nominations and elections are held for Branch officials and an opportunity for discussing local problems with which the Branch is directly concerned is provided. Significantly unlike the theoretical image is the 1/AAA's failure to elicit the participation of a majority of its members.

It becomes of interest, therefore, to examine statistical data on the actual extent of member participation at Branch level to determine who controls the Branch in practice, and thus how successful is the operation of the Union as a democratic organization.

[1] It may be of interest to read the graphic description, by a Trade Union member, of Trade Union life in 1893—particularly the account of a Lodge Meeting—in the Webbs, *History of Trade Unionism* (1920 edition), pp. 444-464.

Chapter 15

WHO CONTROLS THE BRANCH?

AN ANALYSIS OF THE EXTENT OF MEMBER PARTICIPATION AT BRANCH LEVEL

In giving a partial answer to the question: 'Who controls the Branch?' the following topics will be discussed:

I   ATTENDANCE AT BRANCH MEETINGS
II MEMBER PARTICIPATION IN BRANCH ACTIVITIES
III MEMBER PARTICIPATION IN ELECTIONS AT BRANCH LEVEL

I ATTENDANCE AT BRANCH MEETINGS

'What's the attendance at Branch meetings?' is a common question, the answer to which, though seldom available, provides an interesting and indeed significant indication of the extent of member participation at Branch level. Both Tables XXIIa and XXIIb clearly demonstrate the extent of member indifference to 1/AAA Branch meetings.

Of the 154 meetings held by this Branch between May 1942 and June 1949, attendance at eighty meetings was so insignificant that no record was entered in the Minutes. Of the seventy-four meetings for which records are available approximately 80 per cent were attended by no more than 3·5 per cent of the Branch membership (Table XXIIa). Of the fifty-nine meetings falling in this category twenty-eight had records of apathy indicating that less than 2 per cent of the Branch membership were interested enough to attend. The inaugural meeting in May 1942 was the only meeting held during this seven-year period in which more than 20 per cent of the membership appear to have taken part. At only one of the 55 meetings held since December 1945 have there

Table XXIIa

DISTRIBUTION OF 74 MEETINGS OF THE 1/AAA BRANCH
FOR EACH YEAR MAY 1942–JUNE 1949 BY NUMBER AND
PERCENTAGE OF MEMBERS ATTENDING (a)

	1942	1943	1944	1945	1946	1947	1948	1949	Number of Branch Meetings (b)	Number of Branch Meetings as % of Total Number of Branch Meetings
By No. of Members										
1–10	1	3	2	1	–	1	–	–	8	10·8
11–20	3	–	–	1	3	4	14	9	34	46·0
21–30	1	–	–	4	1	5	8	1	20	27·0
31–40	–	1	–	–	2	3	1	–	7	9·5
41–50	1	–	–	–	–	–	–	1	2	2·7
51–60	–	–	–	1	–	–	–	–	1	1·3
61–70	–	–	–	–	–	–	1	1	2	2·7
TOTAL	6	4	2	7	6	13	24	12	74	100·0
By % of Members (c)										
·5– 3·5	1	3	2	3	5	12	23	10	59	79·8
3·6– 6·5	1	–	–	1	1	1	1	1	6	8·1
6·6– 9·5	1	–	–	1	–	–	–	1	3	4·1
9·6–12·5	1	1	–	1	–	–	–	–	3	4·1
12·6–15·5	1	–	–	–	–	–	–	–	1	1·3
15·6–18·5	–	–	–	1	–	–	–	–	1	1·3
18·6–21·5	1	–	–	–	–	–	–	–	1	1·3
TOTAL	6	4	2	7	6	13	24	12	74	100·0

(a) Source: Compiled on the basis of information in: (i) the Minutes of Meetings of T.G.W.U.'s 1/AAA Branch (May 1942–June 1949) and (ii) the Record of Quarterly Changes in Size of 1/AAA Branch Membership compiled by a staff clerk and filed in T.G.W.U. Area 1 Office.

(b) Of the 154 Branch meetings held during this period a record of attendance was kept for only sixty-nine. The total of seventy-four meetings presented here includes five meetings for which the Minutes record 'abandoned for lack of quorum' or 'poor attendance'.

(c) All Branch attendance percentage calculations were determined by taking the number in attendance at a given Branch meeting as a percentage of the total Branch membership at the close of the quarter prior to the one during which the meeting took place.

been more than 6·5 per cent of the membership present. No more than twenty people have been present at 56 per cent of the meetings and only 4 per cent have been attended by more than fifty people. The average number of members attending Branch meetings over this period has remained within closely confined limits above and below twenty-four (Table XXIIb). The maximum average attendance for any year was twenty-nine members out of the 1,184 in the Branch in 1946. A minimum average of nineteen

Table XXIIb

AVERAGE SIZE OF MEMBERSHIP ATTENDING MEET-INGS OF T.G.W.U.'s 1/AAA BRANCH IN RELATION TO TOTAL BRANCH MEMBERSHIP FOR EACH YEAR 1942–1949(a)

Year	Total Branch Membership	Average Number of Members Attending Branch Meetings (b)	Average Attendance as % of Total Branch Membership of the Current Year
1942 (c)	300	22 (6)	7
1943	265	19 (2)	7
1944 (d)	297	—	—
1945	691	24 (6)	4
1946	1,184	29 (6)	3
1947	1,059	27 (12)	3
1948	881	23 (24)	3
1949 (c)	895	25 (12)	3
AVERAGE		24	4

(a) Source: Compiled on the basis of information in: (i) the Minutes of Meetings of T.G.W.U.'s 1/AAA Branch (May 1942–June 1949) and (ii) the Record of Quarterly Changes in Size of 1/AAA Branch Membership compiled by a staff clerk and filed in T.G.W.U. Area 1 Office.

(b) This is an arithmetic mean obtained by adding the number of members attending during a year and dividing by the number of meetings (indicated in parenthesis) for which a Record of Attendance was kept.

(c) Both 1942 and 1949 are incomplete years: (i) the first meeting in 1942 was held in May. (ii) No Minutes after June 30, 1949, were available.

(d) No statistics are presented for 1944 as the Minutes for that year are incomplete.

out of 265 members was recorded for the year 1943. As the size of the Branch increases, the proportion of membership attending meetings appears to decrease. An average of 7 per cent (twenty-two members) of the Branch attended meetings in 1942 when there were only 300 members. In 1947 when there were 1,059 members an average of only 3 per cent (twenty-seven members) had a lively enough interest to attend Branch meetings[1]. It is difficult to conceive of a more conclusive record of a high degree of member indifference to Branch meetings.

All T.G.W.U. officials interviewed—including the General Secretary, an Area Secretary and a District Organizer in charge of 1/AAA members—gave the same answer to a question concerning low attendance at Branch meetings: 'When things go wrong, members flock to the Branches.' None offered as evidence to substantiate this statement anything other than general impressions of meetings attended. Though member interest of this nature would not ensure the successful day-to-day operation of the democratic process in the Union it would at any rate give some indication that members feel that in time of crisis at least their presence at Branch meetings is essential.

There is nothing in the 1/AAA's record of attendance, however, to substantiate this contention. At twenty-one out of twenty-six meetings at which full-time T.G.W.U. officials were present—usually an indication, as the Minutes of the meetings reveal, that the Branch is confronted with an important problem—no more than 3·1 per cent of the membership were in attendance. The largest meeting took place in April 1948, when sixty-seven of the 1,015 Branch members gathered to discuss with three permanent paid officials Colins' unilateral decision to revert to a basic work week of forty-four hours from the forty-hour basic week established in 1937.

[1] A quarterly analysis of Branch attendance in relation to Branch membership is found in Appendix No. 10.

Trades Hall, overcrowded with sixty-seven Branch members, may give an Organizer the impression of a high degree of rank and file interest. A jammed meeting hall can be quite deceptive. It is difficult to believe, however, that these officials were not aware of how unusual was this 'large' attendance at such meetings, and how small were the hall and the proportion of membership present.

Another example is a special mass meeting convened in September 1949, at Southboro Town Hall, by Union signatories of the 1946 works agreement with Colins'. Though it was well advertised that Union officials as well as Branch leaders were to discuss an impending redundancy threatening 178 men and women workers, only 300 of the more than 2,000 Colins' employees were in attendance. Most of the 178 workers subject to redundancy were 1/AAA members. If all 300 present were T.G.W.U. members, a highly unlikely assumption, at best only one-third of the Branch's membership took part in this extremely important event.

These illustrations, when considered with the 1948 Dock Strike material presented earlier, cause one to question the validity, particularly during periods of full employment, of that stereotyped reply which serves to perpetuate what appears to be the myth of a high degree of member interest in Branch activities during periods of crisis[1]. Even if it could be proved that this were not a myth, the problem of eliciting member interest in the day-to-day activities which constitute the continuous operation of the 1/AAA Branch and other Branches, remains to impair the democratic process in the government of the T.G.W.U.

Though such detailed evidence is unavailable for other T.G.W.U. Branches there is some evidence, in addition

---

[1] It may be that Union leaders are describing conditions characteristic of days gone by, when they themselves were active rank and file members:

'Only in the crisis of some great dispute do we find the Branch meetings crowded, or the votes at all commensurate with the total number of members.' Webbs, *History of Trade Unionism* (1920 Edition), p. 465.

to that already presented of a national character, that the 1/AAA's attendance record is by no means unique. Considerable material from various sources has been collected on a cross section of T.G.W.U. Branches.

While only one of sixty-seven candidates for University scholarships under the Union's Educational Scheme, writing essays on the importance of well attended Branch meetings, indicated that attendance at his Branch's meetings was good, thirty-three (50 per cent) wrote of poor attendance and lack of member interest in their respective Branch activities. The thirty-three Branches discussed in these essays were located in ten of the T.G.W.U.'s thirteen Areas and represented members of ten of the twelve active National Trade Groups. Of the thirty-three essayists twenty-five were Branch officials who undoubtedly wrote from personal experience. The Chairman of a Quarryman's Branch in Area 6 had this to say:

> 'During the turbulent period in the South Wales coal fields from 1920 to 1926 I was employed in one of the coal mines of the Rhondda Valley and all Branch meetings were well attended. It did not matter whether the meeting was of the usual routine kind, the members were so interested in Union matters that they invariably presented themselves at all meetings. *The enthusiasm shown in the coal fields during that period is sadly lacking in my locality at the present time. Very often only the bare quorum is present. . . .'*
> (Emphasis added.)

A chocolate moulder and Chairman of his Branch in Area 3 wrote:

> 'Only the past week I have helped enrol thirty new members and it is a practical certainty that not more than 1 per cent of them will take an active part in their Branch.'

A shop steward of a Lorryman's Branch in Area 1, after pointing out that Trade Unionism is taken far too leisurely by a large majority of members, wrote:

> 'In many cases the reasons for poorly attended meetings *and, in some cases they are rarely held at all,* are due to apathy on the part of members.'
> (Emphasis added.)

A collector of a Branch in Area 9 who had been in the Union for over 12½ years described his Branch meetings thus:

> 'From personal experience of Branch affairs I have found that when one attends a Branch meeting where there is an attendance of about twelve (and I have been when there has been less than six), after termination of the business, one has a *feeling of frustration*, that all discussion has been stifled by the thought uppermost in your mind, that you are very much in the minority.'

Additional information on the endemic nature of the disease 'apathy' in a wide variety of Branches is to be found in the unpublished verbatim reports of closed sessions at T.G.W.U. Biennial Delegate Conferences. At the 1947 Hastings Conference a resolution proposing that all new members apply for admission at the nearest Branch and that the practice of issuing cards to new members at District and Area Offices cease, was defeated. An Area 1 delegate, opposing the resolution, said:

> 'I've been a representative of the agricultural workers, those working on farms and in outlying places and there are not 10 per cent of them who have ever been in our Branch room because they live in such a scattered area that it is practically impossible for them to attend a Branch meeting or to come to a Branch at all.' (1947 B.D.C. unpublished Verbatim Report, Minute 45, p. 205.)

Again, in 1947 an interesting debate on a resolution proposing compulsory attendance at Branch meetings revealed how widespread was this apathy. During the course of the discussion before the resolution was defeated at the request of the General Executive Council, a General Workers delegate from a rural district in Area 2 said in opposition:

> 'My members are scattered over a radius of twenty miles and I consider the suggestion is impracticable. . . . It might be all right for urban areas and large boroughs where members are close together but in small areas it is impracticable.'

In support of the resolution two delegates, both dockers, from Area 12 spoke. One delegate said:

'We have 2,100 (members) . . . I've often found an attendance of twenty.'

The other said:

'I wish to speak against the General Executive Council (which opposed the resolution) because our Branch has a membership of 5,564 and I have had six people attending a meeting and four of these have been paid tellers to count the other two votes.' (1947 B.D.C. unpublished Verbatim Report, Minute 33, pp. 155–157.)

No evidence has been discovered on Branch attendance in the T.G.W.U. which in any way refutes the clear-cut impression of apathy at Branch level, recorded above[1]. It therefore becomes impossible to avoid the conclusion that the Branch meeting—if not the Branch itself—as an institution designed to elicit wide-scale member participation has failed to fulfil its function.

In spite of—in the case of super-sized Branches one may argue because of—records of low attendance, Branches do function. It now becomes of interest to ask how many members are in fact responsible for the continuous operation of a Branch and who they are.

II   MEMBER PARTICIPATION IN BRANCH ACTIVITIES

An examination of the Minutes of all 1/AAA Branch meetings to determine the number of members participating each year in Branch activities provides a partial answer to the question: 'Who controls the Branch?' For the purpose of this analysis *Branch activities* include the proposing and seconding of resolutions, the making of reports and the initiating of discussions. It should be noted that these activities require more overt participation on the part of the individual members at Branch meetings than mere consent or disapproval as expressed in voting on resolutions or at elections. Elections at

---

[1] The 1/AAA attendance record expressed as a percentage of Branch membership, and the scattered evidence on other T.G.W.U. Branches, fall far below the estimate of 20 per cent made in the P.E.P. Report. (P.E.P.—'Political and Economic Planning'—*British Trade Unionism*, London, 1948.)

Table XXIII

ANNUAL MEMBER PARTICIPATION IN BRANCH ACTIVITIES
—PROPOSING AND SECONDING RESOLUTIONS, MAKING
REPORTS AND INITIATING DISCUSSIONS—AT MEETINGS
OF THE 1/AAA BRANCH OF THE T.G.W.U.
MAY 1942—DECEMBER 1948 (a)
(With Special Emphasis on the number and percentages of Members responsible for at
least 60% of all Branch Activities at 129 Meetings) (b)

Year & (Number of Meetings held)	Number of Branch Activities Recorded (b)	Total Branch Membership (c)	Number of Members Participating in Branch Activities (d)	Number of Members Participating as % of Total Branch Membership	Number of Members Responsible for 60% of all Branch Activities	Number of Members Responsible as % of Total Branch Membership	Number of Members Responsible as % of Members Participating
1942 (13)	28	292	15	5·1	5	1·7	33·4
1943 (19)	27	262	18	6·9	7	2·7	39·0
1944 (—)	—	307	—	—	—	—	—
1945 (25)	114	441	29	6·6	6	1·4	20·7
1946 (25)	117	1,140	23	2·0	7	0·6	30·4
1947 (23)	153	1,083	30	2·8	6	0·6	20·0
1948 (24)	159	954	23	2·4	7	0·7	30·4
Aver. (e)	114		25	4·1	7	1·2	28·1

(a) Source: Compiled on the basis of information in: (i) the Minutes of Meetings of T.G.W.U.'s 1/AAA Branch (May 1942–December 1948). Note that no statistics are presented for 1944 as the Minutes for that year are incomplete. (ii) Record of Quarterly Changes in Size of 1/AAA Branch Membership compiled by a staff clerk and filed in T.G.W.U. Area 1 Office.

(b) Branch Activities include: the proposing and seconding of resolutions, the making of reports and the initiating of discussions. These activities require more positive action at Branch meetings than mere consent or disapproval as expressed in voting. Voting at elections as well as the nominating of candidates for office have been excluded.

(c) Branch membership as recorded at the end of the second quarter (June 30) of each year.

(d) Number of members participating in Branch Activities is: the total number of different members credited in the Minutes of Meetings with the Branch Activities recorded. (i.e., a member may participate in several Branch Activities but is only counted once in this column).

(e) Each average is an arithmetic mean. As the figures for 1942 are for less than a full year they have been excluded from calculations to determine these averages.

Branch level, an important Branch function, are considered separately.

Table XXIII presents statistics on the size and proportion of annual member participation in these Branch activities at meetings of the 1/AAA held since its foundation in 1942. Between 1943 and 1948 (the year 1944 excepted as the Minutes are incomplete) an average of only 25 different members have been responsible for all of the Branch's activities each year. The minimum number of persons responsible for any full year of activity was eighteen—during 1943. A maximum of thirty members responsible for all Branch activities was reached in 1947. As in the case of Branch attendance, the proportion of the membership responsible for its activities appears to decrease as the size of the Branch increases. Though the evidence is by no means conclusive, it is not unreasonable to suggest that between twenty and thirty members are sufficient to maintain the continuous operation of a Branch, whatever the size of its membership.

Does the membership of this active nucleus of from 2 to 6 per cent of the total Branch membership change from year to year or is it primarily made up of the same people? Though it may appear contradictory, the answer to each question is yes. While the rate of turnover is high among these on the circumference, a small number of members at the centre are responsible not only for many years of Branch activity, but also for most of these activities each year. Table XXIVa shows the distribution of members by years of service in the active nucleus of the Branch.

The 136 man-years of activity were carried out by only eighty-two members during the 1942–1948 period. Seventeen members with three or more years of service accounted for sixty-three of the 136 man-years of activity. Fifty-seven of the eighty-two members in this active nucleus served the Branch in this capacity for no more than one year. Though the material available is incomplete, it has been ascertained that at least fifty-six of the eighty-two members also served the Branch as Shop Stewards, Shop Steward-Collectors or Collectors. The active nucleus responsible for all Branch activity each year, in conjunction with the very small Branch attendance of which this small nucleus is the major part, is overwhelming evidence of the extent to which apathy has left to a minority the responsibility for the continuous operation of the Branch.

Table XXIVa
DISTRIBUTION OF MEMBERS BY YEARS OF SERVICE IN THE ACTIVE NUCLEUS OF THE 1/AAA AS OF DECEMBER 1948

Years of Activity	Number of Members Responsible	Number of Man-Years*
6	2	12
5	0	0
4	6	24
3	9	27
2	8	16
1	57	57
TOTAL	82	136

* *Man-years of activity* are measured like work days lost in a strike. If 10,000 men are on strike for three days, 30,000 work days are lost. If twelve men serve the active nucleus of a Branch for three years, thirty-six man-years of activity have taken place.

More startling than the size of this nucleus is the microscopic size of the inner circle responsible for 60 per cent or more of all these Branch activities. (See Table XXIII.) This inner circle has been composed of six or seven members annually with the exception of 1942 when a minimum of five fell in this category. Since January 1946, close to one-half of one per cent of the Branch membership is all that has been required to constitute this inner circle. Over this period only nineteen

different members have served within its circumference.
Brother Gray has appeared on this list for six consecutive
years, Brother Vinson for five years and five other members for three years each. Of this group of seven with
three or more years' service as members of the inner
circle, five have acknowledged membership in the Communist Party during this period, though not necessarily
throughout the entire period of their intensive activity.
All were simultaneously serving the Branch as Shop
Stewards or Collectors.

Table XXIVb

DISTRIBUTION OF MEMBERS BY YEARS OF SERVICE
WITHIN THE INNER CIRCLE OF THE 1/AAA AS OF
DECEMBER 1948

Years of Activity	Number of Members Responsible	Number of Communist Party Members
6	1	1
5	1	1
4	0	0
3	5	3
2	2	0
1	10	2
TOTAL	19	7

It is of interest further to refine this analysis in relation
to resolutions only—a method of communication through
which the Branch may speak for its entire membership
not only to the Constitutional Committees and the
Biennial Delegate Conference of the T.G.W.U., but also
to governmental and other bodies on which it may
attempt to exert pressure.

Table XXVa indicates that for the years since the
close of 1945 an average of less than 1 per cent of the
membership has been responsible for proposing all
Branch resolutions. During this period more than

Table XXVa

ANNUAL MEMBER PARTICIPATION IN PROPOSING
RESOLUTIONS AT MEETINGS OF THE 1/AAA BRANCH
OF THE T.G.W.U., MAY 1942 – DECEMBER 1948 (a)

(With Special Emphasis on the number and percentages of Members responsible for
proposing at least 60% of all resolutions at 129 Meetings).

Year and (Number of Meetings held)	Number of Resolutions Proposed	Total Branch Membership (b)	Number of Members Proposing all Resolutions (c)	Number of Members Proposing all as % of Total Branch Membership	Number of Members Proposing 60% of all Resolutions	Number of Members Proposing 60% as % of Total Branch Membership	Average % of Total Branch Membership attending Meetings (d)
1942 (13)	9	292	8	2·7	6	2·1	9·1
1943 (19)	9	262	9	3·4	7	2·7	6·4
1944 (—)	—	307	—	—	—	—	1·1
1945 (25)	37	441	14	3·2	4	0·9	6·5
1946 (25)	36	1,140	10	0·9	3	0·3	2·4
1947 (23)	34	1,083	13	1·2	4	0·4	2·3
1948 (24)	21	954	8	0·8	3	0·3	2·3
Average (e)	27		11	1·9	4	0·9	4·0

(a) Source: Compiled on the basis of information in: (i) The Minutes of Meetings of T.G.W.U.'s 1/AAA Branch (May 1942–December 1948). Note that no statistics are presented for 1944 as the Minutes for that year are incomplete. (ii) Record of Quarterly Changes in Size of 1/AAA Branch Membership compiled by a staff clerk and filed in T.G.W.U. Area 1 Office.

(b) Branch Membership as recorded at the end of the second quarter (June 30) of each year.

(c) Number of members proposing all resolutions is: the total number of *different* members credited in the Minutes of Meetings with the proposing of resolutions (i.e., though a member may be responsible for proposing several resolutions during the course of the year, he is counted only once).

(d) Based on data in Table on Size of Membership Attending 1/AAA Branch meetings for each quarter. Note that average attendance is based on the number of meetings for which a record of attendance was kept. Except for 1948 this is less than the total number of meetings held in that year. See Appendix No. 10.

(e) Each average is an arithmetic mean. As the figures for 1942 are for less than a full year they have been excluded from calculations to determine these averages. From calculations to determine the average of the last column both 1942 and 1944 figures have been excluded.

60 per cent of the ninety-one resolutions before the Branch for consideration were placed there by no more than approximately 0·4 per cent (i.e., four out of 1,000 members) of the entire Branch membership.

Of the nineteen members responsible for 60 per cent of all Branch activities, eight have been responsible for well over 60 per cent of all the resolutions proposed in the 1/AAA during this six-year period. Of this hard core centre of eight within the inner circle, two members have achieved the distinction in four of the six years covered, one for three years, one for two years, and the remainder for one year only. Six members of the hard core centre have acknowledged membership in the Communist Party some time during their periods of intensive participation.

Table XXVb

DISTRIBUTION OF MEMBERS BY YEARS OF SERVICE WITHIN THE HARD CORE CENTRE OF THE 1/AAA AS OF DECEMBER 1948

Years of Activity	Number of Members Responsible	Number of Communist Party Members
4	2	2
3	1	1
2	1	1
1	4	2
TOTAL	8	6

Of the 146 resolutions proposed over the 1942–1948 period, all but a very few received the unanimous approval of the Branch. Judging from this analysis, and in light of the extremely low attendance records it becomes clear how ludicrously small is the rather stable minority which speaks as well as acts in the name of the ever-changing membership of the 1/AAA Branch.

That similar patterns of Branch government are common to other T.G.W.U. Branches is suggested by many of the essays on well attended Branch meetings. The following statement by the Chairman of a Trolleybus Drivers' Branch in Area 1 is typical:

'In many centres of unrest there is the position where the actual Branch business is carried out and sustained by a handful of loyal stalwarts who recognize the importance of the Branch . . . into these few hands is thrust a responsibility that should be shared by all.'

The material available is, however, insufficient to determine in what proportion of the T.G.W.U.'s Branches the day-to-day activities, like those of the 1/AAA, are carried out by so small an active nucleus. Within this nucleus the primary responsibility for continuous operation of the Branch can be traced to a smaller and more stable minority—an inner circle of Shop Stewards and Collectors who may or may not be members of an easily identifiable political group. It appears, therefore, that the Branch is not the rank and file member's first contact with the Union. At best it is merely the Shop Steward's first contact.

Are the members of the hard core centre and inner circle the elected representatives of the rank and file?

III MEMBER PARTICIPATION IN ELECTIONS AT BRANCH LEVEL

It might be argued that even if attendance at meetings be low and only a small group be responsible for all Branch activities, the democratic nature of the organization may not be impaired, for the locus of power may be in the hands of a duly elected body, ultimately responsible to the membership.

An analysis of six elections for Branch officials held since the Branch's formation in 1942 discredits this argument. (See Table XXVI.) These elections are but additional records of apathy showing how the election as a symbol of democracy may become oligarchy's disguise. At only one of the six elections held between 1942 and

1949 was there a contest providing the membership with an opportunity to make a choice. At only one of the six elections was there a substantial number of members present to make a choice. There was, however, no contest.

In 1945 at the only election in which a contest took place, Brother Strong, a Labour Party man 'fed up' with Communist Party control, made a half-hearted and unsuccessful bid for the Branch Chairmanship. His opponent, Sister Johnson, a Branch member of less than six months standing[1] and an energetic C.P. member, received fourteen of the twenty-three votes cast. Only twenty-three members, more than half of whom were standing for office, out of a Branch of 685 had sufficient interest in the next two years of Branch administration to attend this meeting. It becomes apparent with what ease a small clique could capture the key power positions of such a Branch by 'packing' one important meeting every two years with a ridiculously small proportion of the membership.

The system of nominating candidates has also deteriorated so as to become meaningless ritual. At the 1945 nominations, for example, fourteen people, twelve of whom were candidates for Branch office themselves, also served as movers and seconders of all the nominations. A complete break-down of the system occurred at the nominations in 1947 (already described in the account of a typical Branch meeting) when 'volunteers' were called upon to stand as candidates in these no-contest elections.

At the inaugural meeting in 1942 when enthusiasm was high and the membership low, a maximum of 22 per cent of the Branch were present to nominate and thus elect their leaders. At all subsequent nominations no more than 3 per cent of the membership took part.

---

[1] Within a month after attending her first 1/AAA Branch meeting, Sister Johnson had been elected to fill a vacancy on the Branch Committee.

Table XXVI

MEMBER PARTICIPATION IN SIX ELECTIONS FOR
1/AAA BRANCH OFFICIALS 1942–1949 (a)
(Showing the Percentage of Total Branch Membership Participating
and the Number of Offices Uncontested at each Election.)

Year	Total Branch Membership of the Previous Quarter(b)	Recorded Attendance at Election Meetings (c)	Attendance as % of Total Branch Membership	Number of Offices(d)	Number of Candidates	% of Offices Uncontested
May 1942	195	42	22	8	8	100
Dec 1943	288	—	—	10	10	100
Nov 1945	685	23	3	10	14	40
Oct 1947	1,070	—	—	2	2	100
Dec 1947	1,070	34	3	10	10	100
Nov 1949	895	21	2	10	10	100

(a) Source: Compiled on the basis of information in: (i) The Minutes of Meetings of T.G.W.U.'s 1/AAA Branch (May 1942–June 1949) and (ii) the Record of Quarterly Changes in Size of 1/AAA Branch Membership compiled by a staff clerk and filed in T.G.W.U. Area 1 Office.

(b) The 1942 membership figure is as of the date of formation and the 1949 membership figure is for the first rather than the third quarter of 1949.

(c) As voting is by show of hands at Branch meetings the Attendance Record is the most satisfactory measure of participation in these Branch activities. The following should be noted:

(i) At the May 1942 meeting nominations and elections took place on the same evening.

(ii) In December 1943 and October 1947 (a by-election for Branch Chairman and Secretary) there was no record of attendance.

(iii) In December 1947 though there were thirty-four persons present at the election meeting there were thirty-eight present at the nomination meeting.

(iv) For November 1949 the attendance figure is available only for the nomination meeting.

(d) Branch officers are: Branch Chairman, Branch Secretary, six Committeemen and two Auditors.

'No-contest' is characteristic of almost all other Branch nominations and elections carried out by show of hands at Branch meetings. These include the election of Shop Stewards and Collectors and Delegates to the Southboro Trades Council who are in most cases self-appointed volunteers.

Though the Constitution provides for the election of Branch officials by and from the Branch membership, it would be more accurate to state that in practice these officials are elected by and from the self-appointed members of the inner circle, if not the hard core centre of the Branch. Only 19 per cent of the Branch's inactive population knew that elections were held in 1947. One hundred per cent of the ninety-two interviewed did not vote in this election for Branch Chairman, Secretary and Committeemen. 'No one ever told me about it' was the most common response. The results were of as little interest to this passive population as the election itself. Nine out of every ten members were unable to name their Branch Chairman, and eight out of every ten could not name their Branch Secretary. It becomes obvious, therefore, that the election of Branch Officials in practice has failed to give the rank and file of the 1/AAA the most elementary outlet of participation essential to as well as characteristic of a democratic organization.

That elections in other T.G.W.U. Branches are conducted under similar circumstances is suggested, though the evidence is by no means conclusive, by some of the essays on well attended Branch meetings. Equally applicable to 1/AAA elections is the description by an Area 1 Organizer, a former Branch Chairman, who wrote:

'. . . duly elected officers should be representative of the members as a whole, and not, as often happens, the filling of positions by the faithful few, who are already overburdened because the attendance sometimes warrants the whole room electing itself into some position or other, owing to the absence and disinterestedness of the bulk of the membership.'

The degree of member participation in elections by

ballot adds additional evidence to the extent to which this institution is used to counterfeit the democratic process not only at Branch level but throughout the T.G.W.U.'s organization. Evidence of a national character on corruption at the ballot box has already been discussed. The circumstances under which the December 1947 ballots for Area 1 Representatives to the General Executive Council took place are typical and will serve to illustrate the procedure for holding a ballot election in the 1/AAA Branch.

Sister Johnson, the Branch Secretary, received from Area 1 Office on behalf of the Branch, 1,000 ballot papers for distribution to approximately 950 eligible members. These ballots were divided into thirty packets each containing one ballot for each eligible member of the 'constituency' of the Shop Steward for whom the packet was designated. In all but a very few cases the distribution of these packets did not go beyond Brother Vinson, Convener of Shop Stewards and C.P. member. Both Sister Johnson and Brother Vinson gave almost identical descriptions of the voting procedure that followed:

A few packets were distributed to Shop Stewards who might have been suspicious if they had not received them. A group of Shop Stewards, all members of the inner circle, gathered around a table one evening and with varied coloured pencils proceeded to place crosses by the names of C.P. candiates Papworth and Jones. To give the appearance of authenticity, only 432 of the 518 ballots cast in this way supported the Branch's favourites. This deceptive record indicates that approximately 55 per cent of the eligible membership participated in this election, while close to 1 per cent would be a more accurate figure. Though not recorded in the Minutes, Brother Vinson claimed that on two occasions since the Branch's formation Area 1 Office has disqualified the Branch's ballot vote. The membership and most members of the inner circle were never apprised of this information.

Of the ninety-two rank and file members interviewed eight (9 per cent) claimed to have received ballots to vote in this election. Of the eight giving this reply four were probably mistaken for they claimed to have voted for candidates whose names did not appear on the ballot. The few who saw a ballot said: 'I never heard of any of the candidates. I just took a chance and voted for the one with the largest number of Branches after his name.' It is common practice for C.P. candidates to solicit the largest number of Branches to support their nominations, so that their names dominate the ballot papers.[1] Other groups are not sufficiently organized within the T.G.W.U. to limit the number of their candidates to the number of vacancies in order to prevent a split vote. Not one of the eighty-four members who during the course of these interviews became aware that they had been deprived (because of their own lack of interest and their Branch leaders' failure to inform them that an election was being held) of one of their fundamental rights of membership, subsequently complained of this at a Branch meeting, or, to my knowledge, to a Shop Steward—so strong is the tradition of non-voting in this Branch.

Some of the active members interviewed were reluctant to answer questions about this ballot. The response is of doubtful reliability but is presented because of some interesting comments. Of the nineteen active members interviewed nine (47 per cent) said they received no ballot for the election. One of the most influential non-Communist Shop Stewards, responsible for 12 per cent of the membership, said: 'I believe it is done at the Branch meeting by block voting.' A very energetic and capable Shop-Steward-Collector (not a member of the inner circle), whose household duties prevented regular

---

[1] (i) See Appendix No. 8 for a photostatic copy of the ballot paper referred to.

(ii) It is interesting to note that the 'Representation of the Peoples Act', 1949, Appendix provides that space on a ballot paper is to be equally divided between the candidates.

Branch attendance, said: 'I've not received any ballot papers since I became Shop Steward (three years prior to the interview). I've never heard of the General Executive Council.' The hard core centre need not worry about these 'watch dogs' of democracy. Only three of the nine active members who received ballot papers claimed to have distributed them to their members.

In 1937 Ernest Bevin, then General Secretary of the T.G.W.U., during a debate on the ever-recurring biennial resolution favouring election rather than appointment of permanent paid officials, confirmed how widespread is such corruption at the ballot box. In arguing against the election of officials he said:

'This method of appointment is the cleanest, the best and the fairest that has ever been invented. One would imagine that ballots are run for elections in an absolute state of perfection. I am surprised sometimes when I hear of the very poor attendance of members at Branches and then see the remarkable polls that come in in the returns sometimes. Let us be quite frank with one another. Trade Union ballots—and I would not say this in public—but Trade Union ballots do not reach the standard of a Parliamentary election. Let us be quite honest about it.' (1937 B.D.C. unpublished Verbatim Report, Minute 48, p. 331.)

It is under these circumstances that the subversion of the electoral process goes unchallenged at Branch level. This same method sent Branch members as Delegates to Biennial Delegate Conferences and to seats on Area Trade Group Committees and thus to representation on National Trade Group Committees. It is in this manner that members of the inner circle, particularly in the hard core centre, accumulate Branch and Union functions which serve to perpetuate them in power. Seven of the nineteen active members interviewed were at some time during their Branch career members of the inner circle. Each was at the time of the interview simultaneously filling an average of five Union or Branch offices. While only 1 per cent of the inactive population served in any Branch capacity, the nineteen active members held between them at least sixty-three posts or offices directly connected with their Branch or Union membership. Though it remains accurate to state that the 1/AAA is one of the most active T.G.W.U. Branches, it must be realized that this activity is the result of intensive rather than extensive member participation.

In contrast to this record of apathy it is worth noting that 76 per cent of the inactive Branch members eligible to vote did so in the General Election of 1945[1] (compared with the Southboro vote of 72 per cent of the electorate). If information on the opportunity and responsibility to vote were more widespread, and if the conduct of elections were more carefully supervised in the T.G.W.U., there is no reason why a tradition of voting could not develop which would elicit the interest of the 'inactive' rank and file members. By vesting Union elections from Branch level to national level with the integrity that Government elections rightfully claim, and thereby making the vote meaningful, an opening wedge of member participation in the government of the T.G.W.U. could be effected.

Constant reference has been made to the fact that the hard core centre as well as the inner circle have been Communist-dominated. These members have been singled out only to show how an energetic minority, in this case an easily identifiable one, can gain control of the *loci* of power at Branch level without destroying the facade of democracy.

It was said earlier that by the beginning of 1948 what was a Communist-dominated Branch became a Branch controlled by Labour Party supporters. It is interesting to note that this change was not a result of pressure from the rank and file members. It was a result rather of pressure from the top—from the General Secretary of the T.G.W.U. and from the Secretary of the Labour Party

[1] Of eighty-seven inactive members eligible sixty-six voted in the General Election of 1945. Of eighteen active members eligible fifteen (83 per cent) voted in that General Election.

who made the headlines at the end of 1947 by calling for the removal of C.P. leaders from all levels of Union organization.

These exhortations to go to the Branch and oust the unscrupulous who had gained control did not arouse the rank and file to action. They did arouse the Branch leaders in power, however. As it became increasingly evident that it was fashionable to be anti-Communist in order to remain in the good graces of those on top, Branch leadership, eager to hold on to its power and to continue to climb the hierarchical ladder of Union authority, began to see the light. The leadership of the Branch remained in the same hands. It was not necessary for the Branch to wait until the 1949 elections to undo what had been done at the November 1947 elections. Members of the hard core centre and inner circle announced that they were no longer Communist Party members at a Branch cleansing ceremony in February 1948, when elections for Branch delegates to the South-boro Trades Council took place. Only Brother Gray continues to acknowledge membership in the Communist Party. What was true of the Branch in relation to member participation and the lack of it remains true. Substantially, the members of the same clique are in power, and ballot papers are still marked on a wholesale scale by a minority for the majority[1].

The decision of the 1949 Biennial Delegate Conference to amend the Rules so that no member of the Communist Party shall be eligible to hold any office in the Union[2] is a tacit admission that the campaign to oust C.P. minorities by arousing rank and file interest failed,

[1] In March 1949, 712 ballots were found in the ballot box, indicating a better than 95 per cent vote by the 746 eligible members. These votes, in conjunction with votes from other Branches, sent Brother Vinson, former C.P. Convener of Shop Stewards, and Sister Johnson, now an active Labour Party member, to the 1949 Biennial Delegate Conference of the T.G.W.U. The Branch Secretary, in an interview, stated that her Shop Stewards marked the ballot papers for her. The same was true in the case of Brother Vinson's candidature.

[2] Rules (amended August 19, 1949), Schedule I (2), p. 56.

in many T.G.W.U. Branches and Areas. It became necessary, therefore, where more persistent Communist Party members than those in the 1/AAA were in power, to resort to this more direct method, requiring little if any member participation, to achieve the results desired by yet another minority—the leadership in control. The General Secretary is now assured that he will not be troubled by resolutions embarrassing to the Labour Government and himself. But the problem of apathy remains and the government of the Branch continues by default.

The analysis, thus far, leads to the conclusion that oligarchy is the term which best describes the government of the 1/AAA Branch, if not that of many other T.G.W.U. Branches. The *loci* of power and authority at Branch level appear to rest in the hands of a ludicrously small minority of self-appointed or 'self-elected' lay members, predominantly Shop Stewards. Though accurate, this statement in the final analysis is inadequate, for it fails to take into account the role of the permanent paid official.

Chapter 16

WHO CONTROLS THE BRANCH? (*continued*)

THE PERMANENT PAID OFFICIAL—
UNION 'CIVIL SERVANT'?

The widespread apathy characteristic of Branch membership, though making possible in the first instance control by a very small minority of lay members, ultimately serves to undermine the authority of this very minority, and places control in the hands of the permanent paid official.

The men appointed to these positions are selected for their organizing and negotiating ability, as well as for their intimate knowledge of the Union, of industry and of labour legislation. The permanent paid official is an expert who 'must be tolerant, tactful, willing to explain and at the same time to accept advice . . . in order that he may profit by the experience of others no matter how humble the position they occupy'.[1]

Selected as a Union 'civil servant' to ascertain the facts of a given situation in order best to apply policy determined by the elected representatives of the lay membership, the permanent official, as years of experience enhance his knowledge and authority, assumes the function of policy-maker as well. It is not suggested here that in practice a very clear-cut distinction can be made between the factual elements and the ethical or value elements in the decision process. 'Policy' is a somewhat ambiguous term and is used in this section to denote the values which, from a theoretical point of view, the membership determines should be implemented by the Union official. The administrative decision on how best to im-

[1] *The Union: Its Work and Problems*, Part II, p. 27.

plement these values is left to the official to determine on the basis of the factual elements involved[1]. That the Union should seek a forty-hour work week, for example, is a policy decision which may or may not have been reached after taking into consideration the specialized information that the Union 'civil servant' may provide. The permanent official as negotiator must decide how to implement this policy. It is not within his authority, however, to decide not to seek its implementation.

Two factors, in addition to those which necessitate the division of labour served so effectively by bureaucracy, aid and abet these functionaries in filling simultaneously the roles of broad policy makers and Union servants. One is the confidence and security created by permanency of tenure in office. The second and more significant factor is the awareness of the permanent official that the Branch, and elected representatives generally, act on behalf of an active minority which can seldom effectively rally the majority of the membership to action.

It is not suggested that the official does not act in the best interests of the membership. It is only argued that the final decision as to what policy will best serve the interests of the membership often rests not with the minority group in control at Branch level, but rather with the permanent paid official. The manner in which an important problem confronting the 1/AAA Branch was handled by a permanent paid official illustrates this point.

Colins' Electroparts Ltd. announced, without prior consultation with either the Works Council or the Unions concerned, that the principle of the forty-hour basic work week, voluntarily established by them in 1937, was to be abandoned in favour of a forty-four

---

[1] See Herbert A. Simon, *Administrative Behaviour* (MacMillan Company, 1948), Chapter III, 'Fact and Policy in Decision Making', pp. 45-60.

hour work week[1]. Posted notices gave as a reason for this change the Labour Government's demand for increased productivity. The actual number of hours worked, however, was not in question, for workers averaged even more than forty-four hours a week.

At Branch meetings held between February and June 1948, the active nucleus argued that the acceptance of the proposed change without a fight would be a retrograde step in the Union's struggle for the principle of the forty hour week. At two of these meetings District Organizers were present to hear arguments on which the case might be based in negotiations with management. Three of these permanent officials were present when sixty-seven members—a record attendance—gave their support to the forty hour principle.

The District Organizers later reported that the management would not reconsider its decision and that preliminary negotiations offered no hope of satisfying the Branch's demands. They then expressed an unwillingness to carry the case, as the Branch wished, before the National Arbitration Tribunal. An important area officer, with many years of experience, responsible for more than 50,000 members, agreed therefore to attend a 1/AAA meeting to discuss the problem. He had been briefed by his subordinate, Brother Tims, the District Organizer who had been responsible for handling the negotiations until the meeting of June 14, 1948.

This capable and competent official, with a wider perspective than most Branch members, was able to place this case in a national context. He argued that in view of the economic crisis facing the country, the National Arbitration Tribunal would not uphold the

[1] Though all Union signatories to the agreement were concerned in the negotiations with the management, the T.G.W.U. was responsible for the largest number of workers and thus could take the lead. The other Unions, though first opposed to the change, subsequently accepted it. By leaving out their part in these activities, the case is somewhat over-simplified, though not in so far as the subject of this section is concerned.

Branch's point of view, and advised against allowing the case to reach the tribunal stage. Members of the inner circle argued that even in the event of an unfavourable decision at arbitration, it was worth fighting to serve the ultimate objectives of Trade Unionism. Some rather effective arguments, more directly concerned with the situation at Colins', were presented as well. Most of the thirty-one members in attendance, however, had not made the necessary preparations to argue the case[1].

The Trade Group official continued to take the un-popular line of opposing Branch policy. However, rather than advise the members in terms of frankness of the facts which militated against the Branch's policy, he resorted to short-cut methods calculated at speedily getting the response he desired. When a reference to the Works Agreement was made, he asked to see a copy. Taking advantage of the fact that none was to be found at the meeting, this Union 'civil servant' impressed upon his 'masters' how ill prepared they were. He followed up by tauntingly remarking: 'If there were any real concern for this decision you couldn't get them all [the Branch members] into this room.'

This attempt to ridicule the active minority's concern turned the discussion from the problem facing the Branch to personal gibes. Finally, anxious to bring the meeting to a close, he secured the support of the inner circle by undertaking to consult the Branch prior to signing a final agreement with the management. This undertaking proved to be another device for eliminating discussion and relieving this official of the burden of using his expert knowledge to explain the reasons which made inadvisable any attempt to pursue Branch policy.

At the next Branch meeting the Chairman's report of the events of the previous two weeks clearly revealed in whose hands the *loci* of power at Branch level may ultim-

[1] There appears to be a need at Branch level for a Research Committee or a Branch Research Officer, responsible for investigating the facts of any important case.

ately rest. The management posted notices claiming that an agreement had been reached to accept the forty-four hour week. Branch leaders tore down the notices, protesting to the management that no agreement could possibly have been signed with their approval. The Branch Chairman reported that District Organizer Tims had confessed to him that a final agreement had been made.

Still hopeful of exerting influence, the Branch, in a resolution, expressed its 'extreme displeasure' at the permanent official's failure to keep his pledge of prior consultation, and requested his personal appearance at a meeting to explain this unauthorized action. It might have been predicted, as indeed it transpired, that this Trade Group Officer would be too busy to appear again before the Branch, and that the resolution would have little effect, by those who heard Brother Vinson say in support of this token resolution: 'We talk about the Trade Union Movement being democratic. We must tell the workers why we lost. We lost because they failed to attend Branch meetings and show their strength to the Organizer.'

Whether or not this permanent official's policy decision was in the best interests of the Branch and the Union is not in question. The method and approach used nullified in every way the functions of a Branch meeting both as an instrument of communication between the paid official and member, and as a device for creating a real sense of participation in policy determination—if only for a small minority of the membership. Though nothing so blatant as the example given has occurred at any other time in the history of this Branch, and though there have been resolutions expressing appreciation of the assistance rendered by permanent officials, a series of resolutions complaining of their disregard of Branch decisions or inquiries is to be found in the Minutes of the 1/AAA.

At this juncture it is worth noting that miscalculations on the part of the permanent paid official, assuming the authority to determine policy at Branch level or higher, may result in 'unofficial' strikes. Before World War II the strike was a crude but effective means of communicating to the official the extent of rank and file support. Today the 'unofficial' strike is in most cases a means of communicating non-support. The absence of the 'unofficial' strike, however, is no indication of member support for official policy, for it is likely to occur only among groups of members, unlike those of the 1/AAA, whose turnover is low and sense of community, at least in time of crisis, high.

The usurpation of policy-making authority which apathy at Branch level encourages is reflected on all higher levels of the T.G.W.U.'s organization. At Area level, for example, one of the most responsible officials in the Union frankly admits that so long as he feels he is acting in the best interests of the Union, he does not hesitate to break its Rules. Though his decisions are an expression of a sincere desire to serve the membership, this permanent official's method is to 'present your executive (the elected representatives) with a *fait accompli*; if necessary look to the Rules to explain your action'. This attitude of disregard for the rank and file member as an individual to be consulted on matters of policy, via the Constitutional Committees of elected representatives is precisely summarized by a remark made during this interview: 'We (the permanent paid officials) know what is best and do it.'

At national level as well there is evidence to substantiate the proposition that apathy at Branch level serves to transfer the control of policy into the hands of the permanent paid official. The General Secretary, though an elected official, can be considered in the same category as the permanent paid official. The General Secretary's main function is to execute the policy of the General

Executive Council and the Biennial Delegate Conference, the supreme policy-making body. Like other Union officials, he has security of tenure in office. Even more important than these similarities is the fact that he too is fully aware of the extent to which apathy has in practice deprived the elected representatives, to whom he is in theory responsible, of the support so essential to their successful exercise of authority over the bureaucracy.

There is little doubt that Ernest Bevin, whose comments on T.G.W.U. elections are cited above, was fully aware, as General Secretary, of the failure of the rank and file to make elections meaningful and thus make their elected representatives powerful. Excerpts from two addresses made by Arthur Deakin, the present General Secretary, at closed sessions of the 1947 Biennial Delegate Conference, indicate that he too is apprised of the lack of member interest at Branch level.

On behalf of the General Executive Council Mr. Deakin, in opposing a resolution demanding that Union cards be issued to new members at the nearest Branch, said:

'. . . you cannot expect membership on a basis of requiring every prospective member to go to the Branch for the purpose of entering the Union. (Delegate: "Why not?") The position is simple . . . will anyone disagree with me when I say that more than half the present membership has been enrolled outside the Branches? . . . It will not work, you cannot go to the nearest Branch, the nearest Branch may be twenty miles away.' (1947 B.D.C. unpublished Verbatim Report, Minute 45, p. 206.)

Again on behalf of the General Executive Council, Mr. Deakin said in opposition to a resolution calling for compulsory attendance at Branch meetings:

'. . . I should like the conference to reject the proposal by reason of its impracticability. How could you do it? You have branches with 2,000 members. How could you compel them to attend? How could you fine them? How could you collect the fines? It would be one of the most destructive factors that could be in the organisation.' (1947 B.D.C. unpublished Verbatim Report, Minute 33, pp. 155–157.)

P

The General Secretary, contrary to what he has said to the rank and file and the public, fully realizes that large-scale participation is impracticable if not impossible under present conditions of super-sized Branches and widely scattered memberships in rural areas served by relatively few Branches.

In the light of this, one is entitled to question both why no positive steps have been taken to remove these physical barriers to participation and the wisdom of the General Secretary's statements which serve to perpetuate the myth that in practice there is a place for every T.G.W.U. member in his Branch or of such exhortations in the Union Journal to the rank and file as:

> 'If you would preserve your freedom and liberty of action, then, in the days which lie ahead, it is necessary that you should be very vigilant; that you should attend your branch meetings, get to understand fully the policy and work of your Union, and take a part in shaping that policy, not on the instructions of any political party, but as free men.'[1]

'Progressive administrations, with a tradition of "mass activity" do occasionally call upon the members to be "more active" but the words are really meaningless . . . The whole matter wears a thoroughly unreal aspect because of the widening gap between the realities of the bureaucratic situation and the "mass" traditions carried over from an earlier day.'[2] Though written to describe a situation prevalent in American Labor Unions, these words apply equally well to the T.G.W.U.

As a result of his recognition of these realities the General Secretary has in practice found it possible to assume final authority in policy-making denied him in theory. In opening a debate on election versus appointment of officials, at the 1947 Biennial Delegate Conference, he described his functions in theory:

[1] Arthur Deakin: 'A Challenge to Democracy—And Our Answer', in the T.G.W.U. *Record*, January 1950, p. 207.

[2] Will Herberg: 'Bureaucracy and Democracy in Labor Unions', in the *Antioch Review*, Fall 1943 (From Mr Herberg's mimeographed copy of the article, p. 6.)

'Above all . . . you are the people in this B.D.C. who determine the policy of this organization. Our job is to apply it.' (1947 B.D.C. unpublished Verbatim Report, Minute 22, p. 124.)

In closing this discussion Mr. Deakin more accurately expressed his and the Executive's position to the elected delegates about to determine Union policy:

'Now there is no gap between the officers and the rank and file of this Union. I repeat that . . . I do not want any half-hearted vote on this. I demand from you on behalf of the officers of this Union a clear vote as to where we stand. We either work for you or we shall go on our way and seek something else. This is not a threat, it is simply a statement of fact.' (1947 B.D.C. unpublished Verbatim Report, Minute 22, p. 133.)

This method of convincing B.D.C. delegates is not very different from an offer of resignation, a threat to which the General Secretary might resort when opposed to policy proposed by the General Executuve Council. Though Mr. Deakin may not resort to this threat often, the fact that it is there to be used demonstrates that in the final analysis the control of policy at national level may rest in the hands of the permanent paid official, if only because the elected representatives cannot confidently turn to a well informed membership for support[1].

Thus apathy at Branch level, while conferring power and authority on a small minority of lay members, does, at the same time, deprive this same minority of ultimate control. That is not to say that the active lay minority or its representatives do not take part in the formulation of policy at each level of organization, but rather that the Union 'civil servant' when opposed to this policy can effectively exercise the power of veto. This group of paid officials does not derive its power from the assent of the membership, except possibly in the case of the General Secretary. But even he, once elected, need not, because of the permanency of his position, pursue policies conforming to the trends of membership opinion.

[1] An interesting analysis of the use of the threat by leaders to fortify their leadership position is to be found in Robert Michels, *Political Parties* (The Free Press, Glencoe, Illinois, 1949), Chapter IV.

The vicious circle of results created by apathy defeats the major functions of the Branch to serve generally as an outlet of member participation and specifically as a means of communication between rank and file, the elected representatives and the permanent paid officials. These officials need not convince by frank explanations, for they can accomplish their objectives by resorting to threats and other techniques of creating desired responses. Thus the assumption of the policy-making function by permanent paid officials prevents increased participation. This eating away of the democratic base of the organization ultimately deprives the Union of its nucleus of active lay members who, even if only a small majority, might at least be sincerely encouraged to elicit the participation of rank and file members.

Chapter 17

THE INACTIVE MEMBER

OTHER CHANNELS OF PARTICIPATION AND COMMUNICATION

The Branch is more than the twice-monthly meetings it holds. It is in the case of the 1/AAA some one thousand members. Thus far the degree of member participation in Branch meetings and elections are the two main criteria on which we have relied to determine the extent to which apathy has undermined the democratic process in the government of the Union. There are, however, other channels of communication and participation at Branch level which may, if functioning well, mitigate, though only in part, the failure of the election and meeting as institutions to safeguard the representative character of the Union. We shall consult, therefore, a cross section of 1/AAA members who have seldom if ever attended meetings or participated in elections to determine how well acquainted they are with the supplemental channels of the Union's formal communication system and to ascertain if they are aware of the part they are entitled to play in Union activities. In answering the second part of the query we shall consider whatever informal outlets of member participation may have developed at this level outside the constitutional structure of the organization.

I SUPPLEMENTAL CHANNELS OF THE UNION'S FORMAL COMMUNICATION SYSTEM

It has become quite clear that the Branch meeting as a two-way channel of communication is an unfamiliar way for the vast majority of 1/AAA members. The following media which constitute the most important supplemental channels in the Union's formal communication system will be considered in relation to their effectiveness in developing a membership well informed on Union matters.

A. *The Rule Book and the Members Handbook.*

B. *The Union's Educational Scheme.*

C. *The 'Transport and General Workers' Record'—official Union journal.*

A. *The Rule Book and the Members Handbook*

Both the Rule Book and the Members Handbook are designed to provide each member with the material essential to a knowledge if not an understanding of the Union's Constitution and structure.

Like many Union rule books, the T.G.W.U.'s 140 pages of rules and schedules are written in legal jargon and printed in uninviting small type. This Rule Book is to most members a road block to an understanding of the constitutional process of Union government. A comment by a Union member from Area 12 describes well its ineffectiveness as a means of communication:

> 'I very much doubt if the average member reads more than half of it before confining it to the bottom drawer. I have yet to meet, at any rate, in our industry a member who can quote a rule or in fact produce a rule book at a minute's notice to settle an argument.'[1]

Three-quarters of the 1/AAA's inactive members are neither well acquainted with the contents of the Rule Book nor do they use it as a reference. Though Rule 18 provides that upon payment of the initiation fee each new member is to receive in addition to his card a Rule Book, one out of every three of these members remarked that he had never received one. Close to half the female members, compared with only a fifth of the

[1] 'What Methods Would You Suggest for Dealing with the Problem of Retention of Members?' an essay written for the correspondence course, *The Union: Its Work and Problems*, by a cold-storage worker, Area 12.

male members, have been so neglected. Rather than turn to their Rule Book, many members turn to their Shop Stewards, most of whom claim to use the Rules as a reference[1].

Recognizing the failure of the Rule Book to serve as a popular medium of communication, the Union published the Members Handbook early in 1947. This pamphlet, written in clear and simple language, is attractively bound. Its typography is pleasing to the eye. Area 12's critic agrees that the Members Handbook compensates for the inadequacies of the Rule Book:

'. . . (It) seems to fill the bill for it explains in a nutshell the aims and constitution of the Union and the rights and duties of its members.'

Though in print for a year at the time of this survey, the Members Handbook had been read by only two out of every ten inactive and six of every ten active Branch members[2]. Furthermore, close to a quarter of both the inactive and active members remarked that they had never heard of this Union pamphlet.

Only a third of the membership, half the men and less than 10 per cent of the women (thirty-two of ninety-two interviewed), claimed to have read either the Rule Book or the Members Handbook. As for the distribution of this material, the women members have been the most neglected. Many of those who claimed to have read either or both of these documents have failed, however, to realize, as will be discussed later, the national character of the T.G.W.U., as well as their rights as members. The

[1] Are you well acquainted with the contents of, or do you use the T.G.W.U. Rule Book?

	Inactive	Active
	(92)	(19)
Yes	26% (24)	95% (18)
No	74% (68)	5% (1)

[2] Have you read the T.G.W.U. Members Handbook?

	Inactive	Active
	(92)	(19)
Yes	20% (18)	63% (12)
No	80% (74)	37% (7)

over-all picture remains one of Union failure in providing
sufficient and effective material for widespread understanding, among 1/AAA members, of the structure and
constitutional procedures of the Union.

B. *The Union's Educational Scheme*

The Union's Educational Scheme, particularly its correspondence course, 'The Union, Its Work and Problems',
is another means of informing rank and file members of
the constitutional processes of Union government.
Though every member's card, the Rule Book, Handbook
and each issue of the *Record* carry an advertisement in
bold face type of the Union's educational facilities, three
out of every four inactive members and one out of every
ten active members were not even aware of the existence
of this scheme[1]. Again the women are the least well
informed members of the inactive population.

As has already been pointed out, only a ludicrously
small number of T.G.W.U. members take advantage of
any of the educational opportunities provided by the
Union. (See Table XII.) Only one of the inactive members of the 1/AAA who had heard of the scheme participated in it. He, however, did not complete his course.
Many remarked either that they were too old or too busy
with their families to devote time to study.

It is not unreasonable to ask how this evidence is to be
reconciled with the statement made earlier that the
1/AAA Branch as a unit is one of the most active participants in the Union's Educational Scheme. This is explained in the very same way as was the Branch's
better-than-average representation on higher levels of
Union organization. Four members, all of the hard core
centre and the Communist Party, have been responsible

[1] Have you ever heard of the Union's Educational Scheme?—Describe it

	Inactive	*Active*
	(92)	(19)
Yes	23% (21)	89% (17)
No	77% (71)	11% (2)

for taking part in the correspondence course, full-time University courses, as well as month and week-end schools which constitute the record of high activity attributed to the Branch. In addition, some active members commenced but failed to continue courses either because they felt they were too old to learn other than by experience, or because essays submitted were not returned corrected.

Thus, the Union's Educational Scheme is for the overwhelming majority of 1/AAA members, as it is for most T.G.W.U. members, an ineffective outlet of participation and channel of communication.

C. *The 'Transport and General Workers' Record'—Official Union Journal*

The T.G.W.U. *Record*, the Union's official journal published monthly, is, as has already been noted, a one-way channel of communication. Official Union policy is transmitted from the editorial centre in Union headquarters via the pages of this magazine to members of the Union. Does the *Record* keep 1/AAA members regularly informed of Union policy? Mr. Deakin's answer is in the affirmative. (See Appendix No. 6.)

The Branch receives thirty copies of each issue of the *Record*. The one copy provided for every thirty-three Branch members compares unfavourably with the national figure of one copy for every eight members. These copies are distributed, as is generally the case in the Union, at Branch meetings. Thus, if the journal is to be seen by the rank and file members who do not attend meetings, the active nucleus, i.e., the Shop Stewards, must assume the responsibility for the circulation of these few copies.

As might be expected under these circumstances, close to eight out of every ten inactive members have never read the T.G.W.U. *Record*. In fact, more than half of these members remarked that they had never heard of it.

None of the inactive female members have ever read their Union's journal. Furthermore, a third of the active membership either read less than half the issues published each year, or never read the *Record* at all[1]. There is considerable evidence, though of a fragmentary nature, that the system of distribution of the *Record*, as well as its capacity to arouse interest among 1/AAA members, is by no means unique in the T.G.W.U. For example, a General Workers delegate from Area 5, in commenting on the section of the annual report devoted to the *Record* at the 1945 B.D.C., said:

'Is it not a fact that in many Areas, the *Record* arrives month after month and is laid on the table and at the end of the month the biggest part of them have to be thrown away?' (1945 B.D.C. unpublished Verbatim Report, p. 10.)

The General Secretary, Mr. Bevin, in corroboration replied:

'I have often wondered if we should not have done better with the *Record* . . . if we had sold it to our members. I believe you would like it better if you paid for it and it would be more likely to have a far wider reading public. At present it is limited in circulation to the interested members.' (1945 B.D.C. unpublished Verbatim Report, p. 106.)

Finally, the more recent comment by a Passenger Workers delegate from Area 1 at the 1947 B.D.C.:

'Today I see thousands of *Records* notwithstanding the paper shortage lying in desks, nobody wants them . . . they will not take the *Record* for nothing.' (1947 B.D.C. unpublished Verbatim Report, pp. 97–98.)

The small proportion of readers in the 1/AAA find that the *Record* is an unattractive periodical containing twenty-two pages of uninviting newspaper print and hazy photographs in a poor lay-out. Among those who

[1] Do you read the T.G.W.U. *Record* (the Official Journal of the Union)?

	Inactive		Active	
	(92)		(19)	
(a) Every month	4%	(4)	58%	(11)
(b) Every other month	4%	(4)	5%	(1)
(c) Less than six times a year	14%	(13)	21%	(4)
(d) Not at all	78%	(71)	16%	(3)

read the *Record* at least once a year the general lead articles and the legal section are the most popular. Thus more than half the inactive and active readers receive the Union's official view on major Union problems or policy in the two or three pages of each issue devoted to articles by the General Secretary and other permanent paid officials. A third of the inactive and close to two-thirds of the active readers find the two pages of the legal section interesting. This section contains information on industrial legislation as well as a series of human interest stories recounting the success of the Union's Legal Department in securing industrial injury awards for members. The remaining pages of the *Record* receive little of the 1/AAA readers' attention[1]. These include the six or seven pages divided among the twelve active National Trade Groups for reporting negotiations concerning members of the respective Groups, an equal number of pages devoted to commercial advertising, and the two or three pages of miscellaneous articles on Union personnel, the garden, books and short reports on debates of interest in Parliament[2]. As there are no provisions for printing letters to the editor, the reader cannot discuss his views on policy with other readers, nor can he use this as a channel of communication to Union officers.

Thus, the *Record* too fails to fulfil its function in the formal communication system of the Union. The size of the 1/AAA's allocation and the method of distribution are two factors which make almost impossible the reading of the official Union journal by more than a small minority of the membership. Only half of this small

[1] If so, what parts of the Journal do you read?

	Inactive (of 21 readers)	Active (of 16 readers)
General lead articles	57% (12)	63% (10)
Legal section	33% (7)	63% (10)
Personalia	14% (3)	31% (5)
National Trade Group news	5% (1)	6% (1)

[2] Distribution of material in the 'Record' is based on an analysis of the issues for 1947 and 1948.

minority read the most important policy articles and even fewer read the *Record* regularly. There is some evidence that the situation is not very different throughout the Union.

It is clear, therefore, that the most important supplemental channels of the Union's formal communication system have failed to maintain regular and close contact, even down one-way channels, with the rank and file members of the 1/AAA as well as of many other Branches of the T.G.W.U. Only four out of every ten inactive members have had any contact with one or more of these media. As is the case with Branch meetings familiarity with these channels is limited to a very small minority of the membership—in fact it is with few exceptions the very same minority. Thus, approximately two-thirds of the Branch's membership have remained outside of the Union's formal communication system and effectively outside the government of the organization itself.

II   INFORMAL CHANNELS—DO MEMBERS THINK THAT THEY CAN INFLUENCE UNION POLICY?

A prerequisite of a member's participation in policy determination is a recognition that as a member he is entitled to take part in Union activities. It is not surprising to find that almost all inactive and that even a third of the active members felt that they have never had any influence in a Union decision or matter of policy[1]. It may be argued, however, that so long as a member is well informed of Union policy, fully aware of the outlets of participation, and so long as he feels free to use these outlets, the democratic process in the government of the

[1] Do you think that you have ever had any influence in a Union decision or a matter of policy?

	Inactive	Active
	(92)	(19)
Yes (national concept)	2% (2)	58% (11)
Yes (local concept only)	2% (2)	10% (2)
No	96% (88)	32% (6)

Union is safeguarded, even though a majority of the members do not feel that they have exerted such influence. Though there is considerable evidence that 1/AAA members are neither well informed in Union matters, nor fully aware of outlets of participation at Branch level, it remains of interest to consider their response to questions concerning their right to help decide Union policy.

A fifth of the inactive members, for the most part men, thought that they could in an *individual* capacity help settle policy in the Union. (See Tables XXVIIa and XXVIIb.) The meanings of the term 'Union policy' will be discussed in some detail in relation to the response to the second in this series of questions. For the moment it is sufficient to note that some members refer only to the handling of a grievance by Shop Stewards, and others to issues of an Area or National character. Another fifth of the membership, a larger proportion of female than male members, didn't know and said that they had never given any thought to the influencing of Union policy. The largest group of members—three out of every five—thought that acting in an *individual* capacity they could not help settle policy in the Union.

It is rather interesting to note that two-thirds (twenty-one of thirty-two) of the members who claimed to have read or be well acquainted with the Rule Book or Handbook, believed they could not influence policy, or replied that they had never thought about it. Only one member, however, remarked that he did not believe what he had read in the Members Handbook. There seems to be little correlation between an inactive member's familiarity with either of these media and his response to the two questions on policy[1]. Such statements as the following are characteristic of members giving a negative response

[1] Of the thirty-two inactive members who claimed to be acquainted with the Rule Book or Handbook, only eleven gave an affirmative answer to the first policy question and sixteen gave an unqualified affirmative answer, or one indicating a knowledge of the Union's structure, to the second policy question.

Tables XXVIIa and XXVIIb

(a) DO YOU THINK THAT YOU, YOURSELF (AS AN INDIVIDUAL MEMBER), CAN HELP SETTLE POLICY IN THE UNION?

	Inactive (92)			Active (19)
	MEN	WOMEN	TOTAL	
Yes	28% (17)	6% (2)	21% (19)	95% (18)
No	60% (36)	56% (18)	58% (54)	5% (1)
I don't know (Never really thought about it)	12% (7)	38% (12)	21% (19)	—

(b) DO YOU THINK THAT YOU, ACTING COLLECTIVELY WITH OTHER MEMBERS, CAN INFLUENCE POLICY IN THE UNION?

	Inactive (92)			Active (19)
	MEN	WOMEN	TOTAL	
Yes (unqualified or national concept of the Union)	35% (21)	6% (2)	25% (23)	85% (16)
Yes (local concept)	17% (10)	25% (8)	20% (18)	5% (1)
Yes, possibly, but I wouldn't know how	20% (12)	16% (5)	18% (17)	5% (1)
Yes (total)	72% (43)	47% (15)	63% (58)	95% (18)
No	21% (13)	16% (5)	20% (18)	5% (1)
I don't know (Never really thought about it)	7% (4)	37% (12)	17% (16)	—

to the question 'Do you think that you yourself (as an individual) can help to settle policy in the Union?':

'That is up to the official, I guess we've not had a lot to do with the Union.'

'The leaders are better educated than I am, any decision they make is good enough for me. I'll follow them and give my support.'

'I'm not educated enough, it's like a puff of wind for me to say something. I leave it to the Steward, he's doing a good job. I speak my mind to him.'

'The Shop Stewards have all the power.'

'Whatever our grievances we go through the Shop Steward, that is as far as we can go.'

These results, when considered against the background of material already presented, are in the nature of what one might have expected. The results of the second question, on the other hand, do appear, at least on the surface, somewhat surprising. The majority of inactive members—three out of every five—thought that acting *collectively* they could influence Union policy (Tables XXVIIa and XXVIIb). It has already been noted that the use of the term 'policy in the Union' in this series of questions did not prove to be entirely satisfactory. It becomes necessary therefore to analyse the remarks accompanying each response in some detail, in order to explain these results.

An examination of the affirmative remarks reveals that they fall roughly and almost equally into one of three categories: first, that in which the respondent mistakenly equated 'Union policy' with 'management policy'; second, that in which the respondent, who most often though not always equated 'Union' and 'management' policy, indicated that he was in doubt as to how he could exert influence; and third, that in which the respondent either gave an unqualified response or indicated that he was at least vaguely aware of the structure and the national character of the Union. The negative responses, though not discussed in detail here, fall primarily in the first and very occasionally in the third category.

The word 'collectively', which for the most part was responsible for the increase in affirmative answers, was associated by a large majority of the members with one of their major reasons for joining the Union, i.e., that by joining together they could improve their bargaining position in relation to the management and thus affect this (the management's) policy on wages and working conditions. For many who gave an affirmative answer to this question though a negative answer to the first, it was, therefore, but a confirmation of one of their major reasons for joining the Union. In fact, the interviewer noted that at least three out of every five inactive members associated the Branch or Union only with the factory in which they worked and not with a large national organization as well. It was not uncommon, therefore, to hear remarks such as the following accompanying an affirmative reply, which indicate how insular is the concept of the Union held by many members:

'My voice is insignificant; only a group's voice can be heard. I'm certain we should be able to be heard. The Shop Stewards would take the matter up for you.'

'Yes, in the factory I tell the Shop Steward and he carries it from there.'

'If we had a meeting we might influence the Shop Steward on a grievance.'

'We tell Shop Stewards—they have a meeting and follow up what we have been complaining about.'

'Indirectly, yes, my ideas are expressed at shop meetings. We debate the idea, take a vote and send it higher up.'

In the second category, into which almost a third of the affirmative responses fall, such remarks as the following indicate clearly how doubtful these members are of how to exert influence in the Union:

'If I took the trouble to go to Branch meetings perhaps I could, but never having gone I don't know if it is possible.'

'I believe you can but I have no idea how.'

'You should do. I would take it to the Shop Steward, otherwise I don't know.'

'We could talk it over with our Shop Steward, through her we could find out what to do or something.'

Finally, in the third category are to be found somewhat more than a third of the affirmative responses. It should be noted that many affirmative answers included in this category were made without qualifying comments. The following remarks were the most articulate expressions given of the inactive members' awareness of the structure and national character of the Union:

'Collectively, definitely; the Branch can pass a resolution. If it comes to any more than that no one knows. I guess we trust our Secretary on where it goes from there.'

'Go to the Branch meeting and air your views or go further up.'

'There is no way other than through voting for representatives.'

'If you have a strong point you can put it to your Branch and get them to pass a resolution.'

'Yes, at the Branch meeting, from the Branch meeting to the General Council.'

Before concluding this analysis, it is of interest to note the common thread which runs through both the negative and affirmative responses (excepting those in the third category) to these questions on policy. This common thread is the inactive members' recognition of the Shop Steward as the unit of Union organization with which to maintain contact. In the light of these comments it is not surprising to find that all the inactive members replied, 'See the Shop Steward', when asked how they would bring a grievance or problem to the attention of the Union[1]. In fact the Shop Steward is for most rank and file members their first and only contact with the Union. To them the Shop Steward rather than the Branch is the Union.

The Shop Steward, however, is not and cannot be, according to Union Rules and under the present circumstances, a real substitute for the Branch meeting as an outlet, though only an informal one, of member participation. In the first place, though Union Rules provide that he may be, the Shop Steward need not be and often

[1] *Procedure for Negotiations:* A worker desiring to raise any question in which he is directly concerned must discuss the matter with his foreman, failing settlement he may be accompanied by his shop steward to see the shop manager. (Memorandum of Agreement between Colins' Electroparts Ltd. and Trade Unions.)

is not elected[1]. Being a thankless job, the office of Shop
Steward is filled by almost any member willing to accept appointment. In view of the average member's
indifference towards elections, coupled with a now tradi-
tional disrespect among the active members for the sanc-
tity of the ballot, even where elections do take place, it
would be a misnomer to call a Shop Steward a member's
elected representative. Secondly, with reference to the
shop meeting mentioned in some comments, it does not
serve as a channel for continuously informing the Shop
Steward, and thus the Union, of membership opinion on
Union problems or matters of policy. These meetings are
held during working hours at the management's discre-
tion and are limited to discussing problems facing the
workers—not necessarily Union members—at Colins'.
Likewise, informal discussions during tea and luncheon
breaks are primarily devoted to local grievances, if concerned with Union matters at all. Thirdly, not all Shop
Stewards attend 'Branch meetings regularly, and many
who do, refuse to report Branch discussions and decisions
to their 'constituents'.[2] Consequently, these members,
not well informed on issues facing the Branch and the
Union, are in no position to discuss them intelligently
with their respective Shop Stewards. Finally, the Union
officially recognizes the Shop Steward only as a member
responsible for dealing with 'minor matters arising at the
place of employment'.[3] Thus, neither the shop meeting
nor the Shop Steward in the 1/AAA Branch has in prac-

[1] Rule 9 (4), pp. 27–28.

[2] Only two of the Shop Stewards interviewed—responsible for 10 per cent of the
membership—make a consistent effort to keep their members informed of Branch
decisions. Two Shop Stewards, both members of the hard core centre and responsible for 20 per cent of the membership, refuse to report Branch decisions to their
'constituents'. They argue that every member is entitled to attend and, if interested,
will attend. A quarter of the active population do not attend meetings regularly.

[3] *Shop Stewards:* It is the responsibility of Shop Stewards to deal with minor matters
arising at the place of employment. In many of the agreements held by the Union
in the general trades there is also a recognition that Shop Stewards shall deal with
rate fixing and generally represent the men in the shop. *The Union: Its Work and
Problems,* Part II, p. 6.

tice effectively replaced the Branch meeting as the outlet of member participation that it is in theory.

The fact remains, however, that the Shop Steward is for most members, not just those of the 1/AAA, their only real contact with the Union. This unit of organization at the work place has in practice become a new level in the structure of the government of the Union as well. It has wedged itself firmly though unofficially between the rank and file member and the Branch. The Branch in practice has in turn become the Shop Stewards', not the inactive members' primary contact with the Union[1]. The failure of the Union to integrate the Shop Steward unit within the formal structure of its own organization has served to hinder rather than encourage member participation at Branch level, and to maintain rather than bridge the gap between leader and rank and file.

Briefly, these are the provisions which seem essential to any reorganization scheme for integrating the Shop Steward within the structure of Union government: Firstly, provision should be made for honestly supervised elections by ballot of a Shop Steward for each of the 'constituencies' (for example 50–75 members each) into which a Branch might be divided. Secondly, the Shop Steward should be required to attend Branch meetings regularly as the elected representative of his 'constituents'. Thirdly, higher levels of Union organization should be required to maintain continuous and constant contact with each Branch's Shop Stewards' group, as well as to provide special training to equip these Shop Stewards to perform the duties of elected representatives. Fourthly and finally, the Shop Steward should be required to meet his 'constituents' as a group at regular and frequent intervals, not only to report, explain and discuss Branch activities, but also to provide information

[1] For an interesting discussion of the role of Shop Stewards in British Trade Unions generally, which concludes that 'to many members the Steward is the Union', see P.E.P. (Political and Economic Planning), *British Trade Unionism* (London, 1948) pp. 125–133.

on the major problems facing the Union as a national organization. The Shop Steward would be expected to encourage the active participation of his 'constituents' in Union activities.

By thus decentralizing Branch level organization and by bestowing official recognition on the members' only real contact with the Union it may be possible to create a broad base of well informed members, who would have, and feel that they have, an outlet of communication with all higher levels of Union organization[1]. In turn, these Shop Stewards would, when speaking through the Branch, be able to command the attention of permanent officials fully aware of the fact that these elected representatives do actually represent and have the support of a well informed rank and file. Though this is by no means the solution to the problem of apathy, it does indicate one obvious and possible method of reducing apathy by taking advantage of the existing position of the Shop Steward to create a link rather than maintain the present break in the chain of communication between the rank and file member and his elected and full-time officials at all higher levels of Union organization.

It is clear, therefore, that the supplemental channels of the Union's formal communication system have failed to maintain close and continuous contact with most rank and file members. The Shop Steward under present circumstances has not been able to serve as an informal link between the Union and its members. Thus the formal and informal channels of communication have neither been able to keep the membership well informed nor to mitigate in any appreciable way the failure of the election and the Branch meeting to safeguard the repre-

---

[1] The fear that recognition of Shop Stewards will bring the Communists greater authority in the Union is in part justified, but only because the rank and file are not well informed, and are not in a position to make an intelligent choice. In the long run, it is better to have the Shop Stewards part of the organisation than to have an *ad hoc* authority develop to which members may turn during unofficial strikes, for example, as was the case in the dock strikes already discussed.

sentative character of Union government. Only a small minority of 1/AAA members have been made to feel that they are entitled to take part in Union decisions and policy determination. Fewer still have even a vague picture of the structure of the organization and are able to associate their membership with the large national body with far-reaching power and influence on the community that the Transport and General Workers Union is. For this very reason there is no feeling of frustration prevalent among the 1/AAA's rank and file. They are ignorant of the strength their membership in conjunction with that of others like them bestows upon Union leaders, and of the policies these leaders pursue on their behalf. A certain stability is thereby achieved, at the expense of democratic control, for members not well informed of the meaning of membership do not feel deprived of the opportunity to take part.

Chapter 18

THE INACTIVE MEMBER (*continued*)
THE PROBLEM OF ELICITING ACTIVE
PARTICIPATION

The failure of the Union to elicit the interest of the vast
majority of 1/AAA members at Branch level is patently
obvious. In order to complete this picture of the Branch
in practice it is desirable to consider the reasons or excuses given by these members for non-attendance at
Branch meetings, as well as to consider their reasons for
joining the Union. The analysis of reasons for non-
attendance is presented to disclose various expressions of
apathy characteristic of this membership. The examination of members' reasons for joining the Union is presented to show the very significant difference in the concept of the Union held by active and inactive members.
It is not within the scope of this survey, nor within the
competence of the writer, to determine the sociological
and psychological factors which might explain the apathy
of most members and the activity of some. Rather than
absolute facts, the results of the statistically dubious
'Why' questions indicate trends and tendencies. This
analysis will serve primarily to emphasize, therefore, how
complex is the problem of eliciting the interest of rank
and file members, even once the physical and constitutional obstacles to participation have been removed. It is
with this in mind that we turn first to an examination of
members' reasons for not attending Branch meetings
regularly.

I   REASONS FOR NON-ATTENDANCE
Six out of every ten inactive members have never attended a meeting of the 1/AAA Branch. One out of

every ten has never been to more than one or two meetings. More than half of those who have attended meetings had not been to one at any time during the six-month period immediately preceding the interview. There were no regular attenders among the inactive population[1].

Reasons for not attending Branch meetings regularly have been placed into one of six categories. These categories do not provide a rigid classification, but rather a convenient method of analysis. The response of inactive members—as well as the views of the active members and of permanent paid officials—are to be considered in relation to:

A. Timidity—Sense of feeling out of place at Branch meetings.
B. Inconvenience of time or place of Branch Meetings.
C. Domestic Duties—Family responsibilities.
D. General indifference.
E. Dissatisfaction with the operation of the Branch.
F. Other reasons.

A. *Timidity—Sense of feeling out of place at Branch Meetings*

Of considerable interest, though less frequently mentioned than most, are those reasons placed under the heading of 'feeling out of place.' One out of every seven

---

[1] (a) Have you ever attended a Branch meeting of the 1/AAA Branch of the T.G.W.U.?

	Inactive	Active
	(92)	(19)
Yes	41% (38)	100% (19)
No	59% (54)	—

(11 per cent of the inactive—a quarter of those who have attended meetings—added that they have only been once or twice; 79 per cent of the active members interviewed were regular attenders.)

(b) If yes, when was the last time?

	Inactive (Of 38 Attenders)	Active (Of 19 Attenders)
The last meeting	—	74% (14)
Less than six months ago	42% (16)	26% (5)
Six months—one year	32% (12)	—
One year or more	26% (10)	—

men attributed his non-attendance in part to a feeling that he would be out of place at Branch meetings. In most cases the respondent thought he was not educated enough to speak in front of groups. In some cases he said 'they laugh at us old fogies'. A non-drinking member of six years' standing reported that he would not attend meetings because they were held in pubs and he would feel out of place among drinking men. He did not know that two years prior to the interview the Branch discontinued meetings at the 'Nags Head' and moved to the drier though damper Trades Hall.

In spite of the fact that the Branch Secretary and a quarter of the active nucleus are women, close to half the single women members are under the impression that meetings are primarily for men. One young lady of eighteen who had been in the Branch for two years, though never to one of its meetings, summed up this mistaken attitude:

> 'I once made a date with my girl friend to go but she let me down. I wouldn't go by myself, most of the people are older and they are mostly men.'

Table XXVIIIa

	Inactive			Active
	MEN (60)	WOMEN (32)	TOTAL (92)	(19)
Feeling out of place at a meeting	15% (9)	19% (6)	16% (15)	16% (3)
Believes not educated enough to speak before group	12% (7)	—	8% (7)	16% (3)
Other reasons including: too old, too young, not for women	3% (2)	19% (6)	9% (8)	5% (1)

(Respondents often gave more than one reason. Percentages are of respondents in each population.)

Two-thirds of the men and all of the women who gave reasons of this nature had never been to a Branch meeting. These misconceptions might be dispelled if not prevented by providing that every new member enter the Union by attending a Branch meeting. It should be noted, however, that these reasons were given in combination with other reasons, primarily those in the 'general indifference' category. For the few men who based their reasons on actual experience at Branch meetings, the I/AAA has failed to assist in the development of the social skills essential to the democratic operation of the Union.

B. *Inconvenience of Time or Place of Branch Meetings*

If a member lives a long distance from the Branch meeting place, if he is on shift work or is fatigued after a day at the bench, attendance at Branch meetings, particularly in the evening of a working day, is made extremely difficult, and in some cases impossible. The following table indicates that half the men and one out of every ten women members attributed their non-attendance to one or more of these three reasons. More than

Table XXVIIIb

	Inactive			Active
	MEN (60)	WOMEN (32)	TOTAL (92)	(19)
Inconvenience of time or place	50% (30)	9% (3)	36% (33)	53% (10)
Too great distance from home to meeting place	7% (4)	—	4% (4)	11% (2)
Shift work	23% (14)	—	15% (14)	26% (5)
Fatigue	23% (14)	9% (3)	19% (17)	16% (3)

(Respondents often gave more than one reason. Percentages are of respondents in each population.)

half the active members considered inconvenience of time or place an important cause of non-attendance.

The distance from the meeting place is the least important element in this category. A somewhat more important reason, not mentioned by any of the full-time officials, is the difficulty of arranging meetings to enable members working various shifts to participate in Branch activities. A fifth of those giving this reason remarked that they would definitely attend otherwise.

The most frequently mentioned reason in this category is fatigue. Two of every ten members—predominantly those in the 40-and-over age groups—said that they were too tired to go to meetings in the evening. Fatigue also deprives the member of the opportunity to think about Union problems during his leisure, and thus to be an effective citizen in its body politic. Mr. Deakin and most paid officials attributed low attendance at least in part to general fatigue after war. The relaxation of wartime tensions and the Union's fight for shorter hours and consequently increased leisure should in the long run make fatigue a less important factor, even though the continuous drive for increased production offers a temporary obstacle, until the main physical burden is placed upon machines and not men.

Though more than a third of the members attributed their non-attendance to reasons falling under the heading 'inconvenience of time or place of meetings', only a tenth of the membership gave this as their only reason, and even fewer said that they would attend otherwise. The majority giving this reason combined it most frequently with reasons falling in either the 'domestic duties' or the 'general indifference' categories. No time or place is satisfactory. On at least six occasions since its foundation, the Branch, in an effort to increase attendance, changed the time or place of meetings. Even Sunday morning meetings, eliminating most of the reasons given above, did not result in an increase in attendance. In the light of this, for many at least, these reasons were no more than excuses.

C. Domestic Duties—Family responsibilities

Another third of the inactive membership said that they could not attend meetings because of household duties and family responsibilities. This was the one most frequently mentioned as a member's only reason for not taking part in Branch activities, and was most common among married men under forty and almost all married women.

Table XXVIIIc

	Inactive			Active
	MEN (60)	WOMEN (32)	TOTAL (92)	(19)
Domestic duties or family responsibilities	18% (11)	63% (20)	34% (31)	21% (4)

' (Percentages are of respondents in each population.)

Both the active members and the full-time officials consider this an important factor accounting for low attendance on the part of women members exclusively. The following response from a Branch member of two years' standing is typical:

'I work all day, come home to three children and a husband, I can't leave the family after a day's work.'

A large proportion of married men (37 per cent) feel that they are too tied down by household responsibilities. In addition to those few whose wives will not let them go to meetings, and many more who spend their leisure with their children, there are many who devote off-work hours to painting and decorating, building repairs, poultry and rabbit keeping, gardening, and even shoe-repairing. These activities àre less in the nature of hobbies than they are pursuits carried out to relieve the financial burden of paying others to provide essential services.

It is not difficult to understand that these members do not find the Branch meeting an appealing way to spend the little leisure remaining after a day's work in the factory and many hours of work about the house. It is worth noting, however, that half of the women members of the active nucleus are married and have children under school-leaving age. In fact, two-thirds of the active members, compared with a third of the inactive, have two or more dependants[1]. Furthermore, equally common among the active members—particularly the men— as among the inactive members, are painting and decorating, poultry keeping, and similar time consuming help-around-the-house activities. (See Appendix No. 11.)

Thus even this reason, though no doubt a valid one for many, does not appear to eliminate the possibility of attending Branch meetings once or twice a month. It is, however, a major factor which must be given consideration if a serious attempt to elicit member interest is to be made.

D. General Indifference

All full-time officials, nine out of every ten active members and six out of every ten inactive members attributed non-attendance to one or more of the reasons grouped under the heading 'general indifference'.

It is, of course, recognized that to say a member is indifferent is but another way of saying he is apathetic. It is hoped, however, to disclose in some detail a few of the most frequent manifestations of this negative attitude by considering some of its component elements separ-

[1] Number of children under school-leaving age and dependants.

	Inactive (92)	Active (19)
None	29% (27)	32% (6)
One	34% (31)	5% (1)
Two	17% (16)	26% (5)
Three or more	20% (18)	37% (7)

ately. Table XXVIIId lists these reasons and the frequency with which they were mentioned in the order in which they will be discussed.

Table XXVIIId

	Men (60)	Inactive Women (32)	Total (92)	Active (19)
General Indifference	% 58 (35)	% 59 (19)	% 59 (54)	% 90 (17)
I didn't realize they held meetings	10 (6)	25 (8)	15 (14)	21 (4)
The Shop Stewards give us all the information— They and the Branch are doing a good job	12 (7)	6 (2)	10 (9)	32 (6)
I pay my contributions— The rest is up to the Union	8 (5)	19 (6)	12 (11)	37 (7)
I have other interests— Hobbies, etc.	27 (16) 48% (29)	3 (1) 25% (8)	19 (17) 40% (37)	5 (1) 47% (9)
Frankly I'm not interested	27 (16)	22 (7)	25 (23)	42 (8)

(Respondents often gave more than one reason. Percentages are of respondents in each population.)

The reason most frequently given by women members in this 'general indifference' group was that they did not realize the Branch held meetings. A quarter of the female and a tenth of the male members claimed to be ignorant of the existence of regular Branch meetings. That this ignorance is but an expression of indifference is substantiated in part by the fact that two-thirds of those giving this reason combined it with such remarks as 'Frankly, I'm not interested' or 'I pay my contributions, the rest is up to the Union.' Only one member, on being informed of the existence of meetings, indicated that she would like to attend; another was surprised to find out that what she had joined was the T.G.W.U. Four out of every ten inactive members had no idea of where Branch meetings were held and six out of ten did not know when they were held. Though poor advertising and what appears to be a tendency to neglect women members generally in the provision of information, is in part a cause of this ignorance, it is equally, if not more so, a result of a member's complete indifference toward the organization joined.

All full-time officials and a third of the active membership concurred that a major cause of non-attendance is the success the Union has had in obtaining improvements in wages and conditions. Indifference induced by satisfaction with improved working conditions cannot be overlooked, for there is ample evidence of Union achievements at Colins'. They include not only higher wages and an improved system of handling grievances, but also the cleaning up of dirty jobs and the introduction of such daily services as providing clean overalls. That the management creates apathy by maintaining wage rates above the national Union rates is a reason of a similar nature expressed by a few active members. These reasons are but alternative expressions of the view that a member's interest in Union affairs is limited to local matters.

The inactive members' reasons most closely resembling those of the active members and officials are expressed in terms of satisfaction with the information provided by Shop Stewards that the Branch is doing a good job, or by stating that once contributions have been paid the rest is up to the Union. The inadequacy of the Shop Steward as a continuous and reliable source of information has already been discussed. Satisfaction with the Branch's work or the attitude of the insurance policy holder characteristic of a fifth of the membership are probably more important causes of non-attendance than the results of this survey indicate.

These expressions of indifference are not, however, indications that members are aware of and satisfied with the policies pursued on their behalf outside the factory gates by Union leaders. There is little cause, therefore, for the complacency characteristic of most officials who attribute a member's non-attendance not to a lack of interest in Union matters, but to his satisfaction with local conditions which are not necessarily to be equated with Union policies of a national character of which the majority of the rank and file are ignorant.

The largest number of inactive members giving reasons classified under the heading 'General indifference' either admitted that they were not interested in attending Branch meetings, or that they had other interests to occupy their leisure. Slightly less than half the inactive and active members attributed non-attendance to these reasons.

Three rather distinct attitudes characterize this 'not interested' response. The most depressing, and fortunately least frequent, is that which is an expression of a lack of interest in anything. Members in this very small group have no hobbies and in everyday life as well as Branch life they appear to be apathy personified. Occurring more frequently is that circumscribed attitude of a majority of the membership in relation to the function of the Branch and consequently of the Union. This attitude is clearly revealed in such remarks as 'I'm not interested unless it concerns me or my department.' Finally, the attitude most frequently expressed is typified by: 'After five o'clock I want to forget all about the factory.' This desire to escape the problems of work and the association of fellow workers no doubt results in many members' unwillingness to attend Branch meetings. It too is an expression of the very narrow role members conceive the Branch to play in the government of the Union. The following statement from a fascinating study by F. Zweig suggests the commonplace nature of this attitude:

'From my conversations with workers I gathered the impression that they are little interested in recreations organised by their firms. They like to forget about work and their fellow-workers. . . . Most of the recreational enterprises organised on an occupational basis have an anaemic life. The workers wish to have a change from the atmosphere of their work-places and enjoy the company of people from other occupations. For the same reason the workers' organisations have little chance of making arrangements for their leisure time, because such organisations are set up on an occupational basis, and the workers themselves like to mix not only with other workers from different jobs, but also with better-off people from other strata, whom they consciously or subconsciously regard as superior in their standard of living. . . . Even the best Trade Unionists like to get away from the workers' crowds.'[1]

Since both permanent officials and active members attribute non-attendance to alternative sources of leisure as well, it is worth considering the competition facing the Branch if it is to make a real effort to elicit the participation of members in Union activities. Brother Vinson clearly expressed the nature of a major aspect of this problem when he complained that the mechanization of leisure hindered the development of the social skills essential to an individual's participation in group activities. He said:

'In the old days the family was a training ground for team play. Each one of us helped the other learn as well as provide amusement for ourselves. Now you have only to press a button for music or to hear a funny story. If not the radio, it is off to the movies. It has become so easy to let someone else do the work for you.'

That the cinema was most frequently mentioned by members in response to 'What are your hobbies—your outside-of-work interests?' reveals to some extent the reliance of members on commercialized sources of entertainment. In fact, half of the seven out of every ten members who mentioned the cinema, go between one and three times each week. Fourth on the list of interests is the watching of sporting events, such as football, dog-races and midget auto races. These are but another series of passive leisure interests which attract a large number of members—particularly men. (See Appendix No. 11.)

It would be misleading, however, to infer that the inactive members' interests are limited to these passive

[1] F. Zweig: *Labour, Life and Poverty* (Gollancz, 1948), Chapter X, 'Amusements—Demand and Supply', p. 46.

activities. A third of the membership, for example, devote part of their leisure to handicrafts such as model building, cabinet making, knitting and carpet making. Here the member does things for himself and usually by himself. These activities are often pursued to relieve a financial burden by producing articles for use in the home, as was the case with the even more frequently mentioned activities discussed in relation to domestic duties under the heading 'Help around the house.'

In addition to these major interests a quarter of the male membership mentioned sporting activities in which they actively participate, such as football, boxing, cycling and weight-lifting, and an equal proportion of the female membership devote some time to reading. Next in popularity is the pub, in which the majority of the tenth of the membership who mentioned this spend at least three evenings a week. Among young single members, dancing is an extremely popular pastime.

A very small proportion of the membership devote their spare time to studies. One member attends classes three evenings a week to keep ahead of his son who began asking home-work questions he could not answer. None of the inactive members mentioned Trade Union activities, though a few named political discussions. Nine out of ten inactive and more than half the active members do not belong to other working-class organizations. Though all pay contributions to the Labour Party as Union members, only 2 per cent of the inactive respondents mentioned their membership in the Labour Party.

Thus the inactive members have wide and varied sources of leisure which frequently combine the passive amusement of cinema with the active enjoyment of developing skills in producing articles of use to themselves. Though none of these serve to develop the social skills of communication or the disciplines essential to reflection on problems facing the Union for example, these members are for the most part alert and inquisitive.

R

The Union and the Branch have, however, failed to arouse their interest.

It would be erroneous, moreover, to suggest that because of these activities members have no time to attend meetings. A brief glance at the outside interests of the active members will reveal an equally broad, if not broader, scope. Two of the most active members of the hard core centre for example, in addition to Trades Council and political party activities, attend the movies or variety twice each week, keep poultry and devote time to reading. Though Trade Union activities hold the first position held by cinema on the inactive members' list, help around the house, handicrafts and sports are as frequently mentioned by the active as the inactive member.

Though only a rough picture of the outside interests of the members has been presented, it does serve to emphasize the nature of the problem of eliciting the active participation of members whose indifference cannot in the final analysis be explained simply by the competition of alternative sources of leisure[1].

E. *Dissatisfaction with the operation of the Branch*

Since relatively few members of the 1/AAA Branch have ever attended Branch meetings and since Branch officials are unknown entities to more than 80 per cent of the membership, it is not surprising to find that reasons for non-attendance seldom expressed dissatisfaction with the operation of meetings or with the incumbent officers at Branch level. In fact, less than 10 per cent of the membership explained their failure to participate by suggesting that Branch meetings were dull or that a small clique

[1] The interest of the Trade Union movement in leisure is broadly stated in 'The Problem of Leisure—A Report approved by the Trades Union Congress': 'In so far as it relies for its strength on a conscious community of interest and aspiration, it is concerned that the mass of the population shall not be merely passive recipients of provided entertainments and pastimes. Mental inertia is the greatest enemy of trade unionism as of democracy generally. We are, therefore, concerned that people should be alive and critical in their appreciation of and participation in social activities of all kinds.' (p. 7.)

controlled the Branch. In six out of eight cases this reason was combined with that of general indifference. Not one of the respondents gave reasons in this category as their only explanation for non-attendance.

Table XXVIIIe

	Inactive			Active
	MEN (60)	WOMEN (32)	TOTAL (92)	(19)
Dissatisfaction with the operation of the Branch	13% (8)	—	9% (8)	32% (6)
Branch meetings are dull or discussions off the point	8% (5)	—	5% (5)	5% (1)
A small group controls the Branch —There is no chance of taking part	7% (4)	—	4% (4)	26% (5)

(Respondents often gave more than one reason. Percentages are of respondents in each population.)

Though the Branch was Communist dominated during part of the survey period and in spite of the widespread publicity given in the newspapers at this time to both Mr. Deakin's and Mr. Morgans Phillips' comments on Communist infiltration at Branch level, less than 5 per cent of the membership complained that any clique— including Communists—prevented them from taking part in Branch activities. On the other hand, a quarter of the active membership and all the full-time officials considered this a major cause of low attendance. This belief is clearly expressed as one of the conclusions reached by the T.U.C. in its 1949 statement on Trade Unionism and Communism. In this 'Warning against Apathy', after stating the truism that where democracy is virile militant

Communist tactics cannot succeed, it concludes that where difficulties exist they are caused: 'by the non-attendance of trade unionists at meetings because their time is wasted in dealing with matters outside the proper scope of the meetings, raised by Communists and "fellow travellers." '[1]

That non-attendance explains how a minority group is able to assume control is apparent. What is questionable is the assumption that non-attendance is the result of Communist control. There is no evidence in the 1/AAA to confirm this, nor is there reason to believe in the light of the scattered evidence available on other Branches that apathy is the result as well as the cause of minority domination at Branch level. Nor is there any indication that attendance is low only in Branches dominated specifically by Communist minorities.

It is essential, therefore, that Union leaders question the validity of this assumption. For if it is erroneous, as it certainly is in the case of the 1/AAA, more than the incentive of anti-Communist feeling will be needed to elicit the active participation of the rank and file member in Union affairs.

F. *Other Reasons*

Other reasons mentioned only once or twice during the course of the survey are cited here as an indication of some other factors that ought to be taken into account by the Union if it is to devise a plan for arousing member interest. From the few inactive members these include the fear of 'the sack' as management retaliation for Trade Union activities, and the rather more common reason that unless all workers are Union members and take part in Union activities there is no use fighting so that others may benefit without taking part or paying dues. Some

---

[1] See 'Report of Proceedings of the 81st Annual Trades Union Congress' (Bridlington, 1949), pp. 274–279. In addition, this statement complained that difficulties were caused 'by the withdrawal of Branches from the activities of certain Trades Councils as a protest against their time, energy and funds being devoted to the support of disruptive bodies'. (p. 277.)

active members stressed the reason that, as most Branch activity takes place in the factory, there is no need to attend meetings. Others suggested that the unattractiveness of the meeting place acted as a deterrent to member participation. Though not of equal importance with those already discussed, these reasons are no doubt in some cases valid, and are not to be ignored if member interest is to be more than temporarily aroused.

These then are the reasons given by inactive members, as well as those attributed to them by the active members and full-time officials for their failure to attend Branch meetings regularly. These factors are in many cases valid, in others but excuses. There is no doubt, however, that while this analysis indicates something of the nature of the rank and file members' apathy, it does not explain why some are more active than others.

II   REASONS FOR JOINING THE UNION IN RELATION TO A MEMBER'S PARTICIPATION

Though the workers at Colins' have shown enough interest in the Union to become members, there is overwhelming evidence that they have shown little or no interest in Union activities. Why then did they join? In answering this question members not only indicated what they expected to get out of the Union, but also threw a revealing light on what they as members intended to put into the Union. It is with this in mind that we examine the over-all results in Table XXIX in order to compare the inactive and active members' reasons for joining the T.G.W.U.

A glance at Table XXIX discloses an immediately apparent distinction between the active and inactive members[1].

[1] Of little significance in this survey are those reasons expressed by no more than 3 per cent of the membership. Three per cent claimed they were forced to join the Union; they were under a mistaken impression (created irresponsibly by their respective Shop Stewards) that they were working in a closed shop. It is of interest to note how few members, two out of ninety-two, joined because of a knowledge of specific Union services. Legal aid was the only service mentioned.

Table XXIX

WHAT WERE YOUR MAIN REASONS FOR JOINING THE UNION?

	Inactive (92)	Active (19)
To improve my (or the workers') bargaining position in relation to employer(s)	71% (65)	95% (18)
To improve working conditions	70% (64)	95% (18)
So as not to be different (social conformity)	25% (23)	—
I was forced to join	3% (3)	—
To obtain Union benefits, specifically mentioning such Union services as Legal Aid, Sickness, Strike or Funeral Benefits, or Convalescent Homes	2% (2)	10% (2)

(Respondents often gave more than one reason. Percentages are of respondents in each population.)

A quarter of the inactive membership, though none of the active, joined the Union as an expression of social conformity, i.e., out of a fear of being different. In fact, two out of every ten members gave this and only this reason for joining the Union. In view of the tradition of non-participation in the activities of the 1/AAA the difficulty of eliciting the interest of these members is apparent. In other words, it is suggested that those who joined in order to conform could be expected to participate only if non-participation were equivalent to non-conformity. Such responses as the following are characteristic of Branch members whose joining was but an expression of social conformity: From men:

"I don't know much about it. I just joined. I didn't want to raise a fuss.'

'When asked to join I didn't want to say no. I had no real reason for joining.'

From women:

'I didn't really believe in it, but the other girls joined, so I did.'
'I joined because I don't like to refuse people who ask things of me.'

'The other girls were in.'

'Someone asked me. I said: "might as well"; they nearly all did.'

Reasons of this character tend to be more common among women than men. This tendency is particularly strong among single women, more than half of whom joined as an expression of social conformity[1].

How is this rather large proportion of membership joining for reasons of social conformity to be reconciled with the relatively high annual rates of lapses and arrearage typical of the 1/AAA's membership? It is to be explained at least in part by the fact that the circumstances under which collections take place differ greatly from those under which solicitation for membership is carried out. The enlisting of new members either occurs during a concerted drive to increase membership or at a time when a new worker is employed by the factory. On both of these occasions this type of member feels that all eyes are focused upon him. On the other hand, after becoming a member, he soon begins to realize that the responsibility for maintaining membership is not his but rather that of his Collector or Shop Steward. Furthermore, the attention of the group is seldom if ever focused on those dropping out.

Two major reasons appear to be common to both the active and inactive populations. 'To improve my (or the workers') bargaining position in relation to the employer(s)' was the response of seven out of every ten inactive members and almost all of the active members. Another equally important reason for joining the Union is to improve working conditions. It is readily seen that these two reasons are but different dimensions of the same reply, i.e., the desire to improve one's bargaining position is actuated by a desire to achieve improved working conditions. Thus six out of ten of the inactive and nine

[1] Seventeen per cent (10) of the men, 41 per cent (13) of all women, and 60 per cent (6) of the single women gave this reason.

out of ten of the active members combined these reasons in answering this question.

An examination of the wording of replies falling into these two major categories reveals a fundamental difference, not disclosed in these surface statistics, between the active and inactive members in their concepts of the Union. Close to five out of every six inactive members who gave one or both of these reasons expressed themselves in purely personal or local terms. In contrast to this circumscribed viewpoint is that of two out of every three active members, who expressed themselves in broader terms, acknowledging their duty and the Union's function in relation to an improvement of the welfare of workers generally. What an overwhelming majority of inactive members expect out of the Union, and thus what they conceive it to be, is clearly revealed in the responses of these members:

A male worker, age 29, with six years' service in the Navy and seven years at Colins', who had attended only one Branch meeting in over a year-and-a-half of membership, replied:

'At one time you could be thrown out for any small thing—eating on the job. The Steward asked me. I joined because I thought it a good thing to increase our strength so the governor can't push us around.'

Another ex-Serviceman, age 35, who had been working at Colins' for eighteen years and had never attended a meeting during his one-and-a-half years in the Union, said:

'When I returned from the forces I found the Union had done a lot of good for the workers, like five minutes for washing up and a ten-minute tea break. Furthermore, if you have a grievance, you can see someone about it.'

This personal reason came from a man who had worked at Colins' for twenty-two years and who had been to only one meeting 'out of curiosity' during his four years of Union membership:

'To get a permit to obtain an alarm clock during the war. Only Union men could get an alarm clock, so I joined.'

A 64-year-old worker who had been at Colins' for fifty years and in the Union for three-and-a-half, and who last attended a Branch meeting more than a year before the interview, declared:

> 'I joined so we could have some influence—to get management to take some notice of us. I've wanted to put something forward before, nobody was there to do it.'

A married woman, age 32, a part-time worker who had never been to a Branch meeting in her year-and-a-half of membership, also seeking representation, said:

> 'I joined because I thought it would do some good, they would fight for you if you have a grievance, something you can't do yourself.'

And finally the response of a young woman worker of twenty who had been at Colins' five years and in the Union for three years without attending a Branch meeting:

> 'To sort of help us out, they could do more than I alone.'

In contrast to the narrow local and personal base on which these reasons are founded, are the comments characteristic of two-thirds of the active members. Brother Vinson, age 53, Convener of Shop Stewards, a founding member of the 1/AAA Branch, a member of the hard core centre with over thirty years of Trade Union experience, explained:

> 'I was brought up in an atmosphere of discussion, wondering why the workers were in the circumstances they found themselves. My dad was an active Trade Unionist, my brother, too. We knew the first Labour M.P. from Southboro well. We ate, worked and dreamed about the conditions of the working man and how to change them. I joined to change them.'

Leading Shop Steward Brother Ball, age 39, who had been working at Colins' for nine years and who had missed only four Branch meetings during four-and-a-half years in the T.G.W.U.—a member of the hard core centre—replied:

> 'I joined to support the worker in his common cause. The worker should have the main say in government and industry.'

Shop Steward Sister Finlay, age 40, married, with two children under school-leaving age, a full-time worker at Colins', who had attended Branch meetings regularly since joining the T.G.W.U. two years prior to the survey, added, after stating that every worker must join a Union to safeguard his position:

> 'I started work at 14; things were drastic; only jobs for juvenile labour. At 16 I was sacked, thrown on to the labour market inexperienced. There was no employment for we were now entitled to full pay and more juveniles became available. On the job there was always the threat of the sack. I thought there must be something to safeguard the youngsters. I joined a Union and the Labour Party. I feel that way even more today, for I have two children and I want a better future for them.'

Finally, Brother Bond, age 39, with twenty years of Union experience, formerly Secretary of the Shop Stewards' Committee at Colins' and a member of the hard core centre, explained:

> 'I joined to improve the wages and conditions of the workers. My dad made us class conscious. He took us to Gamages (a leading London Department Store) every Christmas to show us all the toys and then to say: "Your father can't afford them." My dad was a major influence in my joining a Union.'

The significant difference underlying these reasons for joining, which on the surface appear to be similar, is strikingly revealed in these comments characteristic of a majority of the inactive and active members respectively. What catalysts were present to assist the active member in linking his personal experience with the very similar experiences of others, and consequently to link the broad objectives of social reform with the functions of a Trade Union, is not easily determined. For some, long periods of unemployment and for others, the influence of active Trade Unionist parents appear to have been the effective catalysts. But this fails to explain the inactivity and activity of many. For example, one in ten inactive members had experienced periods of unemployment exceeding six consecutive months, while seven out of ten active members had not. Likewise, four out of ten inactive members had fathers who were Trade Unionists, while four out of ten active members had not. There is no doubt, however, that these factors were important influences leading to the active participation of some members in Trade Union activities[1].

It is quite possible, on the other hand, that the response of active members was influenced by their training and experience in Trade Unions. In other words, their broad view of the role of the Trade Union in the nation may be as much a result of their very activity as a cause of it. This serves to emphasize at least the failure of Branch life to act for the majority of rank and file members as the catalyst so essential to their intelligent and active participation in Union activities.

Inadequate as the material presented on members' reasons for not attending meetings and for joining the Union admittedly is, it reveals clearly the very complex nature of the problem of eliciting member interest in Union activities. Though reasons of 'general indifference', characteristic of more than half the inactive population, have not been satisfactorily explained, some of their most important components have been disclosed in order to emphasize the need for further investigation and experimentation. The inconvenience of time and place of meetings, the demands of household duties, and the timidity, particularly of women members and of those who believe they are not educated enough, present for

[1] (a) Were you unemployed for more than six months continuously during the '30's?

	Inactive	Active
	(92)	(19)
Yes	9% (8)	32% (6)
No	91% (84)	68% (13)

(Sixty-three per cent (5) of the inactive and 50 per cent (3) of the active members in the 'yes' group were unemployed for more than a year.)
(b) Was your father a member of a Trade Union?

	Inactive	Active
	(92)	(19)
Yes	41% (38)	58% (11)
No	58% (53)	42% (8)
Reply missing	1% (1)	—

some at least a real obstacle to participation. At present, dissatisfaction with the operation of Branch meetings is a minor cause of non-participation, yet if the interest of more members is to be permanently aroused there is no doubt that meetings must be made more meaningful and the surroundings in which they are held more attractive.

Why these factors have prevented some and not others from actively taking part in Union activities cannot, on the basis of the material available, be explained. There appears to be a rough correlation, however, between a member's reasons for joining the Union and the extent of his participation. Close to a quarter of the Branch's membership, mainly women, who joined for reasons of social conformity, will not participate in Union activities until it becomes 'the thing to do'. On the other hand, close to three-quarters of the membership are a more promising source of increased activity. Immediate personal problems of wages, grievances and general conditions of work actuated their joining. They joined, however, without recognizing the additional strength with which they were providing a powerful national pressure group. It is the responsibility of the Union to widen the scope of its appeal to the rank and file beyond the horizon of mere wage increases or the improvement of conditions at a particular factory. If after careful investigation and experimentation the outlets of participation and the channels of communication were overhauled to assist these members in linking their personal and local experience with the socio-political as well as economic functions of the Union as a national body, the chances of eliciting more widespread participation in Branch and Union activities would be enhanced.

Only by acknowledging the complex nature of this problem and by exerting every effort to solve it can Union leaders and members hope to ensure the democratic operation of their organization.

Chapter 19

CONCLUSION

The image of the Branch in practice emerges from this detailed analysis of the 1/AAA with features which bear no significant resemblance to those of the image of the Branch in theory. The features of the Branch disclosed by this mass of descriptive material are those of an oligarchy parading in democracy's trappings.

Branch meetings are held regularly for a membership so large that if the majority were to attend, effective participation would be impossible. Meetings attract only a small minority of members who, in meaningless elections, assume apparent control at this basic level and undermine the representative character of constitutional bodies at all higher levels of organization. The Branch has become the forum not of the rank and file but of an active nucleus dominated by a hard core centre. Two-way communication is maintained between the Branch and higher levels of organization, and paid officials frequently attend Branch meetings. Yet the Branch fails to fulfil its function as the main channel of the Union communication system, for so few members can and do have contact with it. The Union civil servant, apprised of the rank and file's apathy and of their failure to identify themselves with Branch leaders and the Union, is in a position to and often does usurp the policy-determining functions assigned in theory to elected representatives.

The supplemental channels of the Union's formal communication system are likewise ineffective means of safeguarding the democratic process at Branch level. Either because of their intrinsic inadequacies or because of poor distribution, these media fail to provide the information essential to a member's intelligent and active participation in Union activities. Furthermore, the informal channel provided by Shop Stewards serves as a break, rather than as the link it might become, if officially acknowledged, between the Union and its members.

That the term 'apathetic' applies to the vast majority of these members became immediately evident from the analysis of data on the membership's size, rate of turnover and arrears. In addition to the physical barriers to participation, the constitutional barriers automatically coming into play deprive a large proportion of the membership of the opportunity not only to seek office, but also actively to take part in Union affairs.

The removal of these barriers by changes in the Constitution and by decentralization at Branch level, though essential to the solution, will not in and of itself solve the problem of apathy. This apathy is not easily explained. It can be attributed in part at least to many of the reasons revealed in the survey, such as timidity resulting from inadequate education, the inconvenience of time and place of meetings, time-consuming household duties, alternative sources of leisure and finally, in a few cases, dissatisfaction with the actual operation of the Branch. It is clear, however, that if a member has in some way been able to link his personal experiences as an individual worker with the Union's broad objectives of social reform, he is more likely to recognize his responsibility for active participation in its government.

It must not be overlooked that, in general, the apathetic rank and file member is an alert and inquisitive person. What at present constitutes the Branch in motion has failed to arouse his interest. Branch life has failed in its major task—to develop within the membership the social skills that are best expressed in an individual's capacity to receive communications from others and respond to attitudes and ideas of others, so as to promote well-informed participation in the common tasks of the democratic operation of the Union.

Though as detailed an analysis of Branch life in other T.G.W.U. Branches has not been possible, the very significant evidence on a cross section of these Branches and the conclusive evidence of a national character indicate the widespread nature of apathy in the T.G.W.U. This evidence of a large proportion of the membership in Branches too large to permit effective participation, of an extremely high rate of member turnover, of a low degree of participation in elections as well as of corruption at the ballot box, and finally of the lack of member interest in the Union's educational facilities, makes inevitably characteristic of a large majority of T.G.W.U. Branches the most prominent features of the 1/AAA. In the light of all this, it becomes difficult to avoid the conclusion that the Transport and General Workers Union is an oligarchy at every level of its structure, failing to elicit the active participation of its members.

There is, however, no justification for concluding that in such a mass organization government by oligarchy is inevitable. And it must be acknowledged that weaknesses in the operation of the Union's scheme of democratic organization may also be characteristic of other organizations, such as political parties and religious bodies.

Furthermore, it cannot be over-emphasized that the T.G.W.U. has many great achievements to its credit and has trained many leaders who have contributed their services to the community in an effort to improve the general welfare. The T.G.W.U.'s achievements, numerous and well known both inside and outside the Union, must not be obscured by this critical analysis.

What is lacking is that tradition of democracy which only every-day experience, custom and practice can build within the Union. No doubt the task of building this tradition will be made easier as the ranks of the Union are filled by working men, who, for the first time in Great Britain's history, will have had schooling till the age of 15 or 16 and been given an opportunity not only to think but also to enjoy the leisure which thoughtful reflection requires. The development of a working democracy, however, remains a vital Union problem.

What is essential for the growth of Industrial Democracy is that tradition of democracy which in the long run the Trade Unions alone can and must offer. In becoming an efficient service organization the T.G.W.U. has lost sight of one of its major objectives. In the Union as in industry, efficiency spells division of labour. In treating the rank and file as cogs in the Union's administrative machinery, the psychological nexus between the member, his Union leader and official Union policy has been broken. The individual member has not been taken into consideration; he has not been kept informed through a free and adequate exchange of information; he has not been consulted. Consequently, he has failed to achieve as an individual in his own Trade Union community the status and respect which Unions have sought for the worker in the community at large.

It may well be that the T.G.W.U. is as much in need of Development Councils as is industry. Certainly the T.G.W.U. must with imagination and zeal set out to provide in practice, as it does in theory, procedures and safeguards for effective member participation in the government of the Union, so that members may develop the social skills and confidence necessary for worker participation in industry.

During the period of transition from *laissez faire* democracy to social democracy, it is becoming ever more apparent how wide will be the repercussions if the cure for apathy is not found, particularly if this disease has affected other British Trade Unions. If the Trade Unions shirk their responsibility of training the individual through democratic participation to adapt himself intelligently to the ever-changing personal relationships created by the demands of a social democracy in a highly industrialized economy, the democracy of the socialized society itself may be weakened and undermined. To prevent the workers from becoming once again a defenceless group facing a new elite in this society, and to prevent the Trade Union from becoming an arm of the state which might itself fall victim to the irresponsible though purposeful seekers of power, the democratic base of Trade Unions must be fortified.

APPENDICES

T.G.W.U. TOTAL MEMBERSHIP AND STATEMENT OF INCOME AND EXPENDITURE FOR THE YEARS 1922–1947 (a)

Year	Membership	Income	Expenditure (b)	Total Benefits (c)	Disputes and Victimization Pay	Balance (d)
		£	£	£	£	£
1922	297,460	367,850	358,538	72,627	30,146	9,312
1923	307,273	409,565	391,918	88,501	33,856	17,647
1924	372,560	492,107	562,738	252,503	192,632	–70,630
1925	376,251	507,398	398,328	76,515	8,442	109,069
1926	335,791	520,593	912,710	577,411	506,134	–392,117
1927	319,532	458,246	397,285	82,535	14,713	60,961
1928	315,819	440,610	366,617	65,144	2,158	73,993
1929	422,836	520,110	457,961	107,584	14,979	62,149
1930	422,048	616,794	536,773	136,581	9,560	80,020
1931	408,734	606,723	550,952	148,609	12,166	55,770
1932	372,992	566,722	518,083	125,101	9,842	48,638
1933	378,869	533,684	484,564	116,850	8,833	49,120
1934	433,816	584,138	480,141	118,357	10,534	103,996
1935	493,266	657,102	546,390	151,486	34,724	110,712
1936	561,908	756,627	588,245	166,762	31,196	163,381
1937	654,510	867,232	743,970	264,918	114,132	123,262
1938	679,360	946,794	694,211	171,380	22,703	252,582
1939	694,474	947,030	724,943	190,761	33,887	222,085
1940	743,349	934,355	729,082	182,351	14,081	205,272
1941	948,079	1,017,619	764,249	161,826	2,041	253,369
1942	1,133,165	1,263,613	854,114	179,018	432	409,498
1943	1,122,480	1,493,048	980,810	214,860	35	512,238
1944	1,070,470	1,553,487	1,039,748	234,793	1,975	512,737
1945	1,019,069	1,551,535	1,149,534	237,570	4,265	402,001
1946	1,273,920	1,808,574	1,185,135	240,154	6,616	623,439
1947	1,317,842	2,114,482	1,538,336	281,722	8,485	576,146

(a) From a chart prepared by Area 1 Financial Secretary Mr. Wisker, based on Report and Balance Sheet for the years 1922–1947. Certain adjustments have been made.

(b) Including total benefits.

(c) Including Disputes and Victimization Pay.

(d) The Union's funds as of December 31, 1947, showed a total of £5,188,177 19s. 9½d. (T.G.W.U. *Record*, August 1948).

APPENDIX No. 2

TRANSPORT AND GENERAL WORKERS UNION ANNUAL CHANGES IN SIZE OF AREA 1 MEMBERSHIP DECEMBER 31, 1935–DECEMBER 31, 1947 (a)

Year	Total Area Membership	Lapsed Member- ship as % of Last Year's Total (b)	New Membership (c)	New Membership as % of Current Year's Total	Real New Membership as % of Current Year's Total (d)	Rejoined Membership as % of Current Year's Total (e)	Rejoined Membership as % of New Membership
1934	133,093						
1935	151,384	23·5	49,181	32·4	29·6	2·8	8·6
1936	165,620	27·4	55,230	33·3	29·2	4·1	12·3
1937	180,721	31·0	65,989	36·4	33·0	3·4	9·4
1938	190,513	31·6	67,330	35·3	31·1	4·2	12·0
1939	183,534	37·0	62,619	34·0	30·4	3·6	10·6
1940	172,947	46·0	73,594	42·5	37·8	4·7	11·1
1941	230,205	44·5	133,037	58·1	51·8	6·3	10·4
1942	284,012	46·7	160,725	56·5	50·7	5·8	10·3
1943	276,106	45·6	120,588	43·6	36·8	6·8	15·6
1944	256,929	44·1	94,043	36·5	29·6	6·9	19·0
1945	256,535	40·0	99,584	41·8	34·6	7·2	18·8
1946	350,840	41·5	196,990	56·1	50·4	5·7	10·2
1947	347,012	40·6	136,206	39·3	34·6	4·7	11·9
Aver. %		38·4		42·0	36·8	5·2	12·3

(a) Source: Compiled on basis of information in Area 1 Financial Secretary's Quarterly Returns of Membership 1935–1947. Area 1 is responsible for the T.G.W.U. membership in London and the Home Counties. In 1947 the Area represented approximately 26 per cent of the total national membership.

(b) Lapsed membership: (i) Includes lapses through death. During period 1935–1947 lapses through death represented an average of 0·6 per cent of total Area membership and 1·7 per cent of Area lapsed membership. (ii) Excludes members transferring out of the Area but remaining in the T.G.W.U.

(c) New membership: (i) Includes previously lapsed members who have rejoined the Union. (ii) Excludes members transferring from another T.G.W.U. Area to Area 1.

(d) Real new membership: Excludes previously lapsed members who have rejoined the Union.

(e) Rejoined membership means: Members previously lapsed, who have rejoined the Union.

UNIONS AMALGAMATING WITH THE TRANSPORT AND GENERAL WORKERS UNION BETWEEN 1935 AND 1947

Year	Name of Union (a)	Member-ship (b)	Member-ship as % of T.G.W.U. New Member-ship (c)	Member-ship as % of T.G.W.U. Total Member-ship (c)
1935	National Winding and General Engineers' Society	3,619	2·3	0·6
1936	Electricity Supply Staff Association (Dublin)	300	0·2	0·05
,,	Halifax and District Carters' and Motormen's Association (d)	—	—	—
1937	Power Loom Tenters' Trade Union of Ireland (d)	—	—	—
,,	Belfast Journeymen Butchers' Association	400	0·2	0·06
,,	Scottish Seafishers' Union (d)	—	—	—
1938	Humber Amalgamated Steam Trawlers' Engineers and Firemen's Union	1,321	0·6	0·2
,,	Imperial War Graves Commission Staff Association	500	0·2	0·07
1939	Port of London Deal Porters' Union	500	0·2	0·07
,,	North of England Engineers' and Firemen's Amalgamation	150	0·06	0·02
1940	National Glass Workers' Trade Protection Association	1,400	0·4	0·2
,,	Radcliffe and District Enginemen and Boilermen's Provident Society (d)	—	—	—
,,	National Glass Bottle Makers' Society	400	0·1	0·05
1942	Liverpool Pilots' Association	120	0·02	0·01
1943	Manchester Ship Canal Pilots' Association (d)	—	—	—
1944	Grangemouth Pilots' Association (d)	—	—	—
1945	Leith and Granton Pilots' Association (d)	—	—	—
,,	Dundee Pilots (d)	—	—	—
,,	Methil Pilots (d)	—	—	—
1946	Government Civil Employees Association	60	0·01	0·005
1947	Liverpool and District Carters and Motormen's Union	8,000	1·6	0·6

(a) Source: *Union: Its Work and Problems*, Part I, p. 31; and the Research and Education Department of the T.G.W.U.

(b) Source: Where possible from the statistical statement of the Trades Union Congress Reports 1934–1946 and the Research and Education Department of the T.G.W.U.

(c) Source: See Table II.

(d) No records were available of the size of these Unions. Mr. Norman Richards, of the Research and Education Department of the T.G.W.U. suggests that the size of Unions for which no records were available never exceeded 500.

APPENDIX No. 4

TRANSPORT AND GENERAL WORKERS UNION OFFICERS AND CLERICAL STAFF RELATED TO MEMBERSHIP (a) BY AREA

Area	Total Membership	No. of Officers	No. of Officers per 10,000 Members	No. of Staff	No. of Staff per 10,000 Members
1	347,012	146	4	156	4
2	58,175	17	3	29	5
3	91,701	35	4	41	4
4	61,137	21	3	25	4
5	147,981	41	3	45	3
6	91,940	40	4	29	3
7	110,658	54	5	60	5
8	56,009	20	4	27	5
9	62,092	23	4	34	5
10	33,880	22	6	17	5
11	84,425	33	4	29	3
12	62,302	55	9	20	3
13	61,879	12	2	16	3
P.W.G. (b)	45,493	12	3	10	2
Average per 10,000 (c)			4		4

(a) Source: Based on figures compiled by Mr. A. J. Chandler, Minute Secretary of the T.G.W.U., March 18, 1948.

(b) P.W.G.=Power Workers Group.

(c) Officers and clerical staff of the T.G.W.U. Central Office are eighteen and eighty-one respectively. This does not alter the average figure per 10,000 members in the Table, because, in relation to total membership of the Union, these figures per 10,000 are both less than one.

APPENDIX No. 5

I. THE PROBLEM

To determine the size of membership at any given time eligible to hold office in the T.G.W.U.—i.e., to estimate the number of members who at any given time have been in continuous membership without falling as much as six weeks in arrears for a period of two years (except in the case of the General Secretary—five years—and the Financial Secretary—ten years) prior to the time of election or date of application for an appointed position.

II. RELEVANT DATA AVAILABLE

(A) Size of national membership as of December 31 for each year for the period 1935–1947 inclusive. See Table II.

(B) The size of lapsed membership and the rate, as expressed in percentages, at which members lapsed for each year of the period 1935–1947 inclusive. See Table II.

(C) The size of membership increases and the rate, expressed in percentages, at which members fell into arrears during the final quarter only of each year of the period 1935–1947 inclusive. See Table IV.

III. THE ASSUMPTIONS

(A) The maximum number eligible to hold office at any time could be no greater than the total membership two years prior to the date of an election (five years or ten years in the case of General Secretary and Financial Secretary respectively), i.e., the base membership.

(B) Any member seven to thirteen weeks in arrears and over thirteen weeks in arrears as of December 31 of the base year would be ineligible to hold office in the year of election or appointment.

(C) The percentage rate of lapses in membership in years can be applied to the entire membership without making an allowance for greater or fewer lapses amongst new members or old members.

(D) Because lapses are approximately four times as great as the size of membership over thirteen weeks in arrears in the final quarter of the year prior to that in which the lapses take place, it is assumed that the percentage rate of lapses includes the percentage rate of these falling thirteen or more weeks in arrears. Therefore the percentage rate for falling thirteen or more weeks in arrears must not be included in any calculations where the subsequent year's lapses are accounted for.

(E) Though the percentage rate of falling into arrears is for a single quarter only, it is not possible to estimate with accuracy the percentage rate of those falling into arrears for an entire year without counting members who fall into arrears for two or more times each time they do so. In order to assure an over-estimation of those eligible to hold office and to reduce the possibility of counting a member more than once as being ineligible, it has been assumed that a single quarter's average be used, thus, no doubt, accounting for an over-estimation of the size of membership eligible for office.

IV. THE FORMULA

On the basis of the above assumptions the following formula was devised, in which E is equal to the number eligible to vote in an election year. See Table V.

1. $E_2 = a - b$

$x = c\%.E_2$

2. $E_1 = E_2 - x$

$z = d\%.E_1$

3. $E = E_1 - z$

KEY: *a*   Total national membership as of December 31 of the base year (i.e., two years prior to date of election). See Table II.

b   Total membership seven to thirteen weeks in arrears in the base year. See Table IV.

$c\%$ Total percentage rate of lapses in membership and of falling into arrears for seven to thirteen weeks in base year plus one year. See Tables II and IV.

$d\%$ Total percentage rates of lapses in membership and of falling into arrears for seven weeks or more in base year plus two years (i.e., the year of election). See Tables II and IV.

V. SAMPLE CALCULATIONS TO DETERMINE THE NUMBER OF MEMBERS ELIGIBLE FOR OFFICE IN 1937. (BASE YEAR 1935)

(All calculations were done with slide rule.)

a =   493,266
b =   53,117
$c\%$ =   33%
$d\%$ =   43%

1. $E_2 = a - b$
   $E_2 = 493,266 - 53,117 = 440,149$
   $x = c\%.E_2$
   $x = 33\%$ of $440,149 = 145,000$

2. $E_1 = E_2 - x$
   $E_1 = 440,149 - 145,000 = 295,149$
   $z = d\%.E_1$
   $z = 43\%$ of $295,149 = 127,000$

3. $E = E_1 - z$
   $E = 295,149 - 127,000 = 168,149$

Thus $E = 168,149$ which is 28 per cent of the 1937 total national membership of 654,510.

APPENDIX No. 6

THE UNION AND THE PRESS
A Reply to Recent Criticisms
By ARTHUR DEAKIN (General Secretary) [1]

I have been studying the newspaper reports and articles about the recent strike of a large number of London dockers, and about the events which preceded and followed it. They are interesting and instructive reading.

Many of the reports, of course, make little attempt to discover the causes of the dispute, or the circumstances surrounding it; the dispute was gladly seized upon as a stick to beat the Government, and a weapon to use against the organised Labour Movement. Other reports, which had no such sinister motive, were scarcely better informed about the way in which our Union is organised, and the work it does. Some commentators, in their anxiety to tell our members how they ought to run their Union in the future, just couldn't spare time to find out what is being done now. Others constantly repeated words like 'vast', 'top-heavy', 'over-centralized' and 'unmanageable' without explanation or examination.

It is not our job to tell the Press how they should present the news, or what steps they should take to ascertain facts before expressing opinions. It is our job to examine their criticisms, to rebut those which are unjustified, and to see what we ought to do to put right, if we find anything wrong.

FIVE MAIN CRITICISMS

On analysis, the criticisms levelled against the Union fall under five main heads:

(1) It is too big.

(2) The inclusion of workers in many different industries means that the special interests of the various groups don't receive adequate attention from experts, or the interests of one group may be subordinated to those of others.

(3) The Union's officers, and particularly those at the centre, are 'remote' and out of touch with the members.

(4) The Union's machinery moves so slowly that members' patience is exhausted before a settlement is reached, and unofficial stoppages are the result.

[1] An article in *Transport and General Workers' Record*, Vol. XXVIII No. 321, August 1948, pp. 56-57.

(5) That there have been a large number of disputes—particularly unofficial disputes—since the end of the war, and that this is because unions are bigger, slower-moving, and more centralised than they used to be.

Well, that's the indictment. Now let's have a look at the evidence. First, the question of size. The strength of a Trade Union depends upon a number of things. The actual number of its members, the financial reserves provided by their contributions, the machinery by which it is governed, the quality and variety of leaders thrown up at all levels, and the standard of services and facilities provided.

On all these counts the larger union is at an advantage, always provided that its constitution is well-designed and flexible. It has greater bargaining power. Its finances are less a cause for anxiety, because risks and loads are more widely spread. It has a bigger field of available talent from which to choose those who are to make and carry out its policy. Administrative costs are relatively lower on a larger unit, particularly in the fields of specialised accounting, research and legal advice. On balance, I think one could say fairly that a union of five hundred members would be too big if its constitution were inadequate, while five million need not be too many, if the structure and administration keep pace with the members' needs. I shall try to show why I think our Union is well-equipped for its task.

ALL SECTIONS EQUALLY REPRESENTED

Next, I want to examine the accusation that the inclusion in our Union of many different groups means that it is a hotch-potch, in which insufficient attention is given to the members' trade interests.

A glance at our constitution is sufficient to dispose of this suggestion. Most careful provision is made, nationally and locally, to ensure that policy is made and carried out by men with a first-hand knowledge of the industry. The rank and file trade group committees and the full-time officers who serve them, exist for precisely this purpose. The fact that lay representatives of all trade groups sit on the General Executive Council means that the subordination of the interests of one group to those of another is impossible, since all sections are equally represented when final policy is decided.

Indeed, the system has very great advantages. Under modern industrial conditions, decisions taken and claims made by workers in one industry or area are likely to affect the position of those in other trades and areas. When people outside the Union begin to demand that it should be split up, it is well for us to remember that 'divide and conquer' is a well-tried maxim.

APPENDICES 283

THE REAL TEST OF CONTACT

The next cry is that we are 'remote' and out of touch with each other. One newspaper solemnly reported that a docker attending one of the open-air mass meetings did not know me by sight. What of it? Our Union is not built upon the Nazi principle of leadership. Our members elected me, and the General Executive Council appointed other officers, to do a job of work. We are responsible to our members, to whom we report regularly. If we fail in our duties, we shall be called to account by the members through their democratically elected committees.

It is this sense of responsibility, this power of calling to account, which is the real test of contact, rather than the recognition of one man by another in a crowd. Not that I underestimate the value of members knowing each other personally. Indeed, I take every opportunity of meeting our people wherever I am; but I am the servant of the member whom I have never met as much as of the one I know well. Every officer of the Union is in close contact with the broad stream of membership, by attendance at branch and delegate meetings, and by sitting with the elected committees which make the policy he carries out.

DELEGATES ARE NOT 'RUBBER STAMPS'

Nor is this policy-making by members a mere formality. The rank-and-filers who are elected are never treated and never consider themselves, as rubber-stamp bodies, existing to endorse the line taken or proposed by their officers. On the contrary, these lay delegates and committeemen know the wishes of the members they represent, they are provided with all the information necessary, and they take decisions in the light of this knowledge. The full-time official is in duty bound to supply facts, to advise and warn where necessary, and to carry out decisions to the best of his ability. He does not *make* policy. Unofficial strikers, or other forms of refusal to honour decisions, are dangerous not because they expose officials to attack, but because they strike at the democratic basis of the Union, and betray the elected lay representatives.

The implications of this democratic method of policy-making are very wide. In the first place, every member must have an equal right to elect and to be elected. Next, the elected bodies must be sufficient in number and suitable in size to allow of decisions being taken with reasonable speed at all levels. Next, provision must be made for co-ordination by an over-riding authority, both on broad issues and on day-to-day matters. Then, the members who elect and those who are elected must have the facts upon which to judge, and they must also have the means of training and developing that judgment. Last—but most vital of all—every member must have immediately at hand the means of exercising these rights and of playing his part.

Unless all these conditions are fulfilled, we cannot claim a really democratic organisation. I think they are all fulfilled by our Union. Our rules give every member equal rights in electoral matters; our network of lay committees is widespread and flexible; the Biennial Delegate Conference and the General Executive Council exercise general oversight; our members are kept regularly informed by letters and reports, and through the pages of the *Record*; our educational facilities—unrivalled in their variety and extent—give every member the means of making an informed contribution. Above all, there is a place for every member in his branch, from which all Union activity springs.

CAUSES OF DELAY IN REACHING SETTLEMENTS

At this point you may say 'This is all very well in theory, but what about the practical side? What about these accusations of long-winded negotiations, failure to keep members informed, waves of strikes, and so on?' That's a fair question, I think, so let's look at the record. After all, the proof of the pudding is in the eating.

First, the charge that negotiations are long-winded. May I say straight away that there is one sure-fire way of achieving a speedy settlement; just accept the first offer made by the employers, however inadequate you consider it to be. But if you think good results are important, and if you think it important also to maintain two-way contact with members, then matters aren't quite so simple, especially at a period of rising wages. It is sometimes necessary to choose carefully the time at which a claim is made; then the process of building up a case and collecting and checking all the relevant material has to take place. Next, dates for meetings have to be agreed and the employers must have time to inform and consult their constituent bodies.

I need not add that at this stage there are conditions which make for delay which are not of our seeking. Sometimes the counter-proposals put forward by the employers are outside of our original terms of reference, or involve something which we feel might be unacceptable to our members. In these cases we ourselves must ask for an adjournment, to allow for consultation with our members.

It must also be remembered that in very few cases are we the only union involved. There may be a dozen others, all of whom use their own individual means for consulting their members. In addition, we think it essential to keep members informed of the progress of negotiations at every stage, by circulars to branches or by delegate conferences.

From this it will be seen that little speeding-up is possible, except at the cost of accepting a poor settlement, and of presenting our members with an accomplished fact. In fact, in most cases there is little cause for complaint. For instance, we are represented on more than 150 national negotiating bodies, and in the year ended December, 1947, these bodies reached agreement on more than 200 separate national issues, apart from those referred to the Industrial Court or the National Arbitration Tribunal. In addition we were parties to more than 300 agreements made by other means.

The public and the Press know little of this steady stream of successful negotiation, or of the constant, patient, undramatic work of interpretation and adjustment to individual needs. They learn only of the isolated occasions in which difficulties occur, and which are 'news' just because they are so rare.

THE SO-CALLED STRIKE WAVE

Now about the 'wave of strikes'. The first thing to notice here is that there is no such thing. The number of days' work lost because of strikes since the end of the war is fewer than one-tenth of the number lost in the similar period after the 1914–1918 war. It is interesting to remember that in that period—1918–1920—our Union was not formed, and in general there were more small 'decentralised' unions—the very remedy now proposed by many of the self-styled 'friends of labour'. Less time was lost because of disputes in 1947 than was the case ten years earlier, in the piping days of peace. More than half the 1947 stoppages lasted less than three days. Nearly two-thirds of the disputes, and nearly one-third of the time lost, occurred in coal-mining.

Of course, we regret that strikes should occur at all, especially at a time when every man-hour is vital. But, before we allow ourselves to be deafened by the hysteria of the 'woe, woe' merchants, let us remember this. The workers of this country, after ten years of war and of post-war exhaustion, are producing on a steadily rising curve. Many of them are tired, and are working with worn tools. These factors, coupled with the anxiety inseparable from the international situation, might well give rise to irritation which finds vent in strikes and stoppages of all kinds. When these occur, there are not wanting anti-Government elements which seek to exploit them. Yet—and I make no apology for repeating this—the annual average of days lost in the three years 1945-6-7 was less than ten per cent.

of the annual average for the period 1918–1932. Will the gentlemen who are so anxious to pillory the Union chalk *that* up to our credit? I doubt it. But, whatever they do, let us remember that we British working men builded better than we knew, when we laid the foundations of the finest Trade Union movement in the world, whose record can stand up to any scrutiny.

A PERSONAL APPEAL

On a sober marshalling of the facts, I think we are entitled to an acquittal on the charges of overgrowth, over-centralisation, unwieldiness and irresponsibility. I believe we are entitled to maintain confidence in our structure, and in the men and women coming forward to serve and lead our Union.

I do not want, however, to encourage complacency. I know well that our very strength and success breed enemies, and I want every member to ask himself what he can do to protect his Union, and to make sure that it stands secure against the attacks which will be made upon it. In particular, I would like to make this personal appeal to every member who reads this. Will you sit down, consider what you have done to help your Branch in the past year, and what you are going to do in the months immediately ahead? Will you think out any suggestions for improving attendance at, and interest in, branch meetings, and in the means we use for consulting and informing our members?

We have suffered considerably by the destruction of branch life through dispersal of our people following the destruction of their homes. This is a handicap, but not one which we must regard as insurmountable.

APPENDIX No. 7

At the 1933 B.D.C. a resolution proposing that the names of movers of motions and the names of those voting for and against be inserted in all Area Trade Group, Area Committee, National Trade Group, and General Executive Council Minutes of Meetings, was declared 'LOST'. Excerpts from the debate are presented to illustrate the opposing views of rank and file and officials anxious to hold on to their power. (1933 B.D.C. Verbatim Reports (unpublished), Minute 22, pp. 214–218.)

BROTHER A. B., Area 7, moving the resolution: '. . . We want to know the names of those supporting various resolutions. We are entitled to that. . . .'

BROTHER F. J., Area 1, seconding: '. . . I think if there is going to be any progress made in the history of this Union that progress will only be made in proportion to the way in which we secure the control of those who are deemed to be our leaders. . . . This necessitates that in so far as the members are concerned they will have to make themselves acquainted with the policy, with the history, with the requirements and with the problems of their job. The present method, the method that has been characteristic of the organisation since its inception, has led to the gravitation of administrative control into the hands of a few people, a few people who are either in the Executive or the Officials themselves. The effect of this, has been that so far as the membership is concerned, a good deal of apathy has arisen.'

THE GENERAL SECRETARY (Mr Bevin) in opposition, said in part: '. . . I never want to see this Union where men sit on a collective body and then go back and say "Please sir, I did so and so". I think when men have to accept responsibility in a collective capacity on an executive they ought not to have an eye to the gallery . . . whether he was in the majority or in the minority he had to accept responsibility for what the Executive did.

'. . . here is another point. I do not think it is fair to men, lay men, who have their living to get and they are not all in secure positions, to have their names pilloried by you. . . . If you are in a conference, if you are the executive, sometimes you have got to take a very unpopular course, may I say that very often the unpopular course is the right course. If the Executive Council has taken a decision, then as an Executive every man should take his gruel for that decision. I believe it is sound and I believe that it is wise. . . . I believe it is wrong to hold men up to examination, sometimes for exercising their honest opinion. . . . Let me point out what is likely to occur. You publish the names, you publish the vote on the big issues and the public gets to know that it is by a narrow majority that you have taken your decision. I have seen big decisions taken with a very limited majority, they have all rolled in and nobody has said, "Please sir, I don't know" whether we were successful or whether we failed and that spirit I trust will be maintained.'

Abbreviated version of a Ballot Paper

TRANSPORT & GENERAL WORKERS' UNION. (AREA No. 1)
ELECTION OF TERRITORIAL REPRESENTATIVES TO GENERAL EXECUTIVE COUNCIL,
1948-1949 PERIOD.

"INSIDE" DISTRICT.

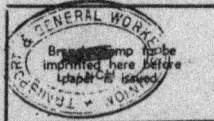

BALLOT PAPER.

NAME OF NOMINEES	NOMINEE'S BRANCH	BRANCHES NOMINATING			VOTE HERE
APPLETON, J. R.	1/943	1/943			
BAILEY, W. A. D.	1/930	1/930			
BAKER, H. W. T.	1/191	1/191 1/410 1/447			
		1/889 1/913			
BARCLAY, A.	1/247	1/247			
BEAUMONT, W. H.	1/82	1/82			
HART, W.	1/55	1/55			
HUMPHREYS, F.	1/928	1/928			
JONES, J. W.	1/498	1/49 1/122 1/149			
		1/156 1/200 1/213			
		1/230 1/265 1/292			
		1/294 1/305 1/306			
		1/307 1/308 1/319			
		1/333 1/335 1/337			
		1/339 1/341 1/342			
		1/346 1/348 1/350			
		1/365 1/376 1/377			
		1/382 1/410 1/420			
		1/426 1/441 1/454			
		1/493 1/498 1/509			
		1/575 1/582 1/583			
		1/686 1/764 1/774			
		1/784 1/827 1/889			
		1/913 1/941 1/1020			
		1/1107 1/1134			
JONES, W.	1/904	1/904			
KANE, J.	1/745	1/745			
PAPWORTH, A. F.	1/382	1/346 1/348 1/350			
		1/376 1/377 1/382			
		1/420 1/426 1/441			
		1/454 1/493 1/498			
		1/509 1/575 1/582			
		1/583 1/686 1/764			
		1/774 1/784 1/827			
		1/941 1/1020 1/1107			
		1/1134			
POPE, R. G.	1/332	1/332			
REES, A. J. A.	1/507	1/507			
REES, J. J.	1/1120	1/1120			
WARD, R. E.	1/188	1/188			
WEBB, H. F.	1/227	1/227 1/232 1/302			
		1/309 1/311 1/316			
		1/318 1/324 1/328			
		1/334 1/337 1/343			
		1/358 1/363 1/365			
		1/537			
WELLARD, J. A.	1/118	1/118			
WHYATT, G. E.	1/1217	1/1217			
WRIGHT, C. E.	1/247	1/247			
WRIGHT, C. H.	1/118	1/118			

You have **TWO VOTES ONLY.** Mark your Ballot Paper thus: X
Any other mark will disqualify.

Greenways. Printers (T.U.) London, N.4.

APPENDIX No. 9

SCHEDULE FOR INTERVIEWING INACTIVE MEMBERS OF A TRADE UNION BRANCH

Key: NH—Never heard of it
NG—Never given me
K—Knows
DK—Don't know or never thought
about it

You

....	1. Age
M.........F.........	2. Sex
M...S...W...D...	3. Married or single, widowed or divorced
CH....DEPS....	4. Number of children under school-leaving age and dependants.
Y.........N.........	5. Did you serve in the armed forces during World War II?
Y.........N.........	6. Were you unemployed for more than six months continuously during the '30s?
....	7. If yes, for how long were you unemployed?
Y.........N.........	8. Did you vote in the General Election of 1945?
Y.........N.........	9. Was your father a member of a trade union?
a...b...c...d... e...f...g...h... i...j....k...l.... m....n....	10. What are your hobbies and outside-of-work interests? *a. Handicrafts; b. Arts; c. Cinema and variety; d. Pubs; e. Help around the house; f. Playing sports; g. Watching sports; h. Study; i. Reading; j. Politics; k. T.U. activities; l. Dancing; m. Nothing; n.......*

You and the Union

....	1. Length of membership in the union
Y.........N.........	2. Have you ever been in arrears for more than six weeks?
a...b...c...d... e...f...	3. What were your main reasons for joining the Union? *a. To improve my (or workers') bargaining position in relation to the employer(s); b. To improve working conditions; c. So as not to be different; d. To obtain union benefits,* specifically mentioning such union services as legal aid, sickness, strike or funeral benefits or convalescent home; *e. I was forced to join; f.......*
Y.........N......... NH......NG......	4. Are you well acquainted with the contents of or do you use the Transport and General Workers Union rule book?
Y.........N......... NH.....NG.....	5. Have you read the Transport and General Workers Union Members Handbook?

T

a...b...c...d... 6. Do you read the Transport and General Work-
NH.....   ers Union *Record* (the official Journal of the
                   union)? *a, Every month; b, Every other month;
                   c, Less than six times a year; d. Not at all.*

a...b...c...d... 7. If so, what parts of the Journal do you read?
                   *a. Personalia; b. General lead articles; c. Legal
                   section; d. National Trade Group news.*

Y........N........ 8. Have you ever heard of the union's educational
                     scheme? Describe it.

Y........N........ 9. If yes, have you taken any of the courses?

a...b...c...d... 10. How would you go about bringing a grievance
...e   or a problem to the attention of the union?
                      *a. Branch; b. Shop steward; c. Area office; d. Trans-
                      port House; e.......*

Y....N....DK.... 11. Do you think that you yourself (as an individual)
                      can help to settle policy in the union?

Y....N....DK.... 12. Do you think that you, acting collectively with
                      other members can influence policy in the
                      union?

Y........N........ 13. Do you think that you have ever had any influ-
                      ence in a union decision or a matter of policy?
                      If yes, in what way did you influence policy?

Y........N........ 14. Did you receive a ballot for the election of
                      Area 1 Representatives to the General
                      Executive Council 1948–1949 sometime in
                      December, 1947?

Y........N........ 15. If yes, did you vote?

You and the Branch

Y........N........ 1. Have you ever held any offices or posts in the
                     union?

Y........N........ 2. Do you hold any offices in the union *now*?

a...b...c...d... 3. If yes, name them. *a. Branch Chairman; b. Branch
e...f...g...h...   Secretary; c. Shop Steward; d. Branch committee;
i....   e. Collector; f. Branch delegate Trades Council;
                     g. Branch delegate Labour Party; h. Works commit-
                     tees; i..............*

a...b...c...d... 4. Do you belong to any other working class organ-
e....   izations? *a. Labour Party; b. WEA; c. Co-op;
                     d. C.P.; e..............*

Y........N........ 5. Have you ever attended a branch meeting of the
                     1/AAA Branch of the Transport and General
                     Workers Union?

.... 6. If yes, when was the last time?

K......DK...... 7. Where are your branch meetings held?

K......DK...... 8. When are your branch meetings held?

K......DK...... 9. When was the last election held for Branch Chairman, Secretary and members of the branch committee?

Y........N........ 10. Did you vote in these elections?

CH...K...DK... 11. What is the name of your branch Chairman?

SEC...K...DK... Your branch Secretary?

a...b...c...d... 12. What are your (or members' in the case of
e...f...g...h... active respondents) reasons for not attending
i...j...k...l... branch meetings regularly? *a. Believes not*
m...n...o... *educated enough to speak before a group; b. Meetings are not for women; c. I'm too young or too old; d. Too great distance from home to meeting place; e. Shift work; f. Fatigue; g. Domestic duties or family responsibilities—I can't leave family after day's work; h. No knowledge of meeting; i. Shop stewards give all the information—they and branch doing good job; j. I pay my contributions—the rest is up to the union; k. I have other interests, hobbies, etc.; l. I'm not interested; m. Branch meetings are dull; n. A small group controls the branch—there is no chance of taking part; o...............*

Comment. DOES THE RESPONDENT APPEAR TO ASSOCIATE THE UNION WITH THE FACTORY ONLY OR WITH A LARGE NATIONAL ORGANIZATION AS WELL?

a........b........ *a. Factory only. b. National organization.*

T*

APPENDIX No. 10

AVERAGE SIZE OF MEMBERSHIP ATTENDING MEETINGS OF T.G.W.U.'s 1/AAA BRANCH IN RELATION TO TOTAL BRANCH MEMBERSHIP FOR EACH QUARTER MAY 20, 1942—JUNE 30, 1949 (a)

Year and Quarter	Total Branch membership	Average No. of members attending Branch Meetings (b)	Average attendance as of total Branch Membership of the previous Quarter	Total No. of meetings held (c)
1942 May (d)	195 (d)	—	—	–
June	292	26 (4)	13·3	4
Sept.	354	14 (2)	4·8	5
Dec.	300	—	—	4
1943 Mar.	240	34 (1)	11·3	3
June	262	—	—	5
Sept.	288	—	—	4
Dec.	265	3 (1)	1·4	7
1944 Mar.	221	—	—	6
June	307	—	—	0
Sept.	257	—	—	2
Dec.	297	3 (1)	1·1	5
1945 Mar.	308	—	—	7
June	441	36 (3)	11·7	6
Sept.	669	22 (1)	5·0	6
Dec.	691	18 (2)	2·7	6
1946 Mar.	936	20 (3)	2·9	7
June	1,140	16 (1)	1·7	6
Sept.	1,185	—	—	7
Dec.	1,184	31 (2)	2·5	5
1947 Mar.	1,119	20 (2)	1·7	6
June	1,083	23 (4)	2·1	5
Sept.	1,070	26 (1)	2·4	6
Dec.	1,059	30 (5)	2·8	6
1948 Mar.	1,015	22 (6)	2·1	6
June	954	30(7)	3·0	7
Sept.	892	17 (6)	1·8	6
Dec.	881	19 (5)	2·1	5

Year and Quarter	Total Branch membership	Average No. of members attending Branch Meetings (b)	Average attendance as of total Branch Membership of the previous Quarter	Total No. of meetings held (c)
1949 Mar.	895	20 (6)	2·3	6
June	—	30 (6)	3·4	6
Total		(69)		154

a. Source: Compiled on the basis of information in: (1) the Minutes of Meetings of T.G.W.U.'s 1/AAA Branch (May 1942–June 1949) and (2) the Record of Quarterly Changes in Size of 1/AAA Branch Membership compiled by a staff clerk and filed in T.G.W.U. Area 1 Office.
b. This is an arithmetic average obtained by adding the number of members attending during a quarter and dividing by the number of meetings (indicated in parenthesis), for which a record of attendance was kept.
c. Of the 154 meetings held, a record of attendance was kept for only 69 meetings. It is of interest to note that Branch Secretaries responsible for these minutes have stated that the absence of an attendance record should be considered an indication of attendance too poor to be recorded. The minutes actually noted 'very poor attendance' or 'abandoned for lack of quorum' on five occasions.
d. The size of membership was first recorded on May 20, 1942. All other quarterly figures are as of the last day of the month, which designates the quarter.

APPENDIX No. 11

WHAT ARE YOUR HOBBIES—YOUR OUTSIDE-OF-WORK INTERESTS (a)?

	INACTIVE			ACTIVE
	Men (60)	Women (32)	Total (92)	(19)
Cinema and Variety	62% (37)	78% (25)	67% (62)	32% (6)
Help around the House*	45% (27)	72% (23)	54% (50)	47% (9)
Handicrafts†	25% (15)	41% (13)	30% (28)	26% (5)
Watching sports‡	30% (18)	6% (2)	22% (20)	11% (2)
Playing sports‖	28% (17)	——	19% (17)	32% (6)
Reading	13% (8)	25% (8)	17% (16)	26% (5)
Pubs	12% (7)	——	8% (7)	——
Dancing	7% (4)	6% (2)	7% (6)	——
Nothing at all	7% (4)	3% (1)	5% (5)	——

	INACTIVE			ACTIVE
	Men (60)	Women (32)	Total (92)	(19)
Arts§	3% (2)	6% (2)	4% (4)	16% (3)
Studying	5% (3)	——	3% (3)	5% (1)
Politics	3% (2)	6% (2)	4% (4)	21% (4)
Trade union activities	——	——	——	69% (13)
The Most Common Combinations				
Cinema and help around the house	28% (17)	53% (17)	37% (34)	16% (3)
Cinema and handicrafts	18% (11)	34% (11)	24% (22)	11% (2)
Cinema and watching sports	20% (12)	6% (2)	15% (14)	5% (1)
Cinema and playing sports	22% (13)	——	14% (13)	5% (1)
Help around the house and trade union activities	——	——	——	37% (7)
Help around the house and handicrafts	10% (6)	28% (9)	16% (15)	16% (3)

a. Many respondents mentioned more than one hobby. Percentages are of the respondents in each population.

* *Help around the house*—Family duties, minding the children, painting and decorating, gardening—allotments, poultry-keeping, rabbit-keeping, boot repairing.

† *Handicrafts*—Cabinet-making, knitting, carpet-making, sewing, wood-working.

‡ *Watching sports*—Football, cricket, boxing, dogs, speedway.

‖ *Playing sports*—Football, cricket, boxing, cycling, motor-cycling, pigeon-keeping, weight-lifting.

§ *Arts*—Theatre, classical music, concerts, composing, painting.

BIBLIOGRAPHY

LIST OF BOOKS, PAMPHLETS AND OTHER MATERIAL USED OR CONSULTED

ARKIN & COLTON: *An Outline of Statistical Methods* (N.Y., Barnes & Noble Inc., 4th ed., 1943).

ATTLEE, C. R.: *The Labour Party in Perspective* (London, Gollancz, 1937).

BARNARD, C. I.: 'Functions and Pathology of Status Systems in Formal Organizations' in *Industry and Society*, edited by William F. Whyte (N.Y., McGraw-Hill, 1946).

COLE, G. D. H.: *A Short History of the British Working Class Movement* (London, Allen & Unwin Ltd., 3rd ed., 1938); 'What Socialism Means to Me' in *Labour Forum* (Vol. I, No. 5, Oct.–Dec. 1947).

CO-OPERATIVE UNION: *So Ill Remembered* (Manchester, 1947).

DEAKIN, A.: 'A Challenge to Democracy—And Our Answer' in the *T.G.W.U. Record* (January 1950); 'The Union and the Press—A Reply to Recent Criticism' in the *T.G.W.U. Record* (August 1948).

DAHL, R. A.: 'Workers' Control of Industry and the British Labour Party' in the *American Political Science Review* (Vol. XLI, No. 5, October 1947).

EVANS, T.: *Bevin—A Biography* (London, Allen & Unwin Ltd., 1946).

GOSNELL, H. F.: *Why Europe Votes* (University of Chicago Press, 1930).

GOSNELL, H. F., and MERRIAM, C. E.: *Non-Voting—Causes and Methods of Control* (University of Chicago Press, 1924).

GOVERNMENT PUBLICATIONS (BRITISH): *Annual Abstract of Statistics*, No. 84, 1935–1946 (H.M. Stationery Office); *Control of Engagement Order*, 1947 (S.R. & O., 1947, No. 2021); *Economic Survey for 1948* (presented to Parliament, March 1948); *Ministry of Labour Gazette* (March 1947, Vol. LV, No. 11; March 1948, Vol. LVI, No. 3); *Ministry of Labour and National Service Report for the Years 1939–1946* (H.M. Stationery Office, September 1947); *Representation of the Peoples Act, 1948*, 11 & 12 Geo. 6, Ch. 65; *Review of the British Docks Strikes 1949*, presented by the Minister of Labour, December 14, 1949 (H.M. Stationery Office, Cmd. 7851); *Societies (Miscellaneous Provisions) Act, 1940*, 3 & 4 Geo. 6, Ch. 19; *Trade Disputes and Trade Unions Act, 1946*, 9 & 10 Geo. 6, Ch. 52; *Trade Union (Amalgamation) Act, 1917*, 7 & 8 Geo. 5, Ch. 24.

HARRIS, H.: *American Labor* (Yale University Press, 1939).

HERBERG, W.: 'Bureaucracy and Democracy in Labor Unions' in *The Antioch Review* (Fall 1943).

HOBHOUSE, L. T. *Liberalism* (Oxford University Press, 1944 Ed.).

JEFFERSON, T.: *Writings, 20 Vols.* (Washington, 1904), Vol. XIV.

KLUCKHOHN, F. R. 'The Participant-Observer Technique in Small Communities' in *American Journal of Sociology* (Vol. XLVI, 1940).

LASKI, H. J.: *Grammar of Politics* (London, Allen & Unwin Ltd., 1934 Ed.); 'Statistics on Member Participation in the T.G.W.U. 1921 Election for General Secretary' (unpublished).

LASSWELL, H. D.: *The Analysis of Political Behaviour* (London, Kegan, Paul, Trench, Trubner & Co Ltd, 1948).

LONDON TIMES: *The House of Commons 1945–1947* (January 1948).

LONDON COUNTY COUNCIL: *Statistical Abstract for London* (L.C.C., 1948) Vol. XXX.

LONDON COUNCIL OF SOCIAL SERVICE PAMPHLETS: No. 5, 'The London Housing Problem' (1928).

LABOUR PARTY PUBLICATIONS: 'Industrial Democracy', Number 1 in the *Towards Tomorrow* Series of Discussion Pamphlets (1948); *The Labour Party Constitution and Standing Orders Approved by the Annual Conference in London 1944* (reprinted 1945); *Labour Discussion Series Number Five—Repeal of the Trade Disputes Act* (issued by the Research Department after the passage of the Act of 1946); *Let us Face the Future —A Declaration of Labour Policy for the Consideration of the Nation* (April 1945); *Report of the Annual Conference of the Labour Party* (1934–1948); *The Communists—We Have Been Warned*, by Morgan Phillips (1947).

MAYO, E. *The Social Problems of an Industrial Civilization* (Boston, Division of Research, Graduate School of Business Administration, Harvard University, 1945).

McCALLUM, R. B. and READMAN, A. *The British General Election of 1945* (Oxford University Press, 1947).

McNEMAR, Q. 'Sampling in Psychological Research' in the *Psychological Bulletin*, Vol. 37, No. 6; *Psychological Statistics* (N.Y., John Wiley & Sons Inc., 1949).

MERRIAM, C. E. and GOSNELL, H. F. *Non-Voting—Causes and Methods of Control* (University of Chicago Press, 1924).

MICHELS, R. *Political Parties* (Glencoe, Illinois, The Free Press, 1949).

MILLS, C. W. *The New Men of Power* (N.Y., Harcourt Brace & Co., 1948).

MORRISON, H. 'Labour for Higher Production'—Address to the 46th Annual Labour Party Conference (May 1947).

NATIONAL ASSOCIATION OF GIRLS' CLUBS AND MIXED CLUBS. *Hours Away from Work* (London, The National Council of Social Service, Inc., 1949).

P.E.P. (POLITICAL AND ECONOMIC PLANNING). *British Trade Unionism* (London, 1948).

RIGGLEMAN and FRISBEE. *Business Statistics* (N.Y., McGraw-Hill, 1938).

ROBERTS, B. *Trade Unions in the New Era* (London, International Publishing Co., 1947).

SAMUELS, H. *The Law of Trade Unions* (London, Stevens, 2nd ed., 1947).

SHELLEY, P. B. *A Defence of Poetry* (London, The Porcupine Press).

SHISTER, J. 'Trade Union Government: A Formal Analysis' in *Quarterly Journal of Economics* (Vol. LX, Nov. 1945).

SIMON, H. A. *Administrative Behaviour* (N.Y., Macmillan Company, 1948).

SLICHTER, S. H. *The Challenge of Industrial Relations* (N.Y., Cornell University Press, 1947).

TAWNEY, R. H. *The Acquisitive Society* (London, G. Bell & Sons, Ltd., 1945).

TEWSON, V. Circular Letter quoted in *Labour—The T.U.C. Magazine* (December 1949).

TINGSTEN, H. *Political Behaviour—Studies in Election Statistics* (Stockholm Economic Studies No. 7, 1937).

TRADES UNION CONGRESS PUBLICATIONS. *Defend Democracy—Communist Activities Defined* (1948); *4 T.U.C. Documents* (approved by Blackpool Conference, 1945), No. 4; *Free Trade Unions Leave the W.F.T.U.* (1949); Reports of Annual Trades Union Congresses, 1946–1949; The Final Report of the T.U.C., entitled *Trade Union Structure and Closer Unity* (1947); *The Problem of Leisure*, a Report approved by the Trades Union Congress (1947); *The Tactics of Disruption—Communist Methods Exposed* (1949); *Trades Councils Guide*, a T.U.C. Handbook (1948).

TRANSPORT AND GENERAL WORKERS UNION PUBLICATIONS. *Annual Report and Balance Sheet* (for the years 1930 and 1935–1948); *Members Handbook*; *Minutes and Record of the First Annual Delegate Conference* (1923); *Minutes and Record of the proceedings of the Biennial Delegate Conference of the T.G.W.U.* (1925–1949); *Minutes and Record of the Proceedings of the National Delegate Conference of Women Members* (London, April 25, 1947); *Rules of the Transport and General Workers Union*, Nov. 1942 (with Amendments attached as of October 23, 1947, and as amended, August 19, 1949); *The Union, Its Work and Problems*—A T.G.W.U. Correspondence Course; *Third Annual Report*, December 31, 1924; *Transport and General Workers' Record* (1935–1949).

TRANSPORT AND GENERAL WORKERS UNION UNPUBLISHED DOCUMENTS. 'Annual Membership Report, December 31, 1946'. 'Annual Reports of the Education Department to the General Secretary and Members of the Educational Committee of the General Executive Council' (1936–1947); 'Financial Secretary's Annual Membership Reports', addressed to the Chairman and Members of the General Executive Council (1935–1947); 'General Executive Council Minutes' (Dec. 6, 1945); 'Liverpool Amalgamation, 1946'; Memorandum: 'Ballot Voting' (Sept. 12, 1944); Memorandum: 'Distribution of Election Addresses' (1945); 'Report and Recommendations of the Committee appointed under the Terms of the Decision in Council Minute No. 1212, dated Dec. 6, 1945, to Conduct an Investigation into the Ballot Arrangements in Area No. 11'; Area Scrutineers' Reports—'Election of the General Secretary' (Nov. 22/23, 1945); Scrutineers' Reports on 'General Executive Council' (for the years 1937, 1941, 1943, 1945 and 1947); 'Statutory Meeting of the T.G.W.U. Finance and General Purposes Committee, 1946'; Table of Statistics entitled 'The Union, Its Work and Problems' (Education Department, 1947); 'The Importance of Well-Attended Branch Meetings' (67 essays by T.G.W.U. Applicants for University Scholarships for the Academic Years 1946 and 1947); 'Verbatim Report of the Biennial Delegate Conference of the T.G.W.U.' (1925–1949).

WEBB, S. and B. *The History of Trade Unionism, 1666–1930* (Printed by the Authors for the Trade Unionists of the United Kingdom, 1920 Ed.); *Industrial Democracy* (London, Longmans, Green & Co. Ltd., 1926).

WOLMAN, L. *Ebb and Flow of Trade Unionism* (N.Y., National Bureau of Economic Research, 1936).

ZWEIG, F. *Labour, Life and Poverty* (London, Gollancz, 1948).

ZEISEL, H. *Say It with Figures* (N.Y., Harper Bros. 1947).

INDEX

For Product Safety Concerns and Information please contact our EU
representative GPSR@taylorandfrancis.com
Taylor & Francis Verlag GmbH, Kaufingerstraße 24, 80331 München, Germany

www.ingramcontent.com/pod-product-compliance
Lightning Source LLC
Chambersburg PA
CBHW050702280326
41926CB00088B/2425